FAMILY VALUES

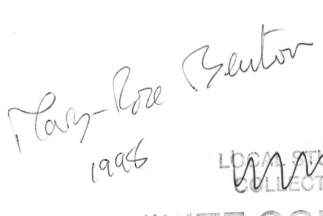

Family photo in studio, early spring 1933
Ruby (*with me on her lap*) and Jack in front, Jimmy, with
Mum's purse to keep him quiet, and Billy
Author's startled exression acquired some three months earlier
— never quite thrown off

Mary-Rose Benton

Family Values

PILLAR TO POST EVACUEE—
EARLY STAGES FOR A TOURING ACTOR

THANET PUBLICATIONS
1998

First published in 1998
by Thanet Publications
48 Windermere Way
Stourport on Severn
Worcs DY13 8QJ

ISBN 0 9532076 0 9

A catalogue record for this book is available from
the British Library

Typeset in New Century 11/12pt by Scriptmate Editions
Manufacture coordinated in UK by
Book-in-Hand Ltd 20 Shepherds Hill, London N6 5AH

CONTENTS

Mum, aged six

CHAPTER ONE

ON YOUR BIKE—1933

A few hours before I was born, I took a bike ride. My mother took the two eldest to school first. Ruby was six, and sat on the carrier at the back. Jack was five, and Ruby remembers having to hold on tightly to him in front of her. His large head held the entire stock of family brains, and was the cause of his frequently toppling over; he had fallen headlong downstairs as a toddler. I hovered somewhere over the saddle, so that made four of us on a bike.

Billy was three, and Jimmy two, so they stayed at home with Daddy, who had TB. By the time Ruby and Jack were brought home from school, they found me in bed with Mum, who told them all that I was to be called Mary Rose. Anyone shortening it to Mary would be in big trouble.

I was never completely sure where she had got the name from. J. M. Barrie's character is the most likely. Less likely is the three hundred and eighty-eight-year-old wreck lying in the Solent, and even less the Duchess of York, who had called her second daughter Margaret Rose. I've had a lifelong battle to stop people outside the family from chopping it in half. I have no problem from the Scots, the Irish, the Americans, nor from people in show business. The first three have a tradition of double names, and those last think it was my own idea.

We didn't need a doctor, luckily. The delivery fee would have been half a crown, and sixpence for the call-out. A wasted tanner for a false alarm, sixpence would have bought two large loaves. Mum had been asked if she wanted her fifth baby to be delivered in the Infirmary, but since that building had, until the previous year, been used as a latter-day workhouse, and as attitudes take longer to change than do institutions, she declined. She had had her first four at home, all within four years, and preferred it that way. The only complication arose when the midwife unscrewed her radiator cap and scalded her arm so badly that she had to come back indoors to dress it.

Ten days later, Germany had a new Chancellor, and the Thousand Year Reich began.

Had I been a boy, I was to have been called Gerald. Dad objected; "We've already got one named after taking a piss, (Jimmy) why name this one after a piss-pot?"

I think of having to take a name like Gerry to school, during World War Two, and breathe a retrospective sigh of relief.

Like many working-class families, we lived in lodgings. No. 1, Buenos Ayres, still stands on the sea front at Margate, and we had the basement rooms. You might think it would be well protected by the area wall from the January gales blowing in from the sea, but a few weeks later the rotten window fell in at last, showering glass on the bed. I had been picked up from it only seconds before. Life is a matter of timing, as the man said when he sat in the electric chair at Sing Sing, on a guided tour. Billy remembers there being a thunderbolt rolling round the room at the time.

"We had toast that day," he tells me. That family joke ranks beside the one about our keeping a pig, which we chased about to make it sweat, then wiped our bread on it. The one about picking mushrooms off the wall came later.

The earliest words I can remember hearing were "Daddy's dead," spoken with an air of detached wonderment by my brothers and sister. So I was nearly two. The taste and smell of emulsions invoke infancy, and puzzled me for years until I was told of the preparation of eggs, milk and other nutrients given to us in the days before penicillin.

I have no memory of our father, because he went into the Sanatorium shortly after I was born, and only Mum was allowed near him. The Sanatorium was also referred to as the Home for Incurables, and would perhaps be termed a Hospice by now.

Harry Benton was born in 1890. He came from Nottingham, from a family background dealing in shoes. There is still a Benton's shoe repairer in Ramsgate. Mum's grandfather was a shoemaker. (Not, as Chambers now has it, a 'snob'. That, she pointed out, was only a cobbler. She had a healthy lack of respect for dictionaries). Harry was sixteen years older than Ruby Clarke, and when young had been to sea. For a time he had been in sail, when the century was in single figures. During World War One he was an Army Sergeant, and before settling down to marriage went across to America to look for work. He went first to Canada, and crossed the Rockies illegally, and according to him, on foot. He

Dad, seated left, with other patients at Preston Hall Sanatorium

worked for Wells Fargo, by that time coachmakers, no longer mail coaches. He joined the Wobblies, the International Workers of the World, until they disbanded.

Back in this country, he answered an advertisement for a job as Head Chef in a high class hotel. He bluffed his way through the interview, got the job, then approached the Under Chef, admitted to him that he couldn't cook, and gave him a portion of his own wages in return for showing him how. I have to assume he was a fast learner, that he delegated the difficult jobs, and that the hotel must have been finding it hard to get staff.

Early in his married life he took two of our uncles, Stanley and Kenny, aged five and three (very young brothers-in-law) for a ride in his Morris Cowley, an open-top four-seater. He stopped at the post office in Cecil Square, in Margate, and told the boys he wouldn't be a minute. They were perched very high up, it seemed to them, staring apprehensively at the gearstick, which was vibrating alarmingly. They were also facing downhill.

Had anyone pointed out to him that it was illegal to leave an unattended vehicle with its engine running, he would have replied, "Only if you get found out."

As he was to buy another Morris Cowley, an eight-seat monster, in which he took a whole crowd of his young kinsfolk for rides, he seems to have been as generous with his time as with his money. I wish I could have got to know him.

Apart from hearing of his death, my only other memory concerning him was the appellation 'Daddy', which stayed frozen in time, as we were all under eight when he died. Long after 'Mummy' became 'Mum', and 'Jackie' became 'Jack'.

Both Mum, and her sister Cissie, had worked as waitresses. Stanley remembers his mother kept busy washing and ironing their uniforms, starching the cuffs and the caps, which sat on the head like a tiara. Apart from directed labour during the War, on munitions, it was the only work that Cissie did. She liked doing it, and was very good at it. She worked in just about every restaurant in the Margate area, all later bombed or taken over.

In an otherwise reserved, quiet family, Stanley and his sister Ruby were very extravert, very verbal. Even when Mum was knee deep in kids, he used to call at the bungalow in the Kent countryside, to have someone to talk to. He would find her putting us to bed, in the general hubbub, and screaming, "Bloody kids!" But he overlooked the noise for the sake of human interchange.

It was this same need for intellectual stimulus that was to lead Mum down many a logical blind alley, furiously arguing her point in the face of the laws of physics. She contended that smoke rose because it 'wanted to', and would not be persuaded that it did so quite helplessly, because it was warm, and lighter than the surrounding air. I was, in adulthood, to get myself embroiled in these disputes, sometimes seeking them out, and becoming as bloody minded in making my point as anyone else in the debate.

* * *

I have always wanted to get back to the sea. When we were evacuated, I was to miss seeing that vast expanse opening the world out to me, and felt closed in and landlocked. It was my earliest influence, that cheap and cheerful town; I love the contrast of a busy urban centre on the edge of the ocean. Like a city on the brink of a desert, it gives both the modern and the primeval. The taste of Italian ice-cream mixing with the salt that settles on the mouth in a sea breeze. The bingo-barking promenade against the ancient wildlife clinging, cold and dark, to the underside of the pier.

Afternoons were spent in the cinema, which my mother loved. While the others were at school, she would take me to the Astoria, in Margate, or to the Regal. Cissie worked in the restaurant above the Regal, and lent Mum her free pass. Sometimes the celluloid would come free of the ratchets, the movement would blur, and the operator would stop the film. Sometimes the film would simply slow down, the heroine's voice would drop to bass, and it would come to a halt in a swishing noise. Taking their chance, boys would whistle loudly until it came back on. But this was my mother's escape—musicals with Ruby Keeler; Bette Davis giving it what for; a Marx Brothers' comedy. An afternoon in the fantasy dark, with the quietest of her brood asking, before falling asleep, "Are we going to get the kids from school yet?"

Although she didn't tell us much about her early life, we did learn from her that they lived near enough to London to spend several hours on the Underground for a penny, riding the whole system, then coming out at the station at which they had got on. It was a cheap way of keeping warm in the winter.

In her early married life, an equally harmless deception was played out by many a working class couple. Knowing they might never be able to afford their own home, they would make appointments to view houses for sale, (Mum once got the key for a newly built house) and would look round them, noting what other classes could afford, and seeing at first hand what it was they aspired to.

She was always self-conscious about our poverty. She would send Jack into a shop in Margate to buy two-pennyworth of pieces of bacon; scraps from the slicing machine, and would wait for him outside. She carried on working as a waitress, preferably silver service, which meant superior leftovers for us. The first time I bought carob chocolate, I had an immediate image of a long, flat, dried brown bean. This must have been one of the many exotic titbits brought home for a treat.

Some friends of Mum's meeting us in Dreamland when I was about three, looked down kindly from a great height and said, politely, "Isn't she pretty?"

I thought 'pretty?'. Shirley Temple; Binkie Stuart—that was pretty. The curly hair and the girly ways. I had straight brown hair, green eyes, and was never girly. Not to make a big production of it. I mention it only to set the scene. I recently went back to Thanet. The Isle of Thanet is a geographical oddity, constituting a hefty chunk of the South East coast, and left off being an island several millennia ago. It is now a District Council area, a post code. Billy and I went back in 1994, and he filled me in on both the geography and history of our early childhood. The following year I went with my partner Denis. This time was by car, so we got off the bus routes and into the countryside to find the bungalow, where we had moved to by the end of 1933. It lies between the A255, Dane Court Road, in the middle of fields and farm, with Northdown Hill away on the east side. For years we had referred to it only as 'The Bungalow', although we remembered its name. When I saw 'Sunnyside' on the gate, my liver and lights shot up into my nostrils as the name leapt forward into the current file of my memory. In fifty-four years, trees and bushes had grown and died and been replaced with more trees and bushes for several cycles, so that what I recognised was only the tilt of the land as it dipped towards the front door.

Ruby will say, "I don't care what anyone says, you can't go back." I love going back. It resolves something, gives the time a shape I can work on. When we went back to Kent, it felt exactly right to do so. There was nothing to mourn. It was not a loss, but a continuation. I have no wish to re-live the time, only to remember it and make it part of the present, and of the time in between. Time travel forms part of my favourite fantasy, but this linking of the past to the present has no element of fantasy in it, it's simply a picture of the whole; instead of chopping time up into chunks—the far past, the middle past, the recent past, it presents time as the running continuum that it is. Besides, I now have the satisfaction of raising two fingers to certain parts of the past, and declaring, "You can't get me now!"

Drapers Mills School, with the re-built Mill nearby, looked, in 1995, as I had remembered it, though I remember nothing of the inside. The chalky smells of school were the same, but without the combination of tarmac and infant pooh which I remembered. The Headmaster showed me what was still there, and told me what had gone. He pointed out the 'temporary' portacabin units, that stood in lieu of proper school buildings. Not much change there, then.

School itself was no problem to me, even when I was kept in to copy words from the board. As far as I was concerned, this was an extension of the daily treat, and I contentedly put the letters down, leaning heavily on the pencil and without leaving spaces between the words.

Hot water was expensive, so we had to get in the bath while it was still hot. I hated the stinging hot water, and walked round and round the table, crying, "I don't want a bath! I don't want a bath!" Billy, Jimmy and Ruby would follow me round, chanting with me in derision, and when I wailed, they would mock me on the same note, like dogs. Once the first impact of hot water had subsided, I didn't want to get out, and wailed again to be allowed to stay. Mum was blessed with an unusual amount of stamina. Just as well.

Ruby, six years my senior, was too old to play with me, though, like most children, she liked to make the baby laugh. She would be left in charge of us all at times, and became pardonably bossy. Jack kept apart, putting off mischief making until he was old enough to call it adventure, and games of dare. Billy and Jimmy, with only fourteen months between them, went about together. So I had Mum to myself. She seemed to me at the time to spend much of her time protecting me from the others.

We had a toy telephone. "Call the Police, Billy," Ruby told him, "to come and take Mary Rose away."

Billy did, I cried, and they both got the buckle end of the strap. What is surprising is that Jack, on occasion, got it too. Good behaviour is no guarantee of escaping punishment. I have heard of mothers who would smack a sleeping child to 'even things up' when the rest of the children had misbehaved.

Charity has never shamed me, only greed. When I spoke, years later, of the halfpenny dinners we were taken to at School, Mum hotly denied it. I never understood her attitude. She certainly had nothing to reproach herself with. We were better fed and clothed by her than I was to be later on, by people of better means. She would let us have fresh fruit, a raw tomato or carrot to eat as we played whenever we asked. The only nutritional mistake she made was to insist that Billy ate all his cabbage up. His constitution couldn't process it, and it would take its revenge exactly twenty-two hours later, and he would have to come home from school for a wash and a change of short pants.

I now assume Mum to have been subject to pre-menstrual rages. Not that she can have had many cycles between having

Mum *(second from right)* with waitresses, early 1930s, at the Bungalow Tearooms, Margate

Ruby and weaning me from breast feeding. This happened abruptly when I was six months, when she caught scarlet fever. Granny took care of me, and the others went into the Cottage Homes, to be separated, bullied and punished for presuming to become parentless. This can't have done much for their behaviour, and on her recovery, Mum coped much as any lone parent of five children would. I dimly remember infant punishment as a response to crying for some other reason. I would be smacked for crying, and there followed as escalation of frantic slapping, and hysteria on both sides, until remorse set in, when I could do no wrong.

She was to tell me that, with a wailing baby on her lap, she would, in sheer exhaustion, join in. Both howling—and *still* the bratling wouldn't stop crying.

* * *

School milk cost a halfpenny a bottle, and we were to raise a hand if we had paid it. I don't remember ever paying it in. Perhaps it had found its way into the shop in The Shallows, at the corner of two country lanes, in exchange for a toffee-apple, but I raised my hand anyway, my desire for the milk overcoming my scruples. To their credit, the teachers never made an issue of unpaid-for milk.

The halfpenny dinners were pretty good. I don't remember if there was meat, but it was a good hot meal of vegetables and gravy, (Billy sat next to Jimmy, where he safely off-loaded the treacherous cabbage on to his younger brother's plate) and we had either a pudding or a slice of bread and jam, followed by a mug of cocoa, without milk or sugar. "What don't fatten, fills," was the opinion of many a mother.

Charity came also, in the form of vouchers for boots. Jack was presented with a pair. The donors believed in doing good by ear-splitting stealth, and the lucky boys were made to parade this generosity in front of the class. Boots were a revealing sign of charity, as the givers chose them over shoes. While this odious attitude never bothered me, a natural communist for whom all wealth was to be shared, it must have been very distressing for those children more alert to the nuances of social superiority.

A group of children, poorer than we were, came to the bungalow for a holiday. They had been sent from London, and it was felt that the sea air and countryside would do them good, and that they would enjoy playing on the sands—we never referred to it as the beach, only holiday makers and the military did that. One of their number was looked down on by the others; they said that he was dirty. Billy took to him at once, for this very reason. Not one to pick on an outcast, he threw his lot in with the underdog, and shared his favourite haunts, his secrets, and his games, with him.

Pranks got played. Billy and Jimmy prodded a wasps nest; the angry insects got out and stung as many as they could. This was all cleared up by a pig farmer, who used to give us marzipan, which would otherwise get fed to his stock. It must have been confectioner's waste. Billy acquired an axe, only for the purpose of proof that he had been up a dark lane where goblins lived.

Billy's partner in prank had a doting mother who declared, "My Albert would never do a thing like that."

"My Billy would," was Mum's acid response.

Jumble sales, then as now, were a rich source of practical goods. (Some twenty years later, I was to pick up an almost complete set of Dickens at twopence a book—little more than one and six the lot). In Margate, Mum bought a carpet sweeper for a few pence, and a trunk for a shilling. In coinage terms, this would be five new pence, but translated into economic worth would be some five pounds. In terms of personal means, however, it would go right off the graph. To make a pertinent comparison: In 1952, I found a pound note in Birmingham Central Library. To put the matter delicately, I needed to go to the loo, and since not all public lavatories provided paper, I looked around for some. Then I saw it, on the floor, green and lovely. I have never so quickly forgotten a bodily urge as I did then, picking up what represented a sixth of my weekly wage as a copy typist. Nowadays, a similar find would amount to some thirty-three pounds, but that would not compare with the difference the pound made to my buying a warm jumper and having my shoes mended.

Only wealth is relative. Poverty is absolute. It begins at precisely the point at which you become cold, sick or hungry through lack of means. This was something known instinctively to whoever left a box of food on the doorstep of the bungalow on the night Daddy died. The last of his children's memories would be that of Jack, aged seven, who saw him brought by car to the end of he short footpath to see Mum. It was the car that stuck in the boy's memory—the first time he had seen a family member in one. On the same night that the telegram was brought to the bungalow, a knock was heard, very quiet but distinct, on the front door of Granny's house in Addiscombe Street, in Margate, followed immediately by a quiet knock on the back door. Thinking it was a prank, someone dashed to the back door while the front door was open, and allowed them to cover the passageway to the back, a covered way through the building. Nobody was there, or to be seen anywhere. They all had an eerie feeling about it, and made a note

Family line-up outside the Bungalow Tea Rooms, Margate
Ruby, Jack, Jimmy, me, Billy

of the time. Over the years, some had remembered it as six o'clock, and some as eight o'clock. But they all agree that it was the same time as that stated on the telegram, when our father had died, on Christmas Eve, 1934.

This family anecdote has only ever been recorded, not analysed. The rest of us are not superstitious, but Mum never had a Christmas tree in the house. This was not because of Daddy dying on the 24th December—her sister Violet had died of diphtheria at seven, when Mum was fifteen. The previous Christmas, 1920, they had for the first time had a Christmas tree, but Violet's death in November 1921, was so close to Christmas, that the thought of having another tree would have been too painful for Granny. Our own mother extended this ban to any evergreens, and would not even have holly in the house. She would also never say Goodnight, and would forestall anyone saying it to her. Christmas trees and Goodnights reminded her both of unhappy Christmases and of the farewells taken at the time.

As for the box of food, did it come from what few neighbours we had? There are two oddly placed Victorian houses opposite, with tiny front gardens, like something from a suburban street, dropped into the countryside, and another bungalow near ours, as well as a farm nearby. Perhaps the people at the Sanatorium had put it together. It might have been sent by Daddy's own people, though if it was, it was their only recognition of their paternal grandchildren.

In 1934, with a rental of some fifteen shillings to pay, and only ten shillings widow's pension, the current form of child allowance in descending order for each child, and with what she could earn as a waitress on the sea front, one suspects, and certainly hopes, that the landlord was not a priority with her. The landlord moved us out when his London home was flooded. Hearing the phrase, "he was flooded out," there came an image into my infant mind of his being swept out of the door on a tidal wave. If only. A landlord, short of somewhere to stay? Poor chap, having to shift a widow and five kids out. He must have been hard up for somewhere to live.

No. 85, Victoria Avenue, is in a cul de sac, which looks out on to farm land at the front. You reach the back by an alleyway which backs on to some ten houses. At right angles to these 'backs' is a broader dirt path backing the houses in the main Victoria Avenue, and leads to Northdown Hill. We had a bathroom and garden in what could be regarded as good working-class houses. It was here that I was sent home from school with German Measles, with Jimmy to take me. We walked everywhere, though I find it surprising that a child sickening for Rubella could walk nearly two miles, across the fields and down the lane.

Because of our being approached by a child-fancier, we were moved to a school in Broadstairs. St Joseph's Convent had been occupied by the Sisters of Retreat, whose *primary* aim was to educate the children of the poor. However by the time we went to St Joseph's, a tin hut was set aside for the children of the Catholic poor, and the Convent was for children whose parents could pay.

I don't remember the episode with the paedophile, but on one occasion, the very day after Billy had been told never to accept pennies from strangers, he was met in the fields by a man who asked him, "Would you like a penny?" Billy stared at him for a second, then turned heel and ran like hell all the way home.

Recovering from German Measles one day, I was well enough to be left on my own for the afternoon while Mum went to work. I eventually got up and wandered round the house. I was going to make the most of having it to myself. I could go round, touching things without being told not to, opening drawers and examining their contents. I wandered downstairs. The kitchen held few charms, except when Mum was making cakes or an apple pie, when I would be allowed to scrape the bowl or eat the peel. The four Coronation mugs on their hooks were testimony to the fact that I had been the only one not of school age at the time. The toffees they had held had been eaten on the way home from school. So royalty had been of some use, however slight.

One of the objects round the house was a stereoscope, which you held to your eyes with an elegantly carved handle, and which gave off a strong smell of metal from the eyepiece. I wondered if some day I would be able to see round behind the three-dimensional objects in the pictures, then set the thought aside, to be answered with all the other mysteries life held. Downstairs, the main room ran the length of the house with a dividing piece, and on the front window sill was a little cardboard mill, a perpetuum mobile, with tiny sacks of sand, and was to me the last word in sophisticated technology. This belonged to Jack. I envied even more the Meccano set that all three boys shared, but it was a complex toy, and would have had to be explained.

I wandered into the glass house, which had been built on to the tiny kitchen. The green trunk was in there. Billy, Jimmy and I used to get into it to play. As I turned from it, thunder began to rumble. Usually, I found storms exciting, but only when there was someone with me, so I moved further indoors, where I couldn't see the lightning.

I found a book, opened it and looked for something familiar. I found the word AND. "A-neh-deh," I said aloud, without knowing what it represented. They hadn't told us that bit yet. I assumed they would, when they were ready. I was more than ready, and keen to know lots of things. I wanted to know how to run my life. It was because I lacked knowledge of the way the world was run that I was so passive, so obedient. I wanted to be on top of the job before I tackled it myself.

Once I did learn to read, I could see what the world was saying, and looked around for things to read; adverts, road signs, cereal packets, shop fronts. The world began to open up in front of me. This was 1939, when the wider world was beginning to close in.

* * *

Mr Bailey was our lodger. He played with us, teased us and trimmed our nails, got tiddly and was great fun.

He came on family outings with us—blackberrying in Nash Court, and nearer home, along the railway embankment. He would come to fetch us back from our rambles, with his bike. He put me on the saddle to steer, and pushed from behind. I sat one evening on the deserted sands with Mum and him teasing me about a five year old boyfriend. I would watch him fill in his pools coupon each week, and wondered what the cryptic code of 1,2,X was supposed to mean. When I asked him why he did it, he said, "I'm hoping it will make me rich." So *that's* how one did it.

Jimmy and I went on our own to a garden fete at Northdown Park, run by the Boy Scouts, and stayed out rather late. Jimmy had won a canteen of cutlery, and held it contentedly under his arm. He would be thought well of for that when he got home. Mum turned up in some agitation, with Mr Bailey, and she put her coat round me in the cool evening, though I didn't feel the chill, as children often do not. It was, I remember, a fur coat, either passed on to her or bought at a jumble sale. On the way home, a furious row broke out between the adults. I never worked out what it was about. It was unlikely to be politics, the finer points of which would have gone right over his carefree head. Surely not religion—our mother's turning to the Catholic Church was not something she felt needed to be defended in terms of logic. It was more likely that she was frantic at our staying out so late, although it was still light. Suddenly, Mr Bailey seized the precious prize from Jimmy's hands and hurled it into the hedgerow. Knives, forks, and spoons went cascading into the hedge which skirted the park. Then he strode off angrily, leaving Mum fuming, and Jimmy and me subdued and wordless, as we trudged home. Goodbye, Mr Bailey.

Billy and Jimmy had prank days. These would mostly be on Wednesdays, when the bins went out. In the days before plastic Wheelie bins, this would involve the removal of the lid with a clang, and kicking the bins over to make sure the rubbish went all over the pavement. They would run up Northdown Hill, shouting at the cars and buses as they swept past. They took their shoes off and shouted, "Saving shoe leather!" Singing, in boy-madness, "Honestly and truly, bagley and booley!" The nature of the beast. Making the most of it until life caught up with them.

At Drapers Mills School, the infants were provided with slippers to wear in school, which saved on shoes, and ensured the children didn't sit in wet shoes in the winter. The British Legion helped out with jumpers and other garments, but shoes remained the problem. The laces broke, and string would have to be used. At one point, Jimmy didn't have any shoes at all. Mum used to take him with her to a masseuse. One week she turned up without Jimmy. The masseuse asked her why. In a quite matter-of-fact way, she explained that as he hadn't any shoes, he couldn't come out at all. (I have a memory of coming home with him and Billy, and Jimmy's feet bleeding from having trodden on some glass). The masseuse was appalled at what Mum told her, and became tearful. Then she wrote out a cheque for her to get shoes for us all.

We had pets to keep. Danny the dog was Billy's, Ruby had the kitten, Queenie. I don't know what Jack and Jimmy had, but the tortoise seemed to be its own person. The goldfish were held to be mine. Danny left part of his tail on the railway line. Billy, Jimmy and I were in on our own when the vet came to collect him; Jimmy huddled the dog to him in a corner and took some persuading. Eventually, the vet coaxed the dog from him and got a blanket from us, then left. We never saw Danny again.

Billy acquired his first cigarettes from a machine outside Whitfield Road Post Office. Two Woodbines and two matches for a penny. He couldn't reach the slot, and a man passing by said, "Your Dad want some fags? I'll put the penny in." Billy took them behind a haystack on Northdown Hill and lit up. Shortly afterwards, he thought it was the end of the world.

A few days later, while he was out with Jack, the same man

passed them and said, "Did your Dad get his fags alright?" Jack asked Billy what the man was talking about; Billy shrugged, and Jack didn't take the matter further. In any case, he wouldn't have told on him. In any event, Billy was put off cigarettes for life.

He, Jimmy and Wilfred Lear, who later joined the Police Force, 'found' some envelopes in the Chapel in Rowley Street, in which contributions were to be collected, to help convert the Heathens. They took these round the houses, asked for contributions, and piously told the donor to seal the envelope. Then they took their haul round a corner, opened the envelopes and divided the spoils. They made about two and six each, which bought about a pound and a quarter of sweets each. As this was before sweets rationing, they lived like little lords while the racket lasted, and until they thought up another one.

There is a pleasing aptness in their having raided the holy coffers. The Heathen would have to wait for salvation. Our own boys had needs, too, even if they were met with sweeties before shoes. Thus they taught themselves the first principle of redistribution. Don't just ask for your rights. Take them.

Christmas Eve, 1938; in the big bed in the front room, between Billy and Jimmy. They would amuse me by enacting scenes from the latest film drama, or Charlie Chaplin foolery, until we all fell asleep. I was still awake when Mum came in to ask me if I would like to have one of Ruby's old dolls put with my presents. I didn't care about dolls and said No, thank you. I liked having a lot of little cheap things, rather than a few big presents. It was the abundance that mattered with me. I liked toys I could manipulate, plasticine, or things that took apart and built up again. Brightly coloured books; books to colour in; crayons and paints; especially paints! Reds you could warm your hands at, blues to swim in, and yellows that lit the world. But this Christmas was to be different. Jimmy and I had been promised a scooter each, something we were not ready to believe in until it appeared. When we went downstairs next morning, there they were, leaning against the table in the front part of the living room, both painted red. We stood there, saying nothing, just staring at them. Bob Bailey's parting gift.

I asked Mum why she didn't play with us, as Mr Bailey had done. It didn't occur to me that she hadn't the time for romping, only for working, feeding us, and putting us to bed. We went quite early, at about six o'clock, which gave her a little time to herself, hence the bedtime stories the three of us played at. We were not old enough to appreciate what a hard time it must have been for our mother. She had enjoyed having children. Pregnancy was always a time of serenity, optimism and promise for her. Once widowed, and with only her phenomenal energy to rely on, she had simply got on with raising us.

I could never be sure why she had joined the Catholic Church. Perhaps for drama and colour. For whatever reason, she had us three youngest baptised. Sister Marie Louise said to me, "Your soul is now as white as your veil."

I had no idea what she was talking about, but I was pleased that she was pleased. She was a warm-hearted person and an excellent teacher. Meanwhile, Billy, the little heretic, stood there with his head wet, wishing a dagger would come flying at him through the window, so that he could go straight to Heaven.

The tin hut school was divided in two in the main part, and a third classroom was made of the kitchen, where there was a large stove. We sat in a semi-circle with the stove at our back. Sister Marie Louise presided. She would bring two slices of bread and butter to school, break it up into pieces, and feed it to us, as if to nestlings. Or maybe communicants. She left none for herself.

She was an entertaining teacher, and I quite liked her lessons on right and wrong. Children are keen to know what the rules are — and she would posit herself in the place of the wrongdoer, for instance; "If I struck Sister Patrick ..." She'd be the first to dare to, for a start. I came in late one day, to find all the desks were occupied. As we were short of desks, the first in got the best place.

Quite expecting to get into trouble if I didn't find somewhere to sit, I said to her, as she was bending over another child's work, "Excuse me, Sister, where can I sit?"

She swirled round in a waft of clean linen, made an obscure gesture with upturned index fingers and thumbs, and snarled, "Sit on that!" That would teach me not to demand basic school equipment.

I had a problem with First Confession. Not only had I to remember all the wickedness I had got up to in seven years, but we had no guidance on what a small child would recognise as sin. We were not encouraged to ask questions that applied to childish naughtiness, like is it a sin to be cheeky, or to get your siblings into trouble; nor even serious sins, like cruelty or indifference. Certainly, my piffling little misdemeanours hardly rated the heroic status of eternal fire-deserving Sin.

In the cold weather, it was common for small children to have a large scarf placed round the neck, outside the coat, crossed over the front, then taken round the back, and secured with a safety pin. It's quite surprising how much warmth this conserves. But I don't remember having gloves, and in the very cold winter of 1939, Jimmy and I were the only children to turn up at the tin hut school. Sister Marie Louise warmed our hands in the folds of her gown, warned us not to put them on the radiator, then gave us tracing paper and pencils and left us to our simple pleasures. We had the entire facilities to ourselves. No sharing desks, textbooks or pencils that day.

Sister Marie Louise used to tell us about Heaven, which sounded like fun.

"Will there be ice-cream?" Jimmy wanted to know.

"Will there be scooters?" I asked.

I didn't want a little thing like death to come between me and my earthly pleasures. Theologically correct or not, she assured us there would be. After all, as far as we were concerned, ice-cream and scooters were indeed, Heaven.

As a Christian festival, I preferred Easter to Christmas. I didn't, it's true, care for the chilling implications of Palm Sunday, when the carpenter was made such a big fuss of when he came into town on the ass, knowing as I did that torture and death were to follow on the next Friday. Commonplace though crucifixion was in 33 AD, I thought it was a disgusting way to 'save' my soul, let alone something to be glad about, especially as it clearly didn't save believers from Hell. They could still go there if they were bad enough—why indeed did their friends pray for their salvation?

Even Sister Marie Louise got it wrong, sometimes. "I'd like you to thank God for not making you a worm," she told me, in her well-meaning way, intending me to count my blessings. I thought, "What kind of God would make something that didn't like being what it was?" It seemed a meanspirited thing to do. I was not impressed with God. He would really have to do better than this.

Nevertheless, it was spring, a time of warm weather, flowers, and optimism. These were the real things. The rest I went along with obediently, and if my elders chose to mistake obedience for respect, they would have to cope with the consequences.

There was to be a procession round the church, Our Lady, Star Of The Sea. The six most docile of us had been chosen to take part. We were to wear white frocks, carry a lily and a basket of flowers, which we were to take out, one at a time, every six paces, kiss it, and place it on the ground. I would believe the flowers when I saw them, and I tolerated the frock.

Well, me of little faith—as we took our places in the front pews, there they were in front of us, six baskets, a glory of pink, white and blue. I couldn't take my eyes off them, all through the gabbled prayers, responses and dead ritual going on around me. I considered, in an objective way, that this was pretty much what Heaven would be like. There was nothing ecstatic in the thought, just a calm expectation that life would continue to be pleasant.

But strewn with petty irritations. I was at the back of the six little girls, and every time I bent down to place a flower on the ground, the servitor behind me nudged my behind with his knee, sending me staggering forward, just holding off from careening into the girl in front of me. I noticed he made no attempt to hang back. Was he apprehensive of all the other servitors collapsing on to him, like dominoes? I gave him a reproachful look—fruitlessly. We ran out of flowers, but kept it up, like robots, with mindless obedience. Then on the last revolution round the church, my lily broke. Symbolic or what?

* * *

Looking out of the back window in early 1940, I saw a khaki-clad figure coming up the path, with a sheepish grin on his face. I jumped up and down.

"It's Mr Bailey," I shouted. "Mr Bailey's come back, and he's dressed like a soldier!"

CHAPTER TWO

VACKIES

Most people born in the early 1930s can remember where they were on the 3rd September 1939. It was a Sunday, I was at home and, as soon as the air-raid warning sounded, Mum took Jack's and Billy's gas masks to them at St Andrews, where they were at choir practice. They hadn't heard the siren, it was drowned out by the hymns. She insisted they put the respirators on; then when she left, they threw them to one side and carried on singing. Meanwhile, I stood on the doorstep, expecting gas and Germans at any minute, and wondering if the gas would damage my skin—I had no idea about breathing the stuff in.

Although for years afterwards, I assumed that the air raid warning that day was of symbolic significance only, as heralding the announcement of War, it was real enough in intent, but a false alarm. The lone aeroplane that had prompted it, Mum always firmly maintained had been carrying the Duke of Windsor back from seeing Hitler.

We no longer played on the sands. They were now barbed wired up and mined, and no-one was allowed on them. We helped Mr Bailey dig the pit for the Andersen shelter; we were issued with an advice list on what to do when the bombs began falling, and were fitted with gas masks. In a hall in Reading Street, Jimmy screamed when they put the horrible thing over his face. He thought they were trying to suffocate him. Billy, too, thought they were up to no good, but was too stubborn to let on. It didn't affect me at all—yet. Children react like animals do, but respond differently to the same threat. With me it was noise, with Jimmy it was having something put over his face, with the sinister smell of rubber, and the talk of being gassed to death. An animal instinctively draws back. This was all he was trying to do.

We had air-raid drill at school, and practised putting on our gas masks. I had now caught Jimmy's terror, because he had

26

said to me, "You've GOT to put it on, or YOU'LL DIE!" So, when Sister Marie Louise gave the word to put them on, I pretended I couldn't get the lid off the canister. Excited voices from the other children came muffled through their gas masks; it was like a game to them, as they urged me to get the lid off. Sister Marie Louise called me over to her, calmly took the gas mask out of the canister and placed the straps over my head.

Seeing my terrified eyes behind the visor, she smiled and said, "There, you see? That's all right now, isn't it?" I nodded. There's a special place in Sister Marie Louise's Heaven for all those like her, well above the salt. And the ice-cream and scooters, too.

It didn't yet feel like a war, and it's a commonplace to refer to the general belief that it would all be over by Christmas. Pranks went on; Sister Patrick bullied, Mum raged, Ruby bossed, and Sister Marie Louise restored my belief in human nature. Not in religion though. That never came to mean anything to me. Billy and Jimmy continued to pay regular visits to hospital—a broken arm, a live coal in the hand, and various injuries sustained in fraternal conflict. Jack was, as ever, detached. It was a family trait, from Mum's side of the family, oddly enough. We never referred to her sisters and brothers as Auntie or Uncle that I remember. We called them by their own names. We didn't care for toy animals, or stories about humanised animals; we preferred tales about children having adventures. I, for one, didn't like Disney's grotesques, and that includes the cute ones. The Wizard Of Oz left me cold—parts of it I found distasteful, a scene in which children emerge out of giant eggs.

"Ugh," I thought, "that's not how children are born."

We all knew we came from Mum's inside, and used to discuss what we must have said to each other as we waited in turn to be born, and of the things we would do once we got out, and how we couldn't wait for the excitement to begin. It didn't occur to me, at least, that we had had to be put there in the first place; I thought we had been in there all together, waiting to emerge, like teeth.

We were not so much intellectually precocious, as that our intellects were encouraged. We had our Saturday penny, the plate came round on Sunday, and a normal childhood continued on its way.

I decided about this time that I wanted to be a carpenter. I wanted to make things—useful things. This was about the only idea I took from Catholicism. I didn't, however, make the mistake of asking if I could be one. I was beginning to learn the rules. Boys did this, girls did that. It seemed unfair to both. Supposing a boy had wanted dolls, dresses and gentle pursuits? Had wanted to keep house? He could have had my share. This was not a heavy matter with me, but it did seem that boys had more fun, even if they did, unfairly, get smacked more often. Billy, Jimmy and I were bathed together, and I noticed their extra bit with envy. I tried to pee standing up, like them, but I accepted my gender with a shrug, and thought little more about it, even acknowledging the advantages. One day in Junior school, a tennis ball made its way towards me in Games, landed with a thud in my groin, and stayed there. I threw the ball into play, feeling no more than foolish. The schoolmasters laughed, and the nuns smirked.

* * *

The jolly times came to an end on the 2nd June 1940, when the school was evacuated. The contents of the tin hut, of the Convent, and schools in Ramsgate, filled the trains going out from Ramsgate Station, where we milled around with French soldiers. We took our own mug, and food for the journey, which we carried in a pillow case, which in turn was to be used for our bed when we reached our billets. Before setting out for Ramsgate, we had had a goodbye service at Our Lady, Star Of The Sea. As we came out, some boys jeered at us because they had seen Mum crying in church.

None of us knew it at the time, not even Mum, but this was to be the last day we would spend together as a family. Our last day getting up in the same house, eating breakfast together, going to Mass together, getting on each other's nerves, Mum seeing us off to school, standing at the gate as we walked along Victoria Avenue to the turn, Billy constantly turning to shout, "Ta ta, Mum!" Mum calling back, "Ta ta, Duck!" several times, till we turned the corner. She kissed us all Goodbye on the 20th June, 1940, and parting came, abrupt as death.

* * *

No parents were told where their children were going, or how long the journey would be. Some were hungry. A boy sitting opposite me in the carriage looked at me eating a bar of choco- late. He was staring at it keenly. "Would you sell me a square for a penny?" he asked.

Since we had brought plenty of food with us, I was happy to do so. I wish I had given him more, and for nothing, but children are literal—he had only asked for one square. He was delighted. He had probably not had breakfast. Children often did not. And still do not. We also had a large bottle of pop. On the train was a Sister Vincent, from Ramsgate, who demanded angrily to know where we had got it from. She wasn't any happier when she was told we had brought it with us. We were to get to know Sister Vincent, at least the boys were. She never hit the girls, but she attacked the boys with anything she could lay her hands on. She even kept the rung of a chair especially for the purpose. I think she may have come from the infamous Sisters Of Mercy, be- cause her favourite phrase was "You BOLD boy!" This is said to have been common to their vocabulary.

When we reached Stafford, we were herded into the market place, and given a packet of biscuits and a bottle of milk. There were hundreds of children, so many of them crying. It must have sounded harrowing, but for me this was an adventure. Leaving my mother was no problem to me. At seven, I was ready to face the world. It is true that I had set up a wail that morning when we had to let the bus go by. Jimmy and I had left the house first, and were told to go and wait at the bus stop for everyone else. I had a thing about missed buses so, when the conductress heard me cry, she stopped the bus and we got on. This was the last time I was to make such a gesture. All such infant devices were put behind me from then on. During the next two years I would look back on this first seven years of life, regulated though it was by a normal range of discipline and almost Spar- tan living, as if it had been a period of indulgence, licence and affectionate cosseting.

Arrived at Stafford, we were taken from the market place to a hall, to await distribution to billets. The official behind the desk, who clearly had better things to do with her time, demanded of Jimmy, who was taller than Billy, though younger, and whom she assumed was the eldest, "Do you want to go with your brother or your sister?"

In his confusion and tiredness, he replied, "With my brother." (We couldn't have been put together, because of the problem of bedroom accommodation).

Many years later, Jimmy told me that he had had it on his conscience ever since, considering all that was to happen to me. What those bustling officials could not get into their insular minds is that working-class children had the same needs as those of more prosperous parents. Because we were used to putting a good face on things, and had the air of capable street wisdom at the very least, it was taken for granted that things were all as they should be. We were obliged to cope, so it was assumed that we could do so by nature, not circumstance, and the justification brought the circular reasoning neatly into play. The Catholic Church in all this, despite Graham Greene's sentimental assessment of it, that whatever its opinion of you, it was never indifferent, was precisely that. Their interest in us never went beyond seeing to it that our morals were commensurate with our class—that we shouldn't do or have anything that was considered too good for us.

I was taken to an address in Coton Fields, by mistake at first to No. 31, Blakiston Street, to an old couple. They seemed rather baffled to have me, but they gave me a meal, and showed me where I was to sleep.

When I woke up the next morning, for the first time finding myself without my family around me, I felt somehow the shine had gone off the adventure. It was all very well spending one afternoon on my own with German Measles, but this experience had a disturbing shape to it. Just one family member would have been enough, to remind me of the old securities, family strife and all. All this was gone, and an alarming vacuum took its place, into which rushed the threat of the new life. My mouth began to go square with dismay; I felt deserted and bleak. In a terrified attempt to stem this tidal wave of grief, I stifled the tears, and busied myself getting dressed, got my small handbag out of the drawer, and went downstairs.

The mix-up in the addresses was sorted out. I met Billy and Jimmy at school, and we compared billets. The question, "What's *your* lady like?" became a general one, and we compared notes on the state of our billets. Some would envy the material possessions of another, a child would be disappointed, and find that it was not as well furnished, or as clean, as the home they had come from. Or it might be cleaner, with better food. After school, I was taken to No. 36, where the Newbolds lived. There was Jessie, her husband Frank, Grandad Newbold, Doreen, who was twelve, and David, at six, one year younger than I was. The house is at the end of a terrace. There is no front parlour, but a main living-room and kitchen. The indoor passageway has on one side the kitchen, on the other the pantry, bathroom, and near the back entrance, the lavatory. There are the usual three bedrooms. The garden, long and narrow, runs down to the backs, a broad footpath between streets and gardens, and where the gardens of the next street back on to it.

I was allowed the loan of Doreen's doll's house to play with, as an introduction. While I was self-consciously moving the pieces of toy furniture about, they all sat and stared at me, watching and assessing what I did. They had heard stories of evacuees, and our strange habits. I was to hear these stories; how we slept in our boots because the rats might bite our toes; how we were little better than savages. Later on, having seen that my manners were quite civilised, they gave up staring and went about their usual family ways. They relaxed and I played with David.

To claim that I was better mannered, better brought up and brighter than they were, is no kind of boast. They were cattle. I was to discover this bit by bit. Too polite to comment, and too immature to judge, I tried to fall in with their ways. I became confident enough to engage in the normal badinage that her own children exchanged with their mother. She said, on one occasion, "Some mothers do have awkward kids."

I followed this with, "Some kids do have awkward mothers." I should have been warned by the look she gave me.

She was soon to thrash all that out of me, and enjoy the process. Meanwhile, I had to learn the patois. "Do you want a piece?" she asked me, once. I stared at her. What the hell was a piece? She asked me again. I stared, still.

"She's an idiot, she doesn't even know what a piece is." I had to figure out for myself that a piece was a slice of bread and butter.

David thought the way I spoke was comical. I read to him from a book, and he laughed when I pronounced the word 'grass' with a long 'a'.

"She talks like the man on the wireless," he said.

I was deputed to read the comic to him as he couldn't yet read. There was a character in it called Goofy The Ghost. I was told I must say Goofy The Fairy, as he was afraid of ghosts. To be fair to him, this was his mother's doing. She used to tell us how, when she was a child, they used to frighten the living daylights out of themselves with ghost stories round the fire in the evening. They were too afraid to go up to bed, she said. I found myself catching some of this, until it was driven from my mind by real terrorism.

I found David to be a good enough playmate, but his mother treated him like a baby. Until he was eight, she took him on her lap. She would play baby games with him, pretending to cry, which prompted him to do the same, and show us all how devoted he was to her. Because she sensed that I was used to being left on my own, she left the two of us alone in the house one day. For some time after his mother had left the house, he kept calling "Mam! Mam!" He kept it up mechanically, while we were playing; while we played with the gramophone, then Snakes and Ladders, he kept calling for his Mam.

He was allowed to swear freely—he belched exuberantly, and said "Guts!" by way of seeking pardon. He was lavatorially uninhibited; he poked at some faecal matter in the toilet bowl with a knife on one occasion. And when he and I took a bath together, he would, after a few minutes, shout through to the living room, "Mam! I've wee'ed!" I made sure to wash my face before getting in.

Aware that I had not lived down to the reputation of the vackies, Mrs Newbold put it about that the old couple had said I licked my plate; she took my Disney mug and said, "That's not yours, that's David's."

When I protested, she shoved her face at me and bellowed, "No, it's not, it's David's. You're stupid!"

Any money I had left after getting my sweet ration, she told me to put on the sideboard. "It'll be all right there," she said loudly, as if I were an idiot, and shot a glance at the others.

I knew she would take it back, but there was nothing I could do.

I heard her telling the others, "She's an idiot, she'll forget about it." She disapproved of my being called Mary Rose. "Who do you think you are, anyway, having a silly posh name like that. You're Mary, so don't you forget it."

She kept me from school to help with the housework and shopping. The only occasion on which she would not bully me was when we were out in the town, as she looked furtively around for school inspectors, on the lookout for those children who had had the good sense to run away. About half the number did, and their parents took them back, in spite of the Authorities' propaganda assurance that we were being cared for by kind Auntie types. They even printed cartoons showing Hitler whispering to a mother, "Bring them back."

I was helping her with the housework one day, when a nun from the school called to see why I hadn't been to school. She found me doing the dusting. Jessie gave a genteel little laugh. "She enjoys doing these little jobs," she twittered.

I hated them. It put me off housework for life.

The nun gave her a sceptical look, told her, "You are to see that Mary Rose goes to school, punctually and every day," then took her leave.

Thwarted in her use of me as a daytime drudge, Mrs Newbold was determined to enjoy at least giving me a sound hiding before falling into line, because she took reprisal. The details are dim, but she was very violent, and kept hitting, and hitting. I thought, "When is she going to stop? She's got to stop soon." But she inflamed herself the harder she hit. She was quite uncontrolled in her relish, and in the strange new words I had not yet heard (my mother's swearing was only lavatorial, never sexual).

Abandoned in the jeering, taunting words she used as she poked me up the stairs with the clothes prop. "Yer've bin petted and pampered, yer mardy bugger—go on, cry, I should!" And I was indeed, crying uncontrollably by now. I had never met this crudity, this mocking derision, as she jabbed and jabbed at me with the prop. And I descended into Hell.

CHAPTER THREE

DE PROFUNDIS

It is by now an established fact that the more severe the abuse, the less likely it is that a child will tell anyone about it. Like soldiers in battle, they grumble about the little things, because the big things are too overwhelming to cope with. I told Billy and Jimmy only about the petty theft of the Disney mug, and they tried to cheer me up by calling Mrs Newbold, 'Mrs Old Scared'. I don't know what they could have done, anyway, or what their own landlady, Mrs Gibbs' reaction would have been, had they told her. That lady's reaction to Mrs Newbold was to consider her vulgar, and she kept away from her. She would not have liked to interfere.

It is only the confident child who runs away—she knows nothing very bad will happen to her when she's caught. I couldn't have walked into Stafford Police Station and said, "Excuse me, my landlady hits me a lot, and starves me, and does other nasty things."

What I had to tell them sounded too Gothic—the child had been reading too much Hans Andersen. Children exaggerate; it's one of those well-known facts. An adult's compassion is aroused only at the sight and moment of the attack, and at the distress shown at the time. All my terrified crying, at the pain of being struck or humiliated, was done, unheard and unseen by my brothers, sister, or the outer world, behind the walls of 36, Blakiston Street. Safely hidden away—the perfect undetected crime. In the light of day, the authorities would give the benefit of the doubt to the attacker; she would have turned on the tears, I would have been returned to her, and the nightmare would have begun all over again, only worse.

People have asked me, "Didn't anyone see the bruises?" Blows to the head don't show bruises; it's surprising how hard a face can be slapped before the blood vessels break, and starvation doesn't become noticeable until the danger point is reached. There are many ways of inflicting pain or physical distress without leaving marks, and psychological attack is particularly cunning in that the victim gets to inflict the physical damage herself.

David and I would play happily enough, but Mrs Newbold would get bored in the evening, and would set the children on to me. They both took turns, one evening, in slapping my face, for the sole purpose of singing "Poor Mary sits a'weeping," when I could no longer hold off the tears.

Their mother called out, in a casual, quiet, sing-song voice, "Stop it, you two." Clearly not intending that they should, but for the look of it.

I thought I had reached the bottom one evening, when I was sitting in a straight-backed chair. We had been on a long walk, and I was nodding off. Jessie was making a joke of it with the others, and I was trying to stay awake, jerking my head back as I nodded. Then she dipped a piece of bread into her cup of tea, and hurled the bread across the room. It hit me full in the face.

"That can't 'ave 'urt yer, yer big titty babby, it's only wet bread!" she shouted, on my reaction. She was angry, not from conscience, but because there were too many witnesses for her to thrash me. It tended, with her, to be a solitary pleasure. "Er's been petted and pampered all 'er life," she would say, derisively. I was, in her eyes, a misery and a cry-baby.

A beaten child, like a beaten animal, will begin to think she has no right to decent treatment. Parallel to this is the case of the indulged child, who sees no reason why life should not bestow even more goodies and licence, and will even be aggrieved at the thought that someone else is better off. There is no judgement in this statement, it's a human reaction. In much the same way, I began to realise that much worse could be done to the powerless than that which I was going through. I had begun by thinking that I had reached the bottom, but now gained the insight that, in matters of child abuse, there is no bottom.

I wonder at Frank Newbold's lack of reaction to all this. He made no attempt to protect me, and put forward only the mildest objection. On most occasions, he was absent, but even when he was there, I have to assume that either he was too weak to intervene, or that it was something worse; that it was part of a pleasure brief between the two of them. I can't be sure, I can only surmise. Either way, she had absolute power over me, and it corrupted her absolutely.

At some point, she began to starve me. I would be given one

slice of bread for breakfast, she would set the food on my plate separately; always a smaller portion than the others. At a party, she kept missing me out as she took the sandwiches round. "'Er's always stuffin' 'er guts," was an accusation made with tedious regularity, along with jokes and jibes about my putative greed. I marvel at how she managed to convince herself; I was a naturally thin child, and didn't need much to eat, a fact that she took full advantage of.

There was no excuse for her on grounds of rationing. Doreen would sit and grumble as she picked at her food, pushing it round the plate. David would shovel it in, chewing with his mouth wide open, and making loud slapping noises with his mouth. No-one was sickened by it, except me. I hated those eating noises, but didn't dare to complain.

She played sadistic games with my food. On Guy Fawkes night, she made me throw away a baked potato, which she said was underdone. "That's bad for you, that is, throw it away behind the shed. Go on, throw it." I was ravenous by now, but didn't dare to disobey. It was a dreadful time.

I ran a fantasy in my mind; I imagined shouting for my mother, loud enough to carry to Broadstairs, and have her come to collect me. Running away was out of the question; by now I was too intimidated. Besides, I wouldn't have known in which direction to go. Billy and Jimmy, bored with Stafford, had made their way southward of the town, but had been picked up at the boundary. There were authorities at the relevant points, waiting to return children to their landladies. (Foster mother was hardly an appropriate term for some of them; they did it for the money and the ration books).

I began to get painful cramps in my stomach, and would sometimes be doubled up. I went to bed hungry, and woke up in the night to find I was chewing the blanket. I now had to scavenge for food. I picked up the stale bread that even the birds didn't bother with, when I went out to the corner shop. Mrs Newbold saw me from the pantry window, where she had gone to spy on me, and shook her fist at me, as a promise of what to expect when I got back. By now, a gaping hole had been blown in my life.

I began to take cabbage leaves through the allotment fence. A man called over to warn me there was lime on them. Concerned for my safety, he may well have thought that it was only mischief that prompted me. I would eat the berries and leaves from hawthorn trees, known to children as 'bread and cheese' bushes. Birds only bother with the berries, but the leaves are edible, too. I found an almost complete apple on the pavement at the corner of Crookedbridge Road and Gaol Road, outside the corner of the gaol, which staved off the worst of it for the day. I picked up discarded chewing gum; found a dropped sweet now and then.

Some neighbours once gave me a bunch of radishes, "for your supper." I wondered if they suspected anything. On a shopping trip with Mrs Newbold, I was given a few scraps of cooked meat by the butcher, at Rolands' in Gaol Road. He put them on the glass counter and said, "Here you are, love." I thought how strange it felt to be spoken to kindly and called 'love'.

Considering how precious the meat ration was, this seemed an extraordinary gift, until Billy explained that Mr Roland was a master-butcher—Billy used to hear the pigs squealing at the back of the house, as they were being slaughtered. So Mr Roland may well have had plenty to spare. At a time when it was wise to eat whatever meat you could, there is piquancy in the thought that nowadays, I can afford not to eat meat.

I had a surprise gift, in the form of an apple, given to me by the teacher after prayers at hometime. "That's for being the only one with your eyes shut," she told me. A prize for a goodie goodie, but I was only glad about the fruit. The prayers meant nothing.

I managed to get a slice of bread from the pantry one morning, and had stuffed as much of it as I could into my mouth, when I heard Doreen coming down the stairs. I shoved the rest under the mat.

"What are you doing? Aren't you ready for school?"

"Yish," was all I could manage, hiding the food in my mouth.

"What are you talking like that for, with your mouth shut?" I was terrified she would find out, and I'd be punished for stealing food, but remained cool enough to look casually the other way, and she lost interest. She must have been stupid to let go an opportunity like that. She was feeling aggrieved with me because she had caught me sticking my tongue out behind her mother's back as I walked through the inner passage, just as she came round the corner into the house. I was facing away from the subject of my derision, but Doreen got the point of the gesture. She marched me back into the house, told her mother, and looked forward to my punishment. But her mother couldn't be bothered this time, and waved the matter aside. This injustice rankled with the girl — she felt discriminated against. David wouldn't have been treated in this manner.

I might have fallen easy prey to men who offered me sweets, but for my taking them quickly, and running, like a feral animal. I was on my way home from school one day, when an old man from one of the cottages opposite the gaol spoke to me as I walked past. "Would you like a piece of cake?"

I was desperate enough by now to say Yes, and followed him into his cottage. As I sat eating the slice of cake, off the ration then, but all the more chancy to get—it would have to be queued for when the word went round—he sat looking at me.

"Would you like a cup of tea?"

"No, thank you."

"Would you like to sit on my lap?"

"No, thank you. I'd better go now."

I ran off, replete, and at tea time, I only just had room for the little that was set out for me.

I was by now developing a facial habit, under stress, which Mrs Newbold found annoying, and she took appropriate action. I later hear her boasting to a friend, "When 'er starts workin' 'er face like that, I slap it till 'er stops." She felt she'd made quite a breakthrough in child management.

I wonder she didn't write a thesis.

* * *

Grandad Newbold ran an allotment and, in return for collecting horse manure from the road for him, David and I were allowed to go with him to his plot and help or hinder, as the case might be. Early on in my stay, like another age by this time, I had mimicked the old chap, while he was out—he was wont to wind his white silk scarf round his neck, put his flat cap on, take his stick and announce, "I'm gooin' to the gardins." I had got all these props on, and was making the others laugh at my mimicry, when Grandad walked in, and caught me at it. He didn't make a fuss. He had more to concern him than a cheeky kid. And I was to have all the cheek and cheerfulness beaten out of me.

Besides, he had enough trouble from David. The boy was playing with a cardboard plate, skimming it across the room. It hit Grandad on the face, and he threw it into the fire. I thought his daughter-in-law would have a fit. She raved at the old man for his sacrilege. The boy might easily have put the old chap's eye out, of course, but that was nothing compared to the heresy of having thrown his toy away. She had, on an earlier occasion, been accused of throwing a knife at Mr Newbold Senior. She had denied it, and said it was a spoon. She later compromised to the extent of declaring it to have been a fork.

I had a mild altercation one day with David. He took a necklace from me which Mum had given me, and he teased me with it. Not one to wear jewellery, nevertheless the trinket was a talisman, and when David refused to let me have it back, it seemed that the last link with home was gone. It was a million years, and a million miles away, and as he twirled the gaudy beads round his head, I was suddenly overcome with hysterical grief.

By a coincidence, the others were listening to a broadcast report about an evacuation to Canada. Jessie Newbold took this opportunity to pretend that this was what I was crying for; the most grotesque lie she ever told. That I was distressed at the thought of leaving her. I was in no state to contradict, either then, or whenever the subject was humorously raised afterwards.

Grandad Newbold, in a tender-hearted mood, offered me one of his peardrops—itself an unusual thing; it was his invariable choice of sweets ration. I accepted it, but could not have eaten it for choking. As I stood there gasping, he offered me another one. The sweets went sticky in my hand while I battled for control.

Smells stay in the memory longer than more subtle reminders, and is the more primitive trigger of emotion. The smell of peardrops; of nail varnish remover; or of anything containing ascetic acid, remind me of the old man's sudden kindness.

Compared with some, I had been lucky. I had at least had seven years of normal childhood, with nothing worse than the rough and tumble of infant hazard. But there were then, and still are, and will always be, those who have been shat on from birth. Our only recourse is vigilance.

* * *

To my great relief, Ruby came to stay at the Newbold's and, I am convinced, saved my life. I was to be grateful for her spirited attitude and childlike bossiness. Mrs Newbold was at first glad to get another girl—they were popular with land ladies who wanted a drudge—but she soon began to feel the restriction on her sadistic games. Although she kept us both short of food, and continued to take every opportunity to humiliate me, the edge was taken off it, and I felt I could cope. "She's tekkin' advantage," she grumbled, of my dependence on Ruby's protection. However, she did find it meant another ten and six a week for the minimum outlay. Since she fed us so little, and Doreen picked at her food, it's hard to imagine what she did with the spare coupons from our ration books. They were, of course, saleable, and more highly prized than adult ration books.

Mum had left Broadstairs by this time, to look for work in Birmingham. When she took time off to come and see us, I could say nothing to her about my treatment. We went for the day to Stafford Castle, all six of us, where we had tea in one of the rooms—some other tourists put their heads round the door, and drew back quickly; they thought we owned the place. A jolly day out, with laughs like this; to try and talk about Mrs Newbold's behaviour would have been to try to describe a nightmare in broad daylight. Everything looked too normal.

After Mum left, Mrs Newbold continued to talk sweetly to Ruby and me, referring to me as 'Mary Rose', and delicately intoning the 'o' in my name. The shreds of gentility left over from the maternal visit were still in place, and for a while she kept it up. Then she reverted to normal, some half hour later, and suddenly screeched; "MAARAAY! Lay the supper!"

She was of an era when even a working class family could afford to have a girl in to skivvy; some wretch from an orphanage, fed on scraps and screamed at. They aped the behaviour of the class above them — people much like themselves, but for a measure of prosperity, and who knew no better.

One night, when Ruby and I were sleepless with hunger, she crept out of bed and got the toy sweets from an old toy sweet-shop of Doreen's. It was pre-War, but the items were still edible. Little candy vegetables, tiny sugar hams, that sort of thing. Ruby once got hold of some money, maybe some coppers for the cinema, and instead she treated herself to some chips and a bottle of Dandelion and Burdoch. A naturally thin child, like me, the unaccustomed load of food, followed by the gassy drink, gave her the most agonizing colic.

Life sometimes achieved a degree of normality. Grandad

Newbold taught me how to play Dominoes, and how to take snuff; not very successfully, as I sneezed it out again, immediately. This encouraged David to shake the pepper pot at my face, and I sneezed violently until my nose bled. That was the first time I ever saw Jessie Newbold concerned about me. It wouldn't do to have the neighbours see blood on my clothes, after all.

The only other occasion was when David tried to get me to swear. "I won't let you have this bun until you say it," he goaded.

His mother said, mildly, "Don't, our David," not wishing it to be seen who was trying to corrupt whom; it didn't fit her fantasy of where I and he had come from.

She liked a drink, and would get back from a pub outing, having wet herself. "It's the laughing that does it," she explained, still in a good humour. She gave me Guinness, to help me to sleep, but I pulled a face at the taste, and she tried me on cider. I liked this, and a small amount could not have done any harm, but it made me get out of bed in the night, losing its purpose.

I enjoyed playing with other children; the more, the better. I preferred the outside community, and perceived safety in large groups. The street games were still formalised affairs at that time. Kerb or wall, developed in the built-up areas; a race by two children at a time, to the kerb and back, then to the opposite wall and back, the partner doing it in reverse. There were eliminating games; such as Statues, anyone found moving when the principal turned round, was out. On The Mountain, a calling game; and selective games, for example, "Anyone wearing green, take one step forward." There was Tag, of course, called Tig in the Midlands. I think we called it It, in the South East. Posh kids called it He, according to Enid Blyton. I often wondered at that, when I read her dull stories. After all, it was a street game—what were Enid Blyton's little snobs doing playing games that street children played? But then, maybe they played it on the meadow, or on their father's estate.

Frank Newbold worked at Bagnall's, which later became Lansing Bagnall, and is now Lansing's. At Christmas, the children of the employees were given a party. The vackies were invited this year. We had had several little treats already, including a film show at a community hall, where they ran the Charlie Chaplin silent film, The Ice Rink. Mrs Newbold was peeved that David wasn't invited. Anything that I had, he had to have, too. I was kept home after being sick in bed one night, having been to Birmingham on the Midland Red, and having staved off the sickness until I fell asleep. So David had to be allowed to stay at home as well, as "It wouldn't be fair," otherwise.

At the Bagnall's party, some bright clerk had written a song for the kids to sing. The end line of the chorus ran, "B-A-G-N-A double L-S spells Bagnall's." The rude little boys had seen that one coming, and bellowed: "B-A double L-S spells Bagnall's!" instead. The men on the platform grinned, and their ladies gave a thin smile.

For all the fuss that was ever made about bad language and vulgar usage, I had heard all the rude words there were, and are, to be known, by the time I began the Junior School. I didn't know what most of them meant, and could not reconcile some of them to my own anatomy, though I had sense enough not to repeat them in front of adults—they in turn took care, with exceptions, not to mention them in front of me, thinking I had never heard them. Isolated words have never offended me, only the hatred expressed in them, and that applies to the most respectable vocabulary.

The Mayor of Stafford presented each of us with a small gift, we had music and games, were entertained by the adults, with more planned for after the meal, then we sat down to a feast, and I ate well for the first time in months.

CHAPTER FOUR

INTERESTING TIMES

"May you live in interesting times"
Old Chinese curse

Ruby and Jack were taken first to Tamworth, to separate billets. So, apart from Billy and Jimmy, we were all split up. The two younger boys went to stay with Frank and Florence Gibbs, an old couple who lived at No. 2, Izaak Walton Street. Jack was taken to the garden of a public house, and the local families were invited to go along and choose their evacuees. He was the last one to be taken. He went to 24, Dormer Avenue, Boleshall, which was on a council estate. The following October he joined Billy and Jimmy at the Gibbses until 1942. The Gibbses were very tolerant—according to Billy, they must have been pretty saintly to put up with them. They had at first asked for two girls, thinking to have a quiet time of it, but had been sent the boys. This happened a lot. There was something of the military mind about it. Ask them what they want, then give them the opposite. Then Jack joined them and stayed for two years.

When the boy next door, Nobby Wilby, had the idea of a concert party to raise money for the Red Cross, they all got together to find performers. The show that I saw in a hut in Izaak Walton Street—piano accordion, songs, sketches, monologues, conjuring tricks, recitations—was the kind of thing that delighted us and quite frankly, was quite as good as that which passed for entertainment on the wireless or on British films.

On the whole a studious child, Jack was getting an education and working at getting his life started. The Gibbses, in tune with the times, assumed with the rest that children obliged to cope were indeed taking it in their stride. They can't have forecast what a jolt it was to him to be told by them on a Friday evening that he would be leaving them the following day.

During the emergency, it was common for these distressing leave-takings to be made so abruptly, but they were taken aback at the effect it had on him. He had come to regard them, not simply as landlady and spouse, but as foster parents.

He was sent to live, for the next two years, with a family in Oxford Gardens. When he left Grammar School and started work in April 1944, the people he was billeted with made it quite clear that he would have to pay his way at fifteen shillings a week, and at the end of the first week, the landlady asked him for the money. He explained that he was paid monthly, at the rate of twenty-eight shillings and sixpence a week, and that he wouldn't be able to pay them until the end of the month, and even then, it would be in arrears. Once again, he was told on a Friday that he would be leaving on the following day. The billeting officer took pity on him and found him a home in Cambridge Street. He stayed there until he went into the Army, to do his National Service, in 1946.

In the hut in Izaak Walton Street, we found the topical jokes about gas masks and the blackout far funnier than any George Formby film. As for ITMA, It's That Man Again, it was all there was, that's all. Tommy Handley had taken the phrase, usually applied to Hitler, in ironic reference. Comedy was one of the casualties of the War. The talent was either fighting or in ENSA, Entertainments National Services Association, or Every Night, Something Awful. Some theatres closed, and at first so did the cinemas. We were advised not to congregate in large numbers. They gradually began business again, and the film companies made propaganda films, some good, but others obviously made by the military. No concession was made, either to artistic subtlety, or to plain speaking. Defeats became 'strategic withdrawals', a rapid retreat was 'redeployment'. Then it would end with such as " ... and so Fritz shows a clean pair of heels, and our gallant men show the Hun a thing or two!" Fade up the jolly music, to the accompaniment of jeers and whistling from the servicemen in the audience. On the Home Front, we would get a Food Flash, or some Make Do And Mend. Several amazing things to do with a carrot, and how to make a small child's frock from two tea towels.

More jollity with; "Look at Auntie Nellie in her gas mask, doesn't she look funny!" The antiquated, Public School accents were a class difference, more divisive then than now, but a difference held in abeyance for the duration. Nothing during a war on your own territory conforms to normal life—like a kicked ant hill, society is rapidly re-organised. Grand people took slum children into their homes, as a simple duty. It became illegal to strike. What was sedititious became High Treason, and a capital offence. William Joyce, the traitor from Ireland, broadcast enemy propaganda from Germany, and was eventually hanged for it. Women were suddenly valued as more than housewives, and were allowed to take the kind of jobs reserved, often arbitrarily, for men. As in World War One, it was re-discovered that women were quite as capable as men in driving, digging and making munitions, and while it lasted, it must have been an extraordinary time for women—suddenly set free from the kitchen.

If the air-raid sirens sounded during a film, the film would stop and a message flashed on the screen, asking those who wished to leave for the shelters to do so in an orderly manner, then the film would go on. One of my great pleasures was to go to the Odeon children's Saturday matinee, for sixpence. We would be shown a Disney cartoon, always in Technicolour, and a cowboy film in black and white. The cartoons were never very good, certainly not up to Tom and Jerry standard, but I loved the Westerns, badly made though they were. You could always tell when it had been filmed Day for Night, because the actors would have their eyes screwed against the glare, in what looked like moonlight. But it was exciting, there was gallop music, I caught the excitement of the boys, who whistled and shouted, and the baddies would come to no good in the end. They were even, sometimes, politically correct enough to show the native Americans in a sympathetic light, being swindled out of their land by the white man with a dodgy certificate. I even liked the documentary shorts, which most kids groaned at as being 'talking films' on account of the constant voice over. They would tell us things I wanted to know, how things were made in a factory. About war work, or the Land Army. I gave up wanting to be a carpenter. I fancied being a farmer. It was something women were allowed to do. Besides, growing my own food, and being self-sufficient appealed to me. It meant empowerment. I must admit though, that I had a very romantic idea of what farming was about. I imagined golden wheat waving in the sunset, not mucking out the pigs, or getting up early in the winter.

At school, we were given some items of clothing, distributed by a charity. I got a pair of shoes. There remains a memory of walking home from school with Jimmy, and just before he turned off for Izaak Walton Street, of his taking the shoes from me and flinging them over the wall of St George's mental hospital, shouting, "We don't want their bloody charity!" He didn't ask me if I wanted it.

Despite the vividness of this memory, when I saw this same wall a short time ago, I thought it looked far too high for a boy of ten to have thrown anything over it. It is a received wisdom that a human body regenerates itself completely over a period of some seven years. The feet that crossed Crookedbridge Road in 1995 were not the same that trudged back from school in 1941, and the eyes that recognised the high wall running along both the gaol and the lunatic asylum would, in fifty-four years, have undergone seven regenerations, cell by cell, so we might assume that the memory-bearing cells do something similar, and maybe lose something in the translation. Or not.

I was malnourished, and got impetigo. This acted as a counter irritant to the nits in my hair, which were driving me frantic. They had been treated with undiluted vinegar and Derbac soap, both of which the little beasties thrived on. Lack of vitamin C made the skin on my knees split in the cold, the blood radiating across the kneecaps. The teachers asked me if I had fallen, and when I told them I hadn't, they conferred among themselves. I knew it was the cold, because it felt like the cold, but I didn't trust them to believe me. I was accustomed to adults believing only what it suited them to believe, and what the limits of their imagination dictated. They did, however, draw the right conclusion, because Mum sent me a pair of woollen knee-warmers, which never stayed up. The other kids laughed at them. Fortunately, I didn't give a flying toss how I looked as long as my clothes were clean and mended.

The vitamin C deficiency affected most children. Billy found the corners of his mouth bled, and when the oranges came in that were to make good the skin damage, he found the citric acid got into the open wounds round his mouth. Provision vessels were being torpedoed and it wasn't only oranges that were not getting through, but bananas, from across the other side of the world, and dairy foods, now that Denmark was occupied. At one point in the War, the cheese ration for a fortnight would have gone on one round of toast.

Clothing was impractical. Girls had to wear frocks in the coldest weather. Boys had to wear short trousers as a badge of their minority. Long trousers on small boys were disapproved of. They were thought to smack of spivvery. Woollen tights would have been ideal, but the prosperous put their daughters in woollen stockings, and the poor didn't matter. I was to acquire a liberty bodice, one that buttoned up, then later on one that you pulled over your head. This was a lightly quilted, sleeveless garment, that went over the vest and under the blouse. We might have a jumper on top of that. We were eventually issued with pixie hoods, but before that, we went bare-headed, like the boys.

"At least you've got extra hair to keep your necks warm," they would say to us.

"All our hair does is to whip against our cheeks in the wet, and that's worse," we pointed out. Mum bought the boys a leather helmet each, modelled on those worn by the flyers in the RAF. They were regarded by their schoolfellows as the elite. A very high ranking thing, keeping your head warm.

* * *

Mrs Newbold was still trying to hit me on the sneak, when she thought Ruby wasn't looking. But she caught her at it. Ruby saw her from the kitchen, through the living room mirror, giving me a sharp pinch, and quietly mouthing something vicious. "Caught you this time!"

Mrs Newbold was furious, and raved on about it being her own house, and she could do what she liked under her own roof, and so on. Then, in a mood of heroic defiance, she threw a pair of pyjamas over the mirror. She was scandalised that Ruby, a mere girl of fourteen, should not only criticise her, a grown up, but that she should break the rules of fair play. We left her to her own degraded sense of right and wrong, and escaped to school.

By now, the tin hut school at Broadstairs had been taken over by the Scouts, and this was its last occupation. The place is taken now by a low-level block of flats. One tree, little more than a sapling before the War, now reaches level with the roof of the flats.

The Home Secretary told us we needn't carry our gas masks any more. The occasional air raid alerts we got in Stafford were no more than a break in lessons. The shelter routine continued. First prayers, then a sing-song, then the All Clear would go. Prayers again, and back to school.

Mum moved up to Birmingham, then settled in a job with the Midland Red. She had wanted to drive a bus, but Digbeth Garage, now the National Express Coach Station, was the only garage that didn't allow female drivers. However, the Midland Red, unlike the Birmingham Corporation buses, did at least go out into the countryside, instead of going back and forth across the city. Ernie Bevin didn't want women working on the buses at all. Fortunately, the union overrode him, and insisted on women getting a wage equal to men's. The idea had slowly filtered through that women, too, have children to feed, and at last Mum was getting a wage to live on.

I can't remember the day in 1942 that I left the Newbold's. There was no dramatic rescue, no grand resolution. But I noticed a sudden improvement in Jessie Newbold's behaviour towards me. Gullible as I was, I thought it was a genuine change of heart, and began to think I wouldn't mind staying there after all. In reality, Ruby had told Mum some of what had been going on, and arrangements were being made to move me on. And so, without knowing it, I escaped the inevitable escalation of abuse that occasionally ends in a child's death, or more often damages it irreparably.

Mrs Newbold was in danger of losing her drudge, the money and the ration book; hence her conversion to sweetness and light. It took the form of gross flattery of everything I did. My putative idiocy was already on hold whenever David had to be read to, so she couldn't fix on that. Instead, because I had just learned how to knit, the neighbourhood had to be told how clever I was, like a monkey that can dance.

"I don't know how she does that—casts on with her thumb," she babbled to friends or to children who called.

"That's not such a big thing," mumbled the girl from next door but one. She had just recovered from pneumonia, and I had called on her at her house, where she lay in bed, with a new Shirley Temple doll, quite a big one. I guessed that her parents thought she might die, hence the doll. I wondered just what a child had to do to gain affection and an expensive present. On my way to school with a friend, we saw a girl who was billeted in Crookedbridge Road being carried out, wrapped in a red blanket.

She had diphtheria, and smiled at us from the arms of the ambulance man. Joan, my friend, said, "Well, I've got a penny she gave me, so if she dies I'll have something to remember her by." It's the sort of thing children do say, although neither of us knew how ill she was. However, she didn't die, and was back at school within a few months' time. I saw another child, who caught polio, got better, but gradually developed a limp, as one leg, though still fit for walking on, ceased to grow. Her gait became more and more exaggerated as she continued growing, until she was bending her trunk sideways at 45 degrees, I couldn't believe how straight and fit she had been, and how casual life's cruelties are. I was to be given, later on, some clothes that had belonged to a child who had died. My friends thought it was morbid, but to me, they were just clothes, which I needed.

1942 was a hot summer, and in the school holidays we rambled over the Staffordshire countryside, getting brown and coming back with armsful of bluebells. It was when we came into the kitchen one late afternoon in early autumn, flushed, thirsty and chattering, and replete with summer's pleasures, that Mrs Newbold remarked, "Look, even Mary's cheered up now."

Even at that age, I wondered what kind of moron she must be, not to have made the connection between my earlier distress and what had been the cause of it. But right now, I was content with life, as we gathered around the sink to wash the gooseberries we had picked, and which we would have with our supper. We were allowed to play outside until nearly ten o'clock in the summer, and as we came off the Rec, and the last of the children would be going indoors, some still in the swimming costumes they had played out in all day, I considered that I was happy.

* * *

After leaving Stafford for the last time, I went with Mum to her digs in Small Heath, near the Haybarn recreation ground. I would play on it on my own all day until the landlady's children came home from school, then we would all go and play on the bank of the River Cole, which was little more than a stream, but a rich playground for imaginative children. The other kids tried to pick on me at first, but with Mum's help, I turned their minds to other forms of play. It's a pointless instinct, the need to pick out a victim, its unhealthy excitements still a lure for the bored child, its function lost in the discontinued rites of early evolution.

Mum took me around to as many friends as she could, to get

me settled enough to get back to school, but none of them had room. I wanted a family round me, a big one, for safety. One place we went to seemed to fill the bill, and as the evening drew on, I tried to ingratiate myself by reading stories to the younger children, all to no avail.

Eventually, one of Mum's fellow workers, another conductress called Winnie Williams, arranged to take me in. She lived with her elder sister, Nellie, and their mother, and although they had two Scottish young women lodging there, on war work, I could be squeezed in, sharing a bed with Winnie. 'Squeezed' was the operative word. All the Williamses were big women, and after the Scottish women left, two vast young ladies from Hull came to stay, to work on munitions. But this would be later. For the present, Mum, Winnie and I went to London, for a holiday.

Ever since I was five, London was the place to which I aspired. I had heard it was big and exciting. Even bigger than Margate. We stayed at Granny's house in Penge, and explored the city by day. As this was 1942, what greeted my eyes was not at all what I expected. I had looked forward to seeing grand stores, huge, elegant parks, bright lights and famous people. The parks had anti-aircraft batteries in place, there were bomb sites, with the rubble cleared and boarded off, blasted shops, with Open As Usual, or More Open Than Usual, chalked on a board; and the bright lights would have to wait for several years. Windows were taped across to take the impact of flying glass. Bus windows had sheets of yellow perforated paper gummed to them for the same purpose. Someone must have made a tidy sum, producing such practicalities. Mum carried a torch, which she neglected to keep pointed towards the ground.

Someone passing us in the dark shouted, "Don't flash that light about, don't you know there's a war on?"

"So that's what all that bloody noise was last night, was it?" Mum shouted back.

When we got back to Birmingham, we were met at the door by Nellie, who told us I couldn't stay after all. Their mother had gone into hospital with appendicitis. I would have to go back to Stafford for a while, so we turned back right then and went back to Mum's lodgings in Golden Hillock Road, which she'd taken because it was nearer to Digbeth.

While I had been away from Mrs Newbold, she had gone to Tenterbanks Road School and spoken to Jimmy through the railings. "Can Mary come back?" she asked him, "We liked her really." Of course she did. She missed the weekly ten and six, and the rest. As Jimmy reports the memory, she had a mouthful of rotting teeth, and he couldn't take his eyes off them.

On my return, she asked me, "Did yer cry in the air raids?"

"No," I told her, unwilling to admit that I was afraid of them.

"I canna understand you," she said, "Yer dinna cry at air raids, and yer didn't blart when next door's dog bit yer, nor when yer gashed yer knee, but I've only got to give yer a tap, or shout at yer, and yer cry like a babby."

Some tap; some shout.

As for air raids, it was only after long exposure to broken nights of appalling noise that I became really terrified. It would cure my constipation every time. Like Pavlov's dogs, we responded to the sirens themselves. As the wail went up, our bowels turned to slush. At the very point at which we were advised to stay indoors, it became necessary to go out to the lavatory. (When I learned that some people had their lavatory indoors, and worse still, in the bathroom, I was shocked. To my prim mind, the only proper place for it was outdoors, where it could be politely ignored).

Whoever designed the air raid siren had a rotten sense of psychology. It sounded like a tormented soul in Hell; an oscillating wail, some five seconds up, five seconds down. We would hear its hateful lament sometimes first in the distance, sometimes nearby, depending on which stations were the more alert. Then the other stations would take it up, one by one. We would hear the far off ones in between the dips and rises of the nearest one, and wonder if we would still be alive within the next three minutes.

The single note of the All Clear, on the other hand, was a symphony orchestra, as each siren took its cue and sent up it Hallelujah of relief. Though frankly, it would have sounded as sweet through the medium of a rusty klaxon.

Mum had got the key to No. 3, back of 27, Adelaide Street, in Balsall Heath, towards the end of 1942. It was a back-to-back house, part of a street length building, interspersed with entries at every four houses, or rather, eight, since the front and the back constituted two houses. Through the entry into the yard, which was held in common by the eight households, four at the front of each court, four at the back, there was a line of four lavatories, two households to a lavatory, and a washhouse, or brew'us, which was common to all. Mum used the sink indoors, instead. This was placed at the top of the cellar, with a cold tap. Above the cellar, the other three rooms of the house were stacked on top of each other. There were, of course, no bathrooms and no gardens to these houses. The bottom room had a gas stove in the corner opposite the cellar corner, at right angles to the stairs door, with just enough room to open it and squeeze through. The food cupboard was at right angles to the window, where Mum left her handbag on the table overnight, in a heatwave, with the window open. The handbag was stolen, and later returned by the Police. It had been handed in to them by a gents' toilet attendant in the city, who had found it in a cistern. Ten shillings had been taken out, and the family photo of the five of us outside the Bungalow Cafe, on the seafront, was streaked, but still recognisable. The only furniture in the bottom room was the table, a straight chair, and the green trunk. The rent, at first, was five shillings a week.

It is mistakenly thought that 'back-to-back' means those houses whose gardens back on to others in the next street. The occupants of these would have been indignant to be classed together with the tenants in Adelaide Street. These were built to house the workers in the surrounding factories, and the streets bore the surname and children's names of someone of such importance that no-one had ever heard of him. There is MacDonald Street, and branching off, Charles Henry Street, Adelaide Street and Angelina Street. Adelaide Street is now a parking lot.

Balsall Heath was, until recently, Birmingham's red light district. In fact, our part was Highgate, but later on in life I referred to it as Balsall Heath. This was inverted snobbery, inherited from my father, and flourished like a scarlet banner. On my birth certificate, under 'Father's Occupation', he had had written, General Labourer, although he was a cook-baker when he could get the work. It just happened that he was a general labourer at the time, and didn't see why he should be embarrassed by it. Since my mother was irked by his attitude, I assume him to have been more of a natural Socialist than she was.

After I had turned my back for ever on the Newbold's, I stayed for a time at a house in King's Heath, where Ruby worked as a live-in childminder and housekeeper. The Woodwisses worked on the Corporation buses, and had two young children, Josie and Terry. Someone for me to play with and to read to. Their mother was a kind woman, who fed me properly, and took good care of me.

When she discovered head lice on her own children and on me, she didn't reproach me with having brought them there, although it's quite likely that I did; she told Ruby about it, and Ruby told her, "Well, I think they use vinegar to get rid of them." Instead of saying "Oh, you know about it, do you?" as someone less caring would have done, she expressed her gratitude and got on with it.

People were often too embarrassed to go to the chemist for help, less still the doctor, so they struggled along with these folk 'remedies' and hoped for the best.

"Ow, it stings!" her own children cried, so she diluted it for them. For all the good it did, she might as well have diluted it for me, too.

When I ran in one day complaining that Terry had been throwing stones at me, she sat him on the table and smacked his legs hard. He howled with dismay at his mother's treachery—turning on her own to protect an interloper. By now nine years old, I felt terrible about it. What a little sneak. He was only a silly kid, after all. I believed I should have handled it myself.

Ruby became dissatisfied with the job, and walked out, taking me with her, to Balsall Heath. The Woodwiss children were left on their own. Mum was out on a turn when we got there, and when Mrs Woodwiss called round to ask what was the reason, Ruby wouldn't answer. "I only want to know why, and why you didn't give me notice," Mrs Woodwiss called plaintively from the yard.

Ruby was more spirited than I was. She had left the Newbold's, shortly before I did, simply by getting on a Midland Red bus in Stafford, and asking to go to Birmingham. She had no money on her, and she must have told the conductor who her mother was, and that her fare would be paid when they got to Digbeth Garage. Jessie Newbold had made her drudge as much as she had me. She would say to Ruby, "I've got my period on, Ruby; do the-housework for me, there's a pal." As she tried this one on about every fortnight, she must have thought Ruby was as stupid as herself.

I stayed at Adelaide Street with Mum, going with her on her turns, unless they were late. On such an occasion, her friend from work, Tommy Moran, called. On instructions, I ignored his knocking, until I was sure of his bona fides, when I eventually unlocked the door and peered out. When I explained things to him, he said, "Has your Mammy left you all on your own now? What a terrible wicked woman she is!" He didn't mean it that way; he was just being Irish. He had been across to the Republic and brought back a load of unrationed goodies, including sweets to the value of an English pound, and which filled a drawer.

To this day, I don't know what we talked about. I had nothing to say, so he rattled on about what a terrible price tea was in Ireland, and would I like a slice of ham. It was something I would have given my soul for a few months ago, but I was not a big eater, and declined.

Mum was delighted to see her friend, and to show me there was nothing wrong with the proffered bonne bouche, she had a few slices herself, and we all relaxed. The fact was, food was still a nervy subject with me. I soon got full up, and had simple tastes anyway.

I enjoyed going with her on her turns. There was a rhythm to it. The bus would leave Digbeth, empty except for the driver, Mum and me, pick up workers till we were full; lumber across to Singer's or Austin's, or whichever, and empty, then rattle along fast out into the country. I'd got my sea legs by now and could enjoy the trip. Schoolchildren would get on later, and after they had dropped off, a few quiet hours' run back and forth over the route, taking people who were out for the day, or shoppers who had missed a Corporation bus and had the extra sixpence to spare.

Trolley buses, horse-drawn milk floats brought out of retirement for the duration of the War, and cars with huge gasbags on top. Plenty of bicycles. Posters asking us, Is Your Journey Really Necessary? Or telling us, Careless Talk Costs Lives. More mysterious ones with the initials, VD printed very large, and an unremembered slogan urging us to Clean Living. I determined to wash my neck more thoroughly. Requests to save paper, tin, and rubber, and to Make Do And Mend, and to beware of the Squanderbug (people on war work were getting better wages than they had ever had, and than they would subsequently have after the War). Pigbins at every twenty houses or so for food scraps and peelings. Railings missing, taken, with worn-out saucepans to be melted down for munitions. A Government initiative of Let The People Sing, between films, the words on the screen, and a bouncing white dot on the syllables for us to follow. I don't remember any audience breaking its British reserve sufficiently to join in. It was bad enough, feeling grim, without the pretence of jauntiness. People did of course let their hair down, but only as the mood swung them that way, from deep depression and terror, to frenetic jollity.

Workers' Playtime on the Light Programme, held at midday at a different factory canteen each day. Dance Halls and cinemas 'Free To Servicemen In Uniform'. Greengrocers with only indigenous produce; fruit only in season. They displayed large colourful placards of tropical fruits, but we resented these tantalising reminders—we'd rather not know what we were missing. Recipes for Woolton Pie. We wondered if Lord Woolton ever ate his recommended pie himself, and doubted it. Money bought more than rations. If you could afford it, you could have an entire week's meat ration on one meal, from restaurants with special dispensation. Hats were the only item of clothing that didn't require coupons, so women tended to treat themselves to one to cheer themselves up. Elastic was almost impossible to get.

It's very easy to forget the mood of the time, and to put, if not a rosy gloss on the memory, then a certain sepia glow, in which everyone was always stoic, and heroic, more likely to share than to cheat, when in reality, we were no worse and no better than we are now. Crisis and emergency exaggerated *both* of these human reactions. The past is a safe place to visit; we know the script and the outcome. But then, we didn't. We thought of defeat, and a Nazi occupation. We couldn't endow the present danger with a Dad's Army jollity—could not foresee the pleasure of revisiting it from the safety of fifty years hindsight.

"Everybody does it," was the justification for getting something from 'under the counter'.

The 'everybody' in this case meaning those who had the means, and the contacts. I felt guilty when I helped Mrs Williams get an extra Swiss roll. We joined a queue at Wimbush's; she gave me sixpence and told me to stand behind her as if I were on my own. When we got home, she told the woman next door about it, and the neighbour said, pointedly, that the last one got sold just before her turn. Mrs Williams brazened it out, and repeated the story of her triumph. The neighbour repeated her gentle grievance. Fact of life—adults embarrass children.

* * *

On Mum's day off, we went into the city. She took me to the Birmingham Art Gallery to see the newly acquired Epstein, Lucifer. On his invisible bike, according to the irreverent critics. There were several contemporary works on a wartime theme. A picture of WAAFS erecting a barage balloon.

"He's cheated," I said, "he's used silver paint for the balloon."

It was a new thing for me to see pictures that were not religious, or allegorical. There was nothing deeper in them than what was represented on the canvas, like the Paul Nash water colour, of aeroplanes and vapour trails, criss-crossing and swirling round the sky.

The pictures of the Virgin and Child bothered me rather, especially the early ones. It didn't look like a baby, more like a miniature adult, making pious gestures with its hands. The Epstein bronze of a new-born baby's head, on the other hand, looked exactly as I felt it should, and was my favourite sculpture. Of the pictures, the pre-Raphaelites appealed to me the most. All that detail to hold the attention—all those items to read. And I had absolutely no quarrel with a work of art that had a message. That was its original function. The one that Mum liked the best was an oil painting of a foundry; she loved bright splashes of colour, and the molten metal emerging from the furnace, showering sparks as it went, gave her the visual excitement she looked for.

The rocks and fossils upstairs stood in defiant contradiction to what the Catholic Church had told me about the creation of the world, and was far more magical. Beetles the size of a small dog, a gigantic amethyst in a geode, explained to me as a jewel formed in a concrete bubble, under tremendous heat and pressure. I thought, "I must come here again some day," a promise to myself I've kept a hundred times.

Mum loved to eat out. It made a nice change to be waited on, so we often went to the affordable restaurants and cafes. This was the first time I had heard the dessert course referred to as a sweet. I had only known it as pudding. It has become fashionable to call it this once again, not always with accuracy, since the word implies a processed mixture—fruit and cream is not a pudding, but ice-cream surely is. These outings would constitute a special treat for Mum; worth her taking it to the limit of her purse to go for waitress service, and the kind of tip she would have appreciated herself.

* * *

All this while, though I was now back with my mother, I had lost human contact with her. The events that had thrown us apart could not be patched together with goodwill. I had forgotten how to be a child—the kind of child she wanted; jolly, mischievous, and readily affectionate. She had known only that I had been unhappy, and not the whole story. I had lost the opportunity to become more like herself. I was this polite, wary alien, older than she was in certain ways, remaining immature and stunted in others. This showed itself in something that happened on a Birmingham to Stafford run. When we reached Stafford terminus, I said I would stay upstairs in the bus until the turn-around.

She looked amused, and to my disbelief, said, "Are you afraid she'll come after you and get you?"

This shut the door on any hope of liaison with her. I can cope better with blustering disbelief. It at least implies an appalled refusal. Surly justification—"Well, you deserved it anyway," is tolerable as indicating a sulky acceptance.

But trivialisation is the worst response. I didn't know how to answer it. Tears would have been too painful, and would have made things messier. I didn't know how to do indignation; and my mouth was finally stopped. I would have to bottle it up; to slam the lid on the pressure cooker and smash the gauge in.

* * *

At about this time, Mum took us all to Jerome's to have a group photo taken. It was in High Street, at the top of the Bull Ring. We were to sit on a bench, in order of age, but Billy hated to conform and wouldn't take his place in the middle of the bench, and sat glowering on the end, turned aside from the camera. In the earlier family picture, the one that found its way into the public cistern, Billy can be seen, out of place on the edge of little Bentons, caught for ever with his mouth engaged in some defiant declaration. Happily, he never changed. The photographer, a patient young woman, must have had a measure of success in getting us lined up, because the picture got taken, and we all got up and went for a meal at Lyons, before returning to our various homes. We had for a few hours become, artificially, a family again—it was now time to return to real life.

Jeromes was bombed the following week, and the photograph was lost to the nation. The building is now a hole in space, a few yards north of the road that sweeps the traffic on to Spaghetti Junction and on its way to London.

CHAPTER FIVE

PENGE—1943

"I was the only child in World War Two to be evacuated to London." Not strictly true, but it's a shame to spoil a good story with the truth, as Mum used to say.

It was decided I should stay with Granny, in Penge, as Balsall Heath was not the best place for a child, and a conductor's working hours were disruptive. Our uncle, Stanley, lived with his mother, and was exempted from military service on account of childhood polio having struck him at the age of two and a half. He remembers nothing of it, nor of ever having the use of his right arm.

Mum used to tell us of how, when he was in fever, he would say, "The birdews are coming, Mummy, here come the birdews," an hallucinatory image that makes me think of Wagner's Valkyries swooping over his cot. His extravert ways helped him to keep up with the other boys.

"He does it to compensate for being disabled," Granny would say, "he wants to prove he's as good as the rest." As indeed he was.

A curious side-effect of the illness was an astonishingly acute hearing. He could hear a beetle scuttle across the floor. "A likely story," declared his sister Ruby, then he repeated every word of a quiet conversation in the kitchen that he overheard from his bedroom. This brought the forceful response, "Huh! You *must* be mad to be able to do that!" This was the nearest she would admit to accepting it.

One of the highlights of his youth was the occasion on which he learned to ride a bike. It's hard to convey the exhilaration on being able to move so quickly, to have suddenly, so much control over his movements—his enthusiasm for the memory remains to this day.

I watched everything he did, fascinated. Simple enough to cut the fingernails of his right arm, which he swung on to his knee, while he cut with his left hand, but he even cut the nails of his left hand himself, holding the scissors between his knees. He lost patience only once that I saw, when he had trouble sewing on a button. He threw the garment down, and jumped up and down, stamping on it.

Granny referred to it as "That time you did your little dance of rage," about the most cutting remark of which she was capable. No-one made the mistake of offering to sew the button for him. He was already furious with himself.

Our two aunts lived with Granny, as well. Cissie, whose husband, Bert, was in the Navy, and Barbara, who was sixteen when I joined them, at the age of nine.

Granny, who wouldn't say boo to a goose, had gone to Stafford for a while; she had a bed-sit at the Vine Hotel, while Stanley went to stay with the all-welcoming Mrs Gibbs. The people in Stafford resented evacuees and were rude to her; they called them bloody refugees. I remember her being in tears when Mum and I called on her once.

A restaurant proprietor had tried to bully her and Cissie by telling them "You can't sit there," several times. Cissie put the pompous oaf in his place by telling him to shut up. They stayed where they were. People didn't pick a fight with the inaptly named Cissie. Mum's favourite story of Granny concerned a newspaper report of a judge who had criticised a prostitute for refusing her services to a man who considered himself to be a gentleman, in the definition of the time.

"What a cheek," my mother's mother had said, "she should please herself who she takes as a customer." In her stand for fair play, she had taken what Mum considered to be quite an enlightened attitude for the time.

I was now living with people I could relate to, in both senses. They understood the family traits I bore, particularly that of detachment; they possessed it in a more marked form than did my immediate family. I think Cissie would have preferred around her a child more ebullient than I seemed to be, but I would need time to get the bounce back in me.

The house has one entrance only, from the street, and no access to the garden except from the house. There are no 'backs' between the streets. I don't remember if it had a bathroom, though it has a front room, which was seldom used, a middle room, which looks on to the narrow side yard and beyond which lies the garden, long and narrow. To the side of the yard is the kitchen, where we had our meals, and the scullery, which served as the kitchen proper. Outside, to the side of the scullery, was the lavatory. The Anderson shelter was at the front of the garden, but Granny preferred to chance it.

"I'd rather go at once, in the comfort of my bed, than catch pneumonia."

Official advice was to put a bed under the stairs—this part was most often standing, when the rest was in ruins. However, the space under the stairs had only room for brooms and brushes.

Life was beginning to look up. Granny was appalled that no-one had bothered to teach me to tell the time, not even at infant school. After that, it had been assumed by other teachers that I must have been taught it, and as I got older, it became less possible to admit it. This was now put right in a matter of minutes. Another landmark arose in my life at this time.

When I had been getting underfoot, Granny said, "Why don't you go and join the library?" So, for a token penny a year, I signed on at one on Anerley Hill. I found it to be an astonishing eye-opener. I wondered why no-one had told me about it before. School books had been chosen for their worthiness—Enid Blyton's was the approved style. I found them dull and mechanical; they were stories that the author found had 'written themselves', and it showed. The stories of Margaret and Mary Baker were little better.

The library was now to yield up the brothers Grimm, Hans Andersen, Noel Streatfield's runaways and ballet girls, little-known authors of schoolgirls 'pigging in the dorm', and a wonderful book about bees, whose chapters alternated between the insect's social life, worthy of David Attenborough, and stories of myth and lore.

Most people who enjoy reading can remember the first book that impressed them. Someone had bought me *Peter Pan*, and I used to sit and read it on the step of the Anderson shelter, or curled up in the corner of the kitchen, with the cat, surrounded by her kittens, as absorbed as she was. Once past the early chapter of nannies and playrooms, Barrie's book had the classic ingredients; leaving home, a quest, a trial, a battle, and home-coming. And a line that jumped out at me—"To die will be an awfully big adventure."

Profound in a different way was *Alice Through The Looking-Glass*. This had the flavour of my own nightmares. Its cruelties were not questioned, nor recompensed. I identified with it. "I'm thirsty," said Alice. "Have a biscuit," said the Red Queen. And from the final pages of *Alice In Wonderland*: "You're nothing but a pack of cards!" words from which I began to take my attitude to life, as a secret reassurance.

* * *

I was given sixpence a week pocket money. Twopence halfpenny would buy a Mars bar or a Milky way, or if I wanted something that would last, two ounces of boiled sweets, though not pear drops. A small bottle of Tizer would be twopence, and the remaining penny-halfpenny would be spent on either the Beano or the Dandy. The choice took some time, and I would usually settle for the Beano; I thought it less babyish. I would sit in the kitchen with these fleshly pleasures and literary delight while Granny did the housework around me. I felt guilty at not helping her but then, she never asked. Had she done so, I would have leapt to help, but I had a complete lack of initiative. It nor more occurred to me to offer to help than to ask for another three ha'pence to buy the Dandy.

Our other two uncles, Kenny, in the Army, and Alfie, an Observer in the RAF, I only saw when they came home on leave. Kenny's image is not clear in my mind, but I seem to remember a rather square face. Alfie was a small man, whose face crumpled up as he smiled, and he smiled a lot. He inherited his lack of height from his father, who was four feet, ten inches. This was passed on to Billy, who is five feet two. Stanley's face I remembered as oval but full; his characteristic gesture of hitching his right shoulder up I always assumed to be compensating for the lack of weight on that side.

When Alfie was on leave, I pestered him to let me take his field glasses out into the garden, which he eventually did. But what I really wanted from that quiet, reserved family was attention, play and fun. I had forgotten how to ask for it, so I resorted to making a nuisance of myself, until my conscience urged me to stop. After that, I went around by myself, between the parks and the library, happy enough to be on my own. I always could stand my own company.

There was a daylight raid on Lewisham on the 20th January, 1943. It was my tenth birthday, and Granny suggested I take my birthday cards to school. It would help me to make friends. In the shelter, a surface building next to a garden, the teacher welcomed the diversion. She seemed more nervous than the children. In the way that adults do, she would have felt responsible if we had come to harm. I had, as yet, little experience of raids. It was, besides, to be the night raids that terrified me; the noise and the dark.

With this captive audience, and my new-found confidence, it was not hard for the teacher to persuade me to show my birthday cards around the class, and to extend the good feeling by getting me to sing a party piece. In the middle of basking in all this, the teacher suddenly shouted, "Down, everybody!" as she dived under the opposite bench.

Then, in the short space of time she believed we all had, she did something that makes me smile even now. She gabbled out the shortest prayer in the canon. "Glory be ... gabble, gabble ... and to the Holy Ghost Amen" then the door blew in against the wall. Considering that we had said prayers as soon as we took our places in the shelter, she need not have tried to save our souls; there wasn't much Hell-bound wickedness we could have got up to in ten minutes, if you don't count my singing.

I was never able to hear the bombs whistling as they came down, and I don't know how ears older and acknowledged to be less keen than mine could distinguish the sound from the rest of the awful din. Adults around me would talk knowledgeably of the hum of the engines, and how they could tell a Wellington from a Dornier. The only sound I could pick out from the rest, apart from the chattering of my teeth from the knocking of my knees, was the sound of a Bofors gun, which sounded like the slamming of a heavy book, with a short echo in its thud. That, and the recognition of Alfie's RAF insignia; Navigator, later called Observer, summed up my entire knowledge of matters military.

This same teacher was among the better ones. She had enthusiasm for her job and loved to talk to the class about the things she was keen on. She would begin with one subject, skip to another and ramble, firing our imaginations with her acquired knowledge. We learned more from that long, meandering dissertation than we ever could from the eyes-to-the-front, serried ranks, dogged rote. I swear that the reason I had such difficulty with arithmetic, apart from being naturally non-numerate, was the insistence of the recitation of the times table. (It might have helped if we had been allowed to *look* at them while we recited). This attempt to thump the figures into our brains was responsible for the numbing effect that prevented my thinking through the sum at all. A concrete link would have helped, though not oranges at a penny-farthing each. The oranges don't represent numerical abstractions. But 'four sevens equal a lunar month', for instance, do. To make me remember a misdemeanour, I had to write out a hundred times ... what? For the life of me, I can't remember. But I do remember being barred from a swimming lesson for having mimicked the teacher, on the bus on the way to the baths.

Not all teachers were as bright as this. One of them had been telling us about Malta, and the ferocious bombing it had been taking. Suddenly, she turned to me and snapped, "Which area in Europe has been the least bombed?"

Caught off balance like this, I heard myself say, "Malta."

The class went wild, which was what she had intended. Bored with her job, she had played the trick of picking out one child, tripping her up with a meaningless question, and getting the rest of the class on her side. The *least* bombed? She hadn't even mentioned it. Besides, what might I have said? Stockholm? Madrid? Dublin? A more sensitised child would have been destroyed by these cheap tricks. Still detached from the rest of the human race, I learned only to despise her.

Betty Turner came running up to me on the way home, and said, "Don't think you're so clever in class, just because you're good at English. I'm good at English and arithmetic!" At least I would escape being the class prig while she was around. I've always been puzzled at hatred directed at someone not well known to the subject. I can understand someone who knows me, hating me. There's logic in it, if not charity. It works in the other direction. To understand is not necessarily to forgive — sometimes the reverse.

The night raids were beginning to get to me. Sometime after the War, when combatants were able to talk and write about it, I read a story written by an airman. The alert sounded, routinely, as the enemy bombers headed for the aerodrome. He was walking along a corridor, at the end wall of which hung a wall map, and which he happened to have in his line of sight as the siren wailed. His mind must have been off guard; the filters shifted slightly, and the terror flooded in at last. Night after night of enemy attack had made their mark. Still too disciplined to take flight, his senses knew he was part of the target as did his brain, and they reacted vividly. As if in the instigation of a fetish, the wall map became part of the experience, and in some Pavlovian sense, carried with it the threat.

Years before I came to read this passage from the airman's story, something similar happened to me. On the Crystal Palace grounds, there was a battery of rockets, in units of about four. These were discharged constantly during an air raid, at a terrifying volume. At the end of an ordinary day, after battling with bullies and long division, I walked into the kitchen, my line of sight taking in the wainscoting on the far wall. It went up to about four feet, and was in vertical slats of brown painted wood. I used to ledge my pencils on the top of it. The sirens went, dread flushed its way through me and sent the miserable tingling through my limbs, as I waited for the drone of engines, the thump of bombs, and the rockets in the Crystal Palace grounds. The three factors, the siren, the wainscoting and the danger, all rushed together in my head, and I was trapped.

Stanley tried to cheer me up with a very rude story about the paper shortage, and by demonstrating his ability to break wind at will. He also recommended I sit in the corner by the chimney breast, for safety, but it only pressed home the point I was trying to ignore. Granny colluded by lighting joss sticks to wave over Stanley. The cat did her bit by shredding a Beano. She was in kitten again. Cissie carried on with normality by making her nightly cocoa, and poured her liquid paraffin on it. I don't know how she could drink it; it floated on top and you could see through it to the cocoa.

While he was outdoors during a raid, Stanley saw a bizarre sight: an anti-aircraft team dragging a Bofors gun through the streets, discharging it at intervals.

It was not until after the War that people generally spoke of their narrow escapes. While you were coping with it your mind was occupied. Besides, you didn't brag about your luck; the gods were listening.

The school made its concession to lost sleep. We were allowed to arrive at school at half past nine. As for history lessons, we were given the impression that Britain, or England, only ever won a battle or a war. Morale had to be kept up and an optimistic slant put on matters. What current affairs we were allowed to know about were acknowledged to be history in the making.

Churchill toured the devastated streets, calling out cheerily to the bombed-out occupants, "Britain can take it!"

"Well, you bloody can," they shouted back, "you're not short of somewhere to live!" They carried on sorting through the rubble.

Having moved round quite a lot, I hadn't had time to make friends. Thrown on to my own resources, I became more aware of adults' behaviour, and noticed the way they talked. I was sitting on the roundabout in the park on Anerley Hill, next to the library, listening to two young mothers on a bench, with their prams by them.

"I only change him if he's dirty. Not if he's only wet. It's good for them. If he's dirty, of course, I'll change him. But if he's only wet, I'll leave him … Being wet doesn't matter. It's good for them."

As she continued to find ten more ways of saying the same thing, I thought, well, she's a grown-up; they are always wiser than any child, and have an absolute right to unquestioning obedience. Besides, I was to be told by my elders how hard grown up life was, and how I would look back and realise how carefree my life had been. I believed everything adults told me, so I dreaded growing up, if it was going to get worse. Children assume that later life will be pretty much the same as it is at the moment, only more so.

Old men used to come and sit in the park. When one of them threw sweets to me as I did handstands on the grass, I moved away. I didn't need the sweets now, I was being properly fed. Fresh fruit and tomatoes when possible, and my favourite foods, Spam and dried egg. A child gets to like what it is brought up on, barring allergies, and a tea of bread and margarine, lettuce and radishes, with a slice of cake, was fine by me. I even had leisure to refuse jam—a year or so before, I ate anything that was offered me, even food I didn't like.

Cough sweets were off the ration, as were dog biscuits, which a surprising number of people found acceptable. They filled a space, had plenty of fibre in them, and may even have contained some cereal nourishment. You could get Horlicks and Ovaltine tablets, also unrationed, which would blunt the craving for sweetstuffs. Sugarless cakes would be made with carrots, and tasted sweet enough with their own natural sugars. Certainly, much of what we ate would not be despised by the smartest vegan now.

Despite the fact that people generally were fitter on war rations, some fat people remained so. Either it was the kind of fat that doesn't shift, or they had access to restaurants and canteens, or had jobs in catering. The few oranges that got through were for children and pregnant women. Shopkeepers near schools, if they had a freezer, would make their own ice lollies from beetroot juice; and very sweet they were, too. At twopence each, children found them more than passable. Boys would, all the same, shout through the shop doorway, "Beetroot juice!" These same fearless urchins would eat every part of the orange they brought to school; pith, pips, peel and all. They could even eat marmalade oranges with a straight face.

Towards the end of 1943, there was a rumour of a new weapon, the V1, the flying bomb, otherwise the buzz bomb or doodlebug. I would have to move on yet again. I had a choice, like Hobson, but no more choice than his was. I could go back to Broadstairs and stay with our previous neighbour, Dolly Whitmarsh, or move in with the Williamses in Birmingham.

Mum, Winnie and I went to Broadstairs for a week to make arrangements to see how I felt about it.

Back in Broadstairs, I was walking with Yvonne Whitmarsh a few streets away, when the sirens sounded. As normal, I began running for home, and Yvonne came strolling after. When she arrived back, she found great amusement in telling the others how afraid I was of air raids, and turned to me, to explain that they were nothing to be afraid of. I looked at Mum, hoping that she would put her right, and tell her that in London the Germans had been bombing the lives and sanity out of us, but she just smiled with Yvonne, as if it were I who was being naive.

The Whitmarsh children were allowed to stay up later than I was, and Mum had a fad for me saying my prayers before I got into bed. She found me already in bed, so I asked her if I could say them right there. Nothing doing. She insisted I got out and knelt down with her, while the Whitmarsh kids giggled behind the door. Fuming inwardly at the humiliation, I was in no state for salvation, whatever that might mean.

If I could date the point at which I became indifferent towards her, it would be at about this time, and on this sort of occasion. Through no fault of her own, she had not been there when I had really needed her, and now I was being treated to, of all things, a show of concern for my moral welfare. I had been forced to formulate this for myself, anyway. I had been introduced to the concept of right and wrong in the most forceful way. I knew, without any holy man telling me, that I was to avoid becoming the kind of person who had treated me with such violence and hatred. I was beginning to be aware of the superficial nature of religion and its self-regarding agonizing. 'Why are we here?' is after all a sloppy way of avoiding the more challenging 'How?' All such questions of Why lead to other whys—why the need for a reason? The shallow response is, revealingly: a reason to behave well, for those who don't otherwise see why they should. Unable to perceive that decent behaviour has its own reason, they prefer threat or reward—and unwilling to take responsibility for their own behaviour, they ask for lifelong parenting, and life long infancy. Having effectively become parentless by the age of seven, all this was irrelevant to me.

Trying to sleep, I became aware of three pairs of eyes peering at me through the door jamb. "We've come to say Goodnight," said Yvonne.

"Oh, Goodnight, then."

They pattered away. I closed my eyes, counting sheep, only to hear the youngest prattling. I heard Yvonne say, "OK let's go down now." After another silence, the baby gave the game away again, wanting to know what was happening. Give me strength! I thought. Piety *and* prurience.

I decided against staying with the Whitmarshes. It wasn't just the kids. Dolly Whitmarsh had that bluff, goodnatured air of the rough and ready that graced Jessie Newbold, and that had taken my mother in and reassured her each time. My suspicions were immediately aroused. I was beginning to catch on.

Before I left London I had a letter from Mrs Newbold. She asked me to come back to Stafford, as David was missing someone to play with. I was to come across women like her, in the flesh and in the files of the Children's Department, People who deal with the world according to the fiction in their own heads.

Towards the end of my year-long stay with Granny, Mum called on us, with Billy. They were on their way to Margate, but Billy had begun to feel train-sick, so they stopped off at Penge. It was good to have someone to share all my solitary haunts with, play war-games with, and play with the cat's latest batch of kittens. We were taken to the city, and Mum decided to go into St Paul's. She was told by an official that no-one was allowed in, but she bull-dozed her way through. We went up to the Whispering Gallery, where I was told, for no apparent reason, to press my head against the wall. I thought there must be an unexploded bomb that we were waiting to go off. I looked below, a long way down, and saw a brazier. Thinking this was the bomb, my heart thudded as I kept close to the wall. The outcome was that I missed the acoustic effect. The Guide's whispered information about the Cathedral's history and present bomb damage simply passed me by.

Before Billy and Mum went on to Margate, I was to go and tell my teacher that I would be moving. Billy came with me, and said he would wait below. The fact was, I was uneasy about doing things in this casual way. I needed it all regulated and approved, to avoid getting into trouble. My nerve gave out. I knew the teacher had only to say, "You missed school this week, go and sit in your place," and I would be stuck there till a quarter past four. Authority was to be obeyed, though never trusted. When we got back home, Granny, in her mild way, was annoyed that she would have to go to the school herself and sort it out. I couldn't have explained, even to her, unless my life depended on it.

Billy was to have my bed, and I would share the big bed, in the same room, with Granny and Barbara. I don't remember hearing them come to bed. Billy and I talked for a long time. At last I had someone to confide in, and who had the same kind of problem communicating with those in power. We talked for a long time about all that had happened since we were last together, going over the big events in our short lives, and making guesses at what plans were being made for our future.

We now lived in a different world. The extraordinary events had left no-one untouched in this global jolt. Then, in a night in which the Luftwaffe left us in peace, we held hands across the gap between the two beds, and slept like Babes In The Wood.

CHAPTER SIX

WITHIN THREE MINUTES

I was standing on a railway platform, on the way up from London to Birmingham, when an express train went roaring through. I thought the very sound of it would destroy me.

I experienced the same reaction when I arrived at the Williamses during the evening, Winnie was singing along to something on the wireless. She had an excellent soprano voice, but I was tired, and the top notes went right through me. I had to keep going out to the lavatory to cry, only to find that the song had not finished each time I got back. Eventually, there was nothing for it. I just cried right there in front of them, something I always dreaded. They were astonished, so I made the excuse of having a headache, and Nellie showed me to my bed. She helped me to undress, something I would rather have done for myself, as normal. I was nearly eleven. There was no blackout up and Nellie was smoking. I expected her cigarette to go in my eye at any moment, in the dark, and said so. She jabbed it around, making a joke of it.

I found the bed to be the softest ever, and had time only to think and worry about getting to speak with a Midlands accent, before I was asleep. I developed this snobbery against local dialect and usage, in response to linking it to people who hated me. If the first stranger I had stayed with had been kind, I would probably have taken on the protective colouring of their accent. This happened with quite a number of children. A schoolfriend at Stafford, Joan Southwood, had settled in so well with her landlady that she called her Mom, not even Mum. She was not very well cared for, and smelt rather, but she could be fun, and there was no malice in her. She was quite non-academic, to the extent that I used to do her sums for her. That indicates how educationally backward she was. I remember Joan, sitting next to me, swinging her legs and humming happily as I did her adding up for her. She told me later that she was

"Going home, for good," and appeared equally accepting of either state, evacuation or home-going.

Once settled in Birmingham, I was taken to the Holy Family Catholic School, originally on Coventry Road, but it had taken one of the bombs meant for the Singer factory, a few hundred yards away on the Coventry side. (We would hear stories of honour between enemies—how the German pilots would swoop over the factory first, to warn the workers that they would be dropping bombs on it).

The Catholics now had to share premises with the Protestants at St Benedict's Road School, and I was now introduced to religious hostility. None of this was expressed between the children; it came only from the teachers and other adults. There were one or two surprises for me. I had gained the impression that Protestants were non-religious, and was told to pray for them, as they didn't know any better. So I was surprised to hear them praying at Assembly. The other surprise was the attitude towards religion itself. The protestants didn't disapprove of Catholic beliefs. But socially, they tended to look down on us. Catholics were perceived, with reason, as being associated with poverty. Mrs Williams' own attitude was summed up in the phrase, "them scruffy Catholics." I seemed to be faced with spiritual superiority on one side, and social condescension on the other. Poor but holy, heretical but well-dressed. I tried to form a choice.

The other big jolt was to discover that the godless Prods were representatives of the nation's official religion, so it wasn't hard to perceive which side was on the defensive. I stopped trying to make sense of it, and looked to the practical advantages. At the Catholic School we were not obliged to bring precious rations for cookery lessons, "for kids to play with," as Mrs Williams so rightly put it. As she was later to complain that they never taught us "how to make a square meal for a man," I had to juggle with her inconsistency as well. Personal hardship was taken into account in other matters, too. We were not asked to provide special clothes for PT, except to make sure we had navy blue knickers—directoire type, not the dainty briefs of today. Neither did we have to make a uniform apron and cap for cookery. If we couldn't spare the food, we did laundry instead. Most of us were in the same position, and there was no loss of face. That was OK by me, it avoided rows and nagging the night before, over taking foodstuffs to school.

What I liked about the Catholic School was the fact that the Headmistress, Mrs Bircher—that really was her name—preferred the arts, and we would begin Monday morning with dancing, art, or singing. I had a guilty feeling that I should be doing arithmetic, about which I was becoming increasingly anxious. I was convinced that I would never make a living unless I could conquer long division. If the teacher had written out the formula (bring down the next number etc.) I might have made headway, because I could never remember what move came next. But, with a class of forty children, they were little more than childminders, and we were factory fodder.

I was taken to the doctor for a check-up at the school clinic, and the doctor asked Mrs Williams how I had come to be in her care. In her simple way, the old lady said, "Well, she was evacuated here."

"Evacuated to Birmingham!" the doctor snapped, incredulously.

The old lady was flustered, and tried to explain it by going on about my father having died when I was four. I didn't bother to correct her, my opinion had not been asked. I wouldn't have known where to start anyway. A seemingly simple question often has to be answered with one's entire life history, each answer leading to another question. I thought what a

Me, aged twelve

snotty cow the doctor was, looking down on the little people from a great, unconcerned height. She was like the nit-nurse, who turned our hair over with knitting needles. Why knitting needles? Why not rubber gloves, tongs and surgical masks? They turned our lives over in their hands, bored, but daintily examining them anyway, with sheer, uncaring nosiness. This doctor kept a depressed-looking dog under her desk. "How very unhygienic," I thought, but realised the dog had no way of protesting.

The Williams had a dog, called Billy. A cheerful mongrel, not much nuisance in the house, but it got dumped on me for taking it for walks. I tied his lead to a fence once, and played with my friends instead, but got discovered. "Be sure your sins will find you out!" For non-religious people, the Williamses were fond of biblical quotations when it suited them.

Before I came to resent the dog for this reason, however, he and I had a traumatic confrontation. I was told he would walk with me to school. What they didn't tell me was that he would obediently stay at the school gate and not follow me in. Nor was there any command that I could give him to 'stay'. So I panicked. I was in fear of getting into trouble at school. I knew how bad 'getting into trouble' could be. So I stood there, in the middle of the road, shouting at him and pointing.

"Go home!"

He stood there, looking at me calmly. Then I started smacking him. He just lay there, tail under, while I frantically hit him, as hard as I could.

A girl just going in called reproachfully, "That's cruel, that is, you wouldn't like it." I ran into school.

Such is our moral vanity, I felt worse about that than about the beatings I had taken myself. It was of a piece with the broken-hearted howlings of Terry Woodwiss when his mother turned on him for chucking stones at me.

That I never mentioned it at Confession is evidence of the fact that we were given no direction on the sin of cruelty—it didn't seem to be included in the list—and only the slightest attention to any other, though they did sit up and pay attention if it bordered on the illegal, like theft. They were concerned at the idea of 'sins against God', which I assumed to mean neglecting to go to Mass, or taking the Lord's name in vain. Rather more puzzling was the concept of 'sins against the self'. Since these were only darkly hinted at, and not explained (they didn't want to put ideas into our heads, after all) I assumed it had something to do with laziness or gluttony—fat chance; or not giving up something for Lent.

From that age I realised that forgiveness was beside the point. It is as irrelevant as revenge, and as sentimental. Although we can explain the workings of revenge—we know exactly what we'd like to do to our enemy—it is revealing that the same cannot be said of forgiveness. It's a made-up thing; a wrong-doer's charter. Its only purpose to make us feel good about having done bad. Better to right the wrong. With this in mind, I tried to compensate the dog by making more fuss of him, but he never walked me to school again. He was convinced he had done something wrong, and didn't know what it was. I could certainly identify with that.

I made further atonement by cleaning him up when he had distemper. It's a canine pneumonia, and very snotty. Every time he sneezed, I had to clean it off the floor, or the legs of the table, and once, off my own leg.

* * *

The raids were not as bad at this point as they had been in London. We still came downstairs when they started but, snuggled up in the bed under the stairs that had been put there for Mrs Williams, and which she shared with me, the noise didn't penetrate as much; the batteries in the park were less noisy than the Crystal Palace rockets, and I even slept through them. Winnie and Nellie would sit in the armchairs, knitting and reading, and listening to the wireless until it closed down.

Mum once walked all the way from Balsall Heath in a raid to see me—about two and a half miles, keeping well away from the city centre, so no bustling Air Raid Warden would shepherd her into a shelter. She loved excitement and had no fear of it, and all three sat round the table, talking until it was over, or until Winnie had to go off for an early turn. She would sometimes leave at about three a.m.

Bomb sites were exciting places to play on. You never knew what you might find, and you got to know the colour of your neighbour's bedroom wallpaper, now open to the street. I had my first lesson in technology; the workings of a front door bell pull were exposed, and we used to pull the cord just to see the wires tugging the bell—a simple handbell. I played with my friend, Jean Taylor, in the crater that had been their Anderson shelter. The house had been hit, too, and the first time I had come to the Williams' it was just an empty gap in the street. It was now once more a house, and all there was to show for the bomb were the new bricks and tiles, the crater in the garden, some aeroplane glass, and a small circlet of bullets. The pilot must have dropped this debris out with the bombs.

Jean's three-year-old sister, Diane, put the circlet of bullets on her head, like a crown. It slipped on to her shoulders, and she couldn't get it off.

"Don't worry," we told her, getting it off her head, as she howled with fear, "nothing will happen." That's how much we knew.

She could have lost her head, and we our hands, but we tossed it aside once it was off, and the bullets remained inert. The unbreakable glass, we stood up against the hedge, and threw stones at it until it broke. The crater was to provide hours of fun, walking across it on the clothes prop. We had been to the circus on Haymills recreation ground, and we were going to be high wire walkers—until the prop broke. This was just before we set fire to the bushes at the end of the garden. This unruly hedge ran the length of the back gardens down Heather Road, so we had to put it out pretty quickly. We got some light planks from her father's shed and beat it out. We didn't play with matches again. Instead, we experimented with a bottle of bleach that Mrs Taylor had left for her daughters to play with. I often wonder if they ever made it to adulthood.

In the Juniors, we had a Miss Coleman, whom the children preferred, because she was so easy going. Until, that is, one day a boy of eleven wet himself. Instead of briskly sending him off for a cloth and a clean up, and at the least asking him if he felt unwell, the mad bitch furiously denounced him as every kind of dirty creature. The following day, after school, I had to come back to the classroom to get something, and found the boy with his mother, talking to Miss Coleman.

"What do you think you are doing here?" Miss Coleman snapped.

I told her.

"Then get it, and be off." She must have taken an earful from the boy's mother, and barked at me to assert her authority. She clearly thought I'd come back to spy on her. I hadn't, but I like to think that the boy's mother put the wretched woman in her place. She had no business being in charge of children. I began to see that Miss Coleman was not so much easy going, as that she had no control over the children, so she picked on the most vulnerable to show how tough she could be. I began to develop a healthy contempt for schoolteachers such as she.

Once into the Seniors, I went to the school the Catholics shared at the Protestant Oldknow Road School. It had been built in the 'twenties on unsuitable soil, and Winnie told me that when she first went there it was level with the road, but that it subsided in a very few years. By the time I went there it had reached a gradient of about one in six, dipping to one in five near the entrance. Some twenty years after that, when I went there for evening classes, there were steps down to the front entrance, which had been the first floor, and the original ground floor was now a basement.

We had to play rounders on it, nevertheless. 'Games' were meant to build character. I think they were trying to make a man of me. Some of the girls were built like blokes. and were as rough. They would go tearing round the tarmac, catching on the clothes of the smaller girls, to get a purchase on the chase. Some of the drill, frankly, was dangerous. There was one which involved a line of us, going round like the hand of a clock. The girls in the middle should have gone much more slowly to let the girls on the outside keep up. but the teacher had put the bigger girls in the middle, and as they strode forward at a gallop, the smaller girls were sent flying, like a whip, into the fence.

Equipment was scarce here, too, especially in the commodity of teachers. One of the girls was put in charge of the class. Mary Quinn was as thick as a brick, but adept at bossing the other girls about, so she was teacher's pet. In the middle of a 'lesson' held by this genius, a girl announced that she had lost a lemon and a half-crown that she had brought with her to school. Mary immediately questioned each of us in turn. As this did no good she searched us all, except herself and the little madam who had mislaid the lemon and the 2/6.

"Let's look through your stuff, Ben'on ..."

She hated me because I could read: she snatched my bag and tipped the contents on to the floor. She did this with everyone else's bag, and scrabbled through them, then let us pick it all up again, then held prayers for the thief to yield up her pelf. This was equally useless. Well, I did say she was thick.

She wasn't going to let this go; she had to have a result, so she picked on a timid girl whose head was heavily bandaged. She had had it lanced of some painful excrescence, brought about by malnutrition and neglect. and was not up to protesting. It was not long before Mary had her in tears.

"There you are!" she cried out in triumph. "you're crying because you're guilty. You go home tonight and say your prayers for being so wicked."

The fact that she hadn't brought the fruit or the money to light escaped her powers of perception.

When the teacher got back to the class, Mary ran to her, excitedly telling her of the 'theft'. She had eagerly reached; " ... and so I searched everybody ..." when the teacher gasped with dismay.

"Mary," she gently reproved her, "you shouldn't have done that."

Mary immediately burst out loudly into tears. It was her best bet.

She got her come-uppance the following day when she was left in charge of both our class and a boys' class. The boys were not going to be ordered about by a girl, that was clear, and they had a field day of riotous behaviour and noise. She was genuinely in tears this time. So what with the school bully weeping, and the boys misbehaving to impress the girls, I found there was some enjoyment to be had at school, after all.

Mrs Bircher was a little redheaded woman who bragged about her short temper. and how it was at least all over in a flash. It took her a good quarter of an hour to enlarge on the details of this facet of her character, with examples, before moving on to an equally riveting characteristic of her personality. She would tell us long-winded jokes about cruelty and sickness, and give us details of illnesses that turned our stomachs. When we had our feet measured, she insisted on measuring her own in front of the class, and exclaiming at how much smaller hers were than some of ours.

"I don't care what kind of feet the shrivelled old hag has got," mumbled Christine Wheatley to me.

We were to have a fancy dress party. Mrs Williams thought I might go as a Hawaiian maiden, and got the raffia to make the skirt. I'm sure she meant me to wear something above the waist as well, but Mrs Bircher was scandalised by the thought of a grass skirt. (She might also have been shocked at the Paganism inherent in the idea. but couldn't bring herself to mention it). Mrs Williams was in her turn so indignant at her idea being disapproved, by a mere Catholic, too, that she forbade me to go to the party. Her denunciation of 'the narrer-moinded old cow' delighted me so, that I dared to laugh out loud. I have to confess, too, that none of this piffle bothered me in the least.

It was part of Mrs Bircher's brief to exclude, and have us beg for inclusion. This happened to one girl, Roma Brennan, who had been one of Mrs Bircher's clique herself. I don't know what Roma had done to upset them, threatened to go as the Pope, at least, judging by the savagery of their exclusion. But she badly wanted to be a part of the jollity, and had her fingers crossed all day on the date itself, hoping that the Important People would notice and have pity on her. They must have loved it, but it did no good.

Mary Quinn was peeved at my being serene through all this nonsense, with my head bent over my work.

"I don't like her attitude," she complained to Mrs Bircher.

"Yes, I know," the Headmistress soothed, ganging up with her. I was undeniably obedient. but held myself aloof from their power games. 'Attitude' in those days meant something different from now. It was always expressed as 'the wrong attitude', and meant a lack of awe towards those in power.

But my stay came to an end when the school nurse discovered head lice on me. She tucked her chin back in disapproval, pursed her mouth up tight like an anus, and said, "You realise what you've got, don't you?"

I said nothing.

Lowering her head in a warning, sideways nod, she said. "Well, there *are* some dirty people about, you know." She let her chin out again and turned, with her knitting needles, to the next child.

This was nothing. I had to take The Note home. The effect was predictable. Mrs Williams did not have the composure to get on with it, treat my hair with paraffin or oil of sassafras, and get me a haircut. This had to be relished. My entire family was denounced as no good and what we needed was a father behind us and what had she done to deserve having me wished on her? A shake of her heavy head from side to side, and the imprecation;

"I must have done something VERY wicked to have deserved you," was to become a tedious mantra, its thudding rhythm a dreaded burden.

Accepted twelve and six a week from my mother, plus my ration book, I thought. But it was, in fact, my doing. I had chosen her guardianship over that of Dolly Whitmarsh, a fact that may have flattered her at first, and initially she had shown a kind attitude, until she realised that I was not quite the slum child she had expected, overawed at their gentility and grateful for being, as she later fantasised, "picked up out of the gutter."

"It's a pity you can't goo 'ome."

I thought so too.

She was old and tired, her health was gone. Not in any state to look after a child. Life had embittered her, and she could not have said why. Any feminist worth the name could have told her exactly why. She had brought up her family according to patriarchal values, worshipped her menfolk, who repaid her by visiting her only at Christmas, and she had blocked her daughters' efforts at marriage. Winnie derided her, whenever she said anything foolish.

"You are daft, our Mother, you're nearly as daft as Mary."

"I could have been anything, if I hadn't married." This was always her cry whenever she felt she had said something stupid. I wondered just what she could have been.

"When I was your age, I was in service, with a little cap stuck on top of me 'ead."

The cap was always part of this statement, as representing her badge of service, her lack of status. She had gone into service at twelve, barely able to read, and with little chance of learning. Her mistress would not call her by her own name, Helen.

"My own daughter has that name. I cannot possibly call you by it. I shall call you Mary. That's quite good enough for you."

Odd, I thought, how the name that almost a third of the girls in the Catholic School had had bestowed on them in affectionate respect should also be cast derisively at one held to be a scullery slut.

I saw written on her ration book, the name Mrs John Williams.

"They've put your name down wrongly," I said to her, "they've put a man's name where your name should be."

"Oh no, that's quite right," she preened herself, "when you get married you get called by your husband's name, all of it."

I found this repellent, and could not at the time have said why. Having been worked like a dray horse by the fine lady who employed her, and generally been prevented from taking any pleasures thought to be above her appreciation, I suppose marriage was her only hope of status and a life of her own. It was the nearest she was to get to it. She had watched the grand people at play, and loved to describe the great parties at which she had served. She would talk about the gowns and the fancy dress, and the jewels, and of one dramatic moment when a lady discovered her own lost jewels on the neck of another woman, and cried aloud at it, causing a sensation.

"The 'ole 'all went deathly quiet," she dramatised.

She had also read *Peg's Paper*, and the penny dreadfuls, in what little leisure she had been allowed, following the words slowly and carefully.

She seemed to have enjoyed having children, because the worst punishment she could think of for a woman was, "She ought to be sterilised." She clearly thought being barren was the worst thing to happen to a woman, setting aside her own daughters' enforced state of childlessness in her mind. She told me, poignantly, of when she got her first council house.

"I sat on the bus, thinking, 'I've got a key! I've got a key.'"

It was commonplace for working-class families at that time to live in lodgings, as it was still when I was born. She spoke of the good things they had eventually been able to afford; how they bought the children's toys from Barnby's, a high-class toyshop in Birmingham, and of the twenty-first birthday party held for their eldest son, in a public hall. The cine camera he acquired, which went up in flames at the first projection, and of the bucket of water they had standing by, as per instructions. I heard about the cycling clubs that the sons and daughters had belonged to in the 'thirties, when it was all the rage; and of the young woman who got tired, refused to go on, and threw a tantrum, hurling her bike into the road and stamping on it to break it.

Most revealing was an anecdote about Winnie. She took her to Lewis's store, as a toddler, about 1919. The child saw a large teddy bear, costing a pound, a working man's weekly wage. She demanded it, and screamed until she got it. It surprised me that her mother told me this, and so often, considering how she despised anyone else whose children made a fool of them. She would, on the other hand, speak sturdily of how 'the Dad' ruled the house with a rod of iron. I saw through this eventually, on hearing further stories of how the girls 'wrapped him round their little fingers' and the boys eluded punishment by subterfuge and deceit. Like the adherents of mythical family values in any age, they tyrannised the obedient, made excuses for the uncontrollable and sentimentalised them, then picked out the easy bits and flourished them as evidence of what a splendid job they had made.

I'm sure she mistook me for her own children when they were young.

She would issue the threat, "All that lot's coming off tomorrow, my girl."

She meant my hair, which was already too short to be cut any further. Winnie had had long, blonde curls, and it was evident that this harmless threat was made, with rancid boredom, every time her mother lost control over her, which was often.

When she said it to me the twentieth time I said, "Can I have the sixpence to have it done, then, please?"

She whacked her hand across my head and snapped, "Shurrup, or I'll slap yer mouth up!" There would clearly be no point in bringing elegant friends to the house for her approval.

Although I aimed at being genderless, I was not at war with my own nature, as I blundered towards adolescence. I could, however, have done without Winnie bathing me, right up to the age of sixteen. There was no point in my asking for privacy. There would have been an indignant uproar, and a questioning of my peculiar motives. I was their property, to be peered at, prodded, and made an object of less than wholesome interest. From the bathroom, I heard Winnie sniggering with the others at the changes taking place in my body. This, with Nellie's facetious remarks, and their mother's sternness about the matter, must mean there was something ugly about what I was growing into. At once nasty and foolish. I wondered if it happened to other girl's bodies, and whether they had to shave off the shameful body hair.

There was no single point at which something went 'snap'. It was more like a click, a switch quietly tripped out in my mind. I knew I couldn't gain their affection, and I switched off my feelings. A Buddhist detachment split me off from all that troublesome effort, in which it no longer mattered. Nothing mattered. Click.

There were cheerful times. VE Day came; I no longer feared imminent death. The Thousand Year Reich was over. Like me, it was twelve years old. But it died, and I didn't. I always loved a party, and there was one in every street. The bonfire was collected; people contributed prunings, sometimes a whole tree. Money was collected, and food vouched for. It was decided whose piano was to be brought out, and who should play it. I won a total of two and six, winning races, and found having a meal out in the street a strange and welcome experience. The bonfire was lit, the piano played, and the singing started. As the night became cooler, fewer and fewer of us were left standing round the embers, and I was allowed to stay up late. Special licence had been granted for the bonfires, and public money set aside to repair the damage and replace the tarmac. A man got drunk, did a Fred Astaire impression, went flying and got a bloody nose. Also, the War was over, and I no longer feared death within three minutes. What more could a girl want?

V.J. Day wasn't quite the same, even though more money had been collected, and the organisation was more brisk. It was as if we had already celebrated, and the jubilation was over. Besides, someone had made a dummy of General Tojo and put it on one of the bonfires.

This had upset Mrs Williams, but Winnie told her, "Don't be so squeamish, our Mother."

A bit of a hanger and flogger, was Winnie. But I know what the old lady meant. It was not just compassion for the wrongdoer, but she sensed a scapegoat. It echoed in her remorse to me when she had attacked me harshly, as it did towards the man picked out to hand over to the Americans to hang. I had a similar forbearance to spare for her, too.

Most of her anecdotes began; "When I was at the Women's …" or; "The woman in the next bed …" and concerned the list of illnesses she had borne, aggravated by her habit of comfort eating, and which was to kill her. In the cold weather she would say, "I'll never be warm again." In the oppressively hot, "I'll never be cool again."

Every night, as she settled her wrecked body to sleep, I would hear her sigh and say, "Thank God for a good bed." Besides which, anyone who had had an infant such as Winnie, a spoilt thug from the start, deserves some measure of lenity.

There was always a party at Christmas. Nellie played the piano, we had a turkey and two chickens, which all came with head, feet and feathers still on, and hung, dripping blood on to the kitchen chair, for a couple of days. The in-laws came, and placed their share of rations on the kitchen table. The Williams' house was quite modern, in that they had an electric stove and kettle. The puddings were made in the coal-fired boiler in the bathroom, which contained only that and the bath, which had only a cold tap. As the Christmas pudding was being apportioned out in the kitchen, we would hear the chink of threepenny bits as one coin was placed on each plate, to make sure everyone got one, instead of stirring them into the mixture before making them, and letting the guests chance it. We played silly games, and sang sillier songs. With so many children there, seven grandchildren, and the little boy from next door, I would feel part of a family again.

Jean Taylor told me about a young woman who gave tap dancing and acrobatic lessons. This was all the rage at the time; girls were suddenly doing handstands and cartwheels in the playground, and in the way that these things progress, the speed of which no-one seems able to explain, it had spread countrywide within a surprisingly short time. We decided to give it a go. I asked for, and got, surprisingly without any trouble, the shilling a week that it would cost. I didn't, after all, get regular pocket money, and had to ask each time for what was needed. The class was held in one of the infant classrooms at St Benedict's Road School, and we practised at home—the acrobatics on the grass, the tap dancing on the concrete yard, getting ready for the day when we would become famous. After only a few lessons, however, Jean told me the young lady had gone away to entertain the troops, so we would have to be famous for something else.

I caught the flu for the first time when I was twelve, and was put in the bigger of the back bedrooms, where there was a fireplace. While I was ill, Mrs Williams stopped nagging. She was very attentive, up and down the stairs, bringing coal, hot drinks, cool drinks, and anything she could think of to tempt my appetite. She had a chance to be a mother again, and was once again doing her favourite job, her chosen fulfilment.

When I was well enough to put my nose above the quilt, I was allowed to read a large compendium of collected temperance magazines. This was a major step in my literary development. It had serials, short stories, competitions and puzzles, and would no doubt be a collector's item now. Not all of it was concerned with temperance. The children's serial was about a little girl who had run away in disgrace for losing her baby stepbrother, and her search for him, and her eventual regaining of her stepmother's love. Once again, I found all the mythic archetypes and format; the quest, the trial, the ordeal, the light relief, the last minute crisis, and the homecoming.

John Williams Snr. had no doubt joined the Temperance movement as being part of the social reform that embraced both that and the Labour Movement. He kept an allotment, and he had plotted the tiny front garden to hold a lawn, split by the diagonal path, and holding on its borders a lilac and a laburnum tree, with wallflowers under the bay window. In the back garden flourished the flowers he had set in some time before he died. Mrs Williams told me their Latin and folk names. She told me that he had built the wall with home-made bricks in front of the Anderson shelter, so that his wife could lean against it as she backed down into the shelter. This being at the end of the back garden, he had placed a rockery in front of the wall, and at the foot of that was a Blenheim apple tree. At the very back, backing on to the garden of a house in the next street, it had become a miniature woodland; admired as looking "just like the Lickeys" scaled down, with tall bushes, golden rod and wild flowers. Soil had been placed on top of the shelter, and short-stemmed flowers encouraged to grow there.

In front of the apple tree were the lawns, separated by a tiny pond and home-made bridge. Flowers grew at the foot of the hedge running down to the yard, and there was a side path alongside the lawns. That left the steps down to the concrete yard. A working man had taken as much pride in individual cultivation as he had in the co-operative of the Socialist ideology he became part of. On a less grand note, I may well have slept in the same bed that Keir Hardie, as the Williams' guest, once slept in. Now there's a thing. Mr Williams had built up his savings by running a 'Club'—which I learned was really a pub, so he must have joined a Temperance Lodge at a later date.

The council house itself is of a familiar pattern. The front gate and path to the entry, and the entry itself, is held in common by the next-door neighbour, and branches off by two tall gates into the separate yards. There was a living-room and kitchen — no front parlour. The front door led straight up the stairs, with the living-room opening on to the right. So the lobby under the stairs formed part of the same space as the coal bunker and the lavatory, which you had to go outside to reach. There was a lean-to jutting out from the lavatory, which housed the mangle and such things as the lawn mower and garden tools. The house had the usual three bedrooms, the largest at the front, a smaller one and the smallest at the back. The largest and the middle sized bedroom both had fireplaces backing on to each other with their twin chimneys. In any age, these could be considered to be good, working-class dwellings.

Mrs Williams told me one morning as I was eating breakfast,

that she was going to insure me. I asked her what that meant. "It's for money to bury you with."

I thought she meant that she would bury the money with me, and wondered what was the point of that.

She misinterpreted my blank look, and said, defiantly, "Yes, your mother disapproves as well. But I insured all my own children, and you are going to be insured as well."

At the time she was rearing her own children, it was commonplace to lose a child, and for the poor, it was also likely that they lacked the money to bury them decently.

I preferred to think that this was all she had in mind, and not that she was trying to make money out of me. Mum thought differently, as she was to tell me, and that there was a little sum to pick up when the policy matured. As it happened though, Mrs Williams would discover that she was unable to insure any child not a blood relative.

I played with, and looked after, two of the Williams' grandchildren, Josie and Michael, five and six years younger than I was. When they stayed overnight, we would share the big bed, and I would tell them a bedtime story. I lost this knack of making up a story as I grew up, and I could only relate a known story from a book. I used to have the care of them, to take them out, to the park, or on a long walk, and often walked them much farther than they were used to; and they would drag after me on the way home, bad tempered and throwing sticks at me as I strode on ahead.

Winnie would spread a newspaper on the kitchen table, get the fine-tooth comb, and indulge in her current treat, searching my head for nits. Her relish of it, relayed to Nellie in the living-room, when she spotted a big one, was greeted by a delighted shout of laughter from her sister. I wished them both dead on the spot; Winnie for humiliating me, and Nellie for what passed for satire on her behalf.

I was once more put in my place; inferior to them—flea bound and therefore stupid. At least they didn't get nits in their hair. Until, that is, Nellie got them anyway, and had to postpone going into hospital for that reason—or so I was told. I was at fault for passing them to Nellie, but, curiously, Nellie was not to blame for catching them from me, as I was for having caught them from the one before me. I don't think they even thought as deeply as that about it.

The best bit of logic Mrs Williams could come up with was to accuse me; "You must have been putting your head close to them dirty kids at your scruffy school."

I imagined them talking about me to their fellow workers; "We've got this dopey kid at our house, who catches nits and talks like the man on the wireless." It would be on a level with the dialogue that passed across the supper table, no doubt.

Every autumn Nellie would say, "Nights are drorin' in." And six months later; "Nights are drorin' out."

They listened to Have A Go on the Light Programme—for the curious, it was several degrees worse than Blind Date—making their comments; then they would listen to the repeat, and make exactly the same comments again. It can be imagined how the long winter nights flew by in this atmosphere of Wildean repartee.

Winnie criticised the way I lay in bed at night. "She poses in her sleep," she would say, with contempt. Then, "Our Josie and Michael snuggle down properly, all nice and cosy."

There was nothing I could do about this latest fault in my behaviour. I was asleep at the time, and even if I lay in the approved way at first, once I was asleep I would throw the clothes away from my mouth. I was having trouble breathing, and would wake, coughing violently. I was taken to the Chest Clinic, but declared negative of TB, so maybe it was psychological. All other expression was suppressed, so my lungs decided for me. And so, if I was found at night with my arms above my head, Winnie would say, "She's been posing again."

She continued bathing me every Friday, bitterly inveighing against my skinniness. She would give me a sudden thump on my naked back, as a punishment for not being "nice and plump, like our Josie and Michael." She even had a fad for going on a diet, which involved the lot of us, including the two vast ladies from Hull. They were kind to me, and silently deplored my being knocked about, but didn't protest. They were afraid of Winnie, and didn't like to criticise the old woman. Their very size was a reproach to her, as much as my leanness was.

So we all had to go without Sunday tea. As I was never allowed to eat between meals (I didn't dare ask), and had no pocket money, it meant going without food from dinner time until supper at about nine o'clock. At mealtimes, I was set a small amount, with my skimpy appetite in mind.

Blanche, the bigger woman, used to sneak me a biscuit or two on these Sundays, to prevent my passing out. Her friend Lena would give me some of her sweets ration. To our general relief, Winnie's will power gave in, her temper improved, and we were all allowed to eat normally again.

Poor Winnie, railing against her size, not much more than a well-proportioned ten stones in any case, would declare, "Well, I'd rather be fat and happy than thin and miserable."

'Thin' was usually accompanied by the adjective 'painfully' with great stress on it. Ricocheting between resentment and acceptance, envy and derision, she would make the same joke about playing The Bluebells of Scotland down my spine, like a xylophone, under the impression that a joke became funnier with each repetition. Nellie would back her up with a facetious laugh at short notice. Their mother would chip in with; "I wouldn't mind, but she EATS!"

This had a rising, almost questioning, inflection. She was confusing me with someone else again. Winnie took to describing me as "you great, 'ulking thing," and my shoulder blades stuck out like wings.

"We come from big stock."

"Our Winnie ought to have extra rations, like men on heavy work."

"She's big across her shoulders because she has to keep stretching up to ring the bell." These were the more memorable pronouncements and bizarre justifications for something which, nowadays, we don't feel needs justifying. Certainly, Winnie was not lazy. Unlike her driver, she was on the trot all the time, running up and down stairs for the fares, and when she walked anywhere, she strode, whereas I dawdled.

The only time I fought back, it had a surprising outcome. I had finally burst out with

"Well, I'd rather be thin than FAT!" Winnie only blustered loudly, she didn't hit me. Her mother placated her, but to my astonishment, didn't give one word of reproof to me. So that was all it took. Descending to their level. They nagged through sheer inertia. It was something they could get away with, and there was no-one to stop them. I certainly didn't know how to stop them at it, beyond pointlessly trying to please. The harder I tried, the worse things had got. They only despised me for it.

Aware that I should be told the Facts Of Life, Winnie asked me next bathtime, in a stern voice specially adopted for the occasion, what we had been taught in biology that week.

I said, "Bleeding."

Aha. It had gone suddenly quiet in the living-room. The voice grew sterner.

"What sort of bleeding?"

"Arterial."

"Oh."

I prattled on, pleased that she was taking an interest in what passed for my education, but she didn't seem to want to know about Harvey's discoveries after all.

It must have been hard luck on Winnie that her one benign action towards me misfired badly. She put my hair in curlers. As she wound the hair around the metal clips, I became more and more distressed. By the time she had finished, I was in tears and cried in a corner. It wasn't much better when the curlers were taken out a few hours later. I didn't dare go out, with my hair sticking out in that unaccustomed way, and I kept miserably pressing it down to straighten it. I found the whole thing such a contrast. I had got used to coping with their hatred, then I was suddenly faced with this grooming, this apparent caring. They had never so much as provided me with a pair of nail scissors, and I had to peel my nails in a rough attempt to trim them. I would use the kitchen scissors, surreptitiously, when no-one was looking.

I didn't feel entitled to ask for a manicure set. I was, after all, a burden on the family purse; "Set a beggar on 'orseback, and 'e'll ride to 'ell." The half hour diatribes would come at me in a thudding sing-song, reducing me finally to tears.

"That's right, now cry, I should."

And now, suddenly, I was expected to be the engaging, affectionate, and jolly twelve year old that they in their turns had been. They were quietly baffled at my response.

The only other reason for my extreme reaction to this rite of passage is that I had not, after all, accepted being one or other gender. While I was pre-pubertal, I was genderless, and that was fine by me, neither did I crave to be a boy. But this was crossroads time, or rather, one way street. There was not the acceptance then of multiple facets to human nature that there are now. And there are many. I recall my mother striding about in boys shoes during the War, but she also enjoyed being female, and had no quarrel with her anatomy, except in the 'twenties, when she believed her breasts were unfashionably large, and these "great lumps of flesh" embarrassed her. I would have been just as distraught had I been a boy in body, but still genderless in mind, going through whatever they are put through in adolescence. It was the polarity that jarred.

It was at the age of twelve that I made the big discovery that everyone makes, and copes with or not, some as early as five, some as late as eighteen. That I would one day have to die. I was drifting off to sleep one night when the thought struck me. I sat bolt upright in bed, my heart thumping. There would be a day when I would wake up, and it would be the last time I would do so. I would clean my teeth for the last time; have breakfast, dinner, then tea; the last meals I would ever have. I gave the matter all of three minutes' thought, then put it to one side, all the more determined that, since life is so short, then I would make it mean something.

At no time did it occur to me that religion should play a part in coping with existential fears. It just never crossed my mind. Not even when my life had been in danger. Nor, more to the point, when I had been in despair. The "No atheists in foxholes" argument, I saw as merely a vulgar threat from the godly. Nothing the Church offered had opened my eyes to life's possibilities, not even that which it was good at. I would have to discover Sacred Music, Bach and Mozart for myself.

I was to learn of simpler pleasures, though. At Christmas, 1945, I was taken, with all the Williamses and Billy, to see Babes In The Wood, at the Alexandra Theatre. It was the first pantomime I had ever seen. I had heard Panto on the wireless, and been puzzled by it. Instead of the children's story that I expected, I heard Raymond Baxter chuckling over the slapstick, grown-up dialogue, and unexplained laughter when the Dame was doing something too questionable to be broadcast. At these points Mrs Williams would say, "I bet they're doing something funny now," to keep up the spirit of things. Between scene changes, we would hear two seedy old comics making jokes in front of the curtain. These went right over my head.

I was to ask the teacher if I could leave early. I sat at my desk, fidgeting. Every so often, I would raise my arm.

"Not yet, Mary Rose," Mr Doyle would say, patiently.

Then at last he nodded at me, and I was out of the classroom, running all the way home, to find everyone in a good mood. We had tea, then walked to the bus stop. On the way, I was given a bar of chocolate, saved from the sweets ration, to eat during the performance.

I had never seen anything so magic. Better than a cinema

screen, this was real, and bigger. I glanced at Mrs Williams, who was smiling in absorption at the chorus of little girls, tap dancing — she loved anything to do with children. These were Betty Fox's Babes, before 'babe' came to mean grown woman. Kirby's Flying Ballet; colour, music, fun and a happy ending.

As we waited at the bus stop, I said to no-one in particular, "Have you noticed, when you shut your eyes you can see the costumes and the colours all over again?"

I no longer wanted to be a farmer. My mind was made up this time. I was going on the stage.

CHAPTER SEVEN

BLOODY CRANKS

Once I'd left the Holy Family School, and started at Bierton Road Secondary Modern, I could hardly attend the Holy Family Church any more, so I was sent to St Benedict's Church, which I think was High, halfway between Catholic and Protestant. The Minister, Father Rhys, asked me if I had taken my first Holy Communion. I'd been going to St Benedict's for several weeks by this time, without going to Communion, and to prevent his asking me why not, I said I hadn't had the sacrament yet. I'd got an idea that it was sacrilegious to have this done more than once, rather like marrying twice, but since it was only the Church's view that I would go to Hell, and not like getting into real life trouble, I let it go.

I took my First Confession again. Again, I mentioned only those sins which I felt Father Rhys could cope with. I left out cruelty and hatred, but put in a few of the more orthodox ones to pad it out with. This too, was a sin, but the fact is, if I had followed his instructions to "go in peace and try to sin no more," and then turned up the following week to tell him I hadn't got anything to confess, he wouldn't have believed me, and would have thought I was trying to be funny. The Church wanted sinners, and couldn't function without them. Such was its cynicism that the confessional was regarded as a spiritual lavatory. People queued up in the pews, waiting to relieve themselves of their carefully cultivated guilt; would come out clean, and could start sinning all over again. The Church and its congregation were in love with sin and guilt. I found it all very unsavoury. I was not rebellious, so no attempt was made to save a sheep not obviously astray. Only the Prodigal was of any interest—his dutiful brother didn't count. It was this ultimate cynicism that was to enable me to shake off the Church. To be just, it never exploited my emotional needs. But then, it had never addressed them.

Of real value, though, was the Girl Guides, which was run at

St Benedict's by Miss Bamford, who never insisted we call her Captain, and who taught us camping skills, camp songs, country dancing and basic astronomy. We were spared the study of Craft Skills Badge, Cookery Badge, or any other home-disrupting stuff. The really important thing was to meet other girls, and swap life experience and advice.

As for Guide Camp, I hadn't realised how much I needed to get away from 'home'. (I never felt entitled to use the word after June 1940, except at Granny's house. I lived where I did only on sufferance.

By the time we got to the camp site, it had rained so heavily that we had to come back, on the same lorry that brought the Scouts back from their week on the site. We finally made it by the following Tuesday, and had just four days to enjoy. But that four days was a window in my childhood. I shared the lives of girls whose lives were the polar opposite of mine. We shared a tent and talked into the night. We got nature study at first hand, learned to cook after a fashion, and had tea with the local vicar. Scary stuff, for him anyway. We had jokes played on us and vice versa, made up daft poems, and played like puppies. These naive pleasures were the last word in exotica to me. On the way back from the tap down the lane, we met a group of girls from a local orphanage, and overheard them making envious comparisons between our casual clothes and their own grim uniform. Girls living out their lives in disgrace by proxy. Put in a home for having been born.

We took supper in the sunset. Had camp fires and fancy dress parties, using only what we'd brought with us and what the hedgerows provided. In the middle of an afternoon of this merry play, I looked up to see Winnie walking across the field with Josie. Damn it all, this was my holiday. I could see those two any time. But I had to give up several hours of my short holiday to go to tea with them in Malvern. Slightly mollified by the extraordinary gift of a ten shilling note, I resumed what was left of the week.

Whenever I smell bruised grass, the dusty smell of hay and the blackcurrant aroma of hedgerows; of paraffin and wet canvas, or hear the clank of a dixie against a tin plate, I time-travel down Worcestershire lanes to 1946, walking back in the summer evening with eleven others; ravenous for baked beans. Waking in a rainy night, cosy on our palliasses, while the rain bucketed down on Miss Bamford going round, slackening the guy ropes. Reminders that for a few days, life relented.

* * *

The Williamses never had a national Sunday paper, just the Sunday Mercury. They were very strict about that. Except when there was a particularly lurid murder, in which case they made a tolerant exception. The Camb murder had taken place, in which James Camb, a cabin steward, pushed the body of a woman through a porthole. On the Sunday on which it was printed, the News Of The World was spread out on the table. They were all broadsheets in those days, so it took up the whole of the table.

"Don't you go reading any of that, do you hear?" I was told, then they all went out for the afternoon, and I had the house to myself.

Items for the tea-table had been placed on top of the newspaper, so I couldn't have folded it up without rearranging things that didn't belong to me. I did what was expected of me. I read it. It was of a piece with their method of getting me to Learn About Life. Well, that would come in handy should I find myself on board with a psychopath.

One afternoon, with the table set for tea, I took a spoonful of sugar out of the sugar bowl, and was just putting it into my mouth when Mrs Williams came up the front garden path and saw me through the window. Instead of waiting till she got into the entry, and running out of the front door, I lost my head and went into the lobby under the stairs, where she dragged me

With friends at Guide camp, 1946
Beryl Bayliss (*left*), Sheila Danks (*right*)

out and thrashed me. The two events seem linked. Wallow in sordid murder, but don't take food without asking.

I used to go round to Jean Taylor's house in the evening when her parents went out, taking Diana. One evening I went when the Williamses were all going to the pictures.

I was told to be sure to be back in the house by eight o clock. Jean was terrified of being left on her own. She was dreading my going back round to 281 and leaving her to her fears. When eight o'clock came I said, "I'll have to go now, or I'll catch out." She begged, bullied and jeered me into staying.

I was hard-hearted, I was a coward for being afraid of the old woman; I was selfish and never considered other people's feelings.

At nine o clock she suddenly said, "I can hear them coming down the street, quick, run for it."

I dashed out and ran down the road, two houses down. I had just made it to the bedroom and was pulling my nightgown over my head when Mrs Williams burst in and began flailing about me with her fists, in complete silence.

Jean asked me about it next time I saw her. I told her what had happened.

"Still, never mind," she said, "that's all over now, isn't it?"

"Not really. She won't trust me any more now—she's told me so."

"Oh," said Jean, faintly.

And the old woman certainly wouldn't trust me. She was triumphant at having found me out as a deceitful, lying brat, and would take carte blanche for even stricter behaviour. Jean didn't want to know me after that. In itself a blow, because, from dinner-time till six o'clock, when Nellie came home, I didn't get anything to eat — I always had to wait till Nellie got home, and I used to rely on Jean making me two slices of toast after school, to stop me gagging with hunger. There would be no more inter-prandial toast now.

We had swimming lessons from school, at Green Lane Baths. We were lined up, waiting to go out one day, when a girl came running along the side, slipped, grabbed my arm, and we both went in. I was near enough to grab the rail, and she could already swim. Someone went to our homes to get dry clothes, while the gym mistress rubbed us down. We went into the office for a hot drink, and as we sat there, covered in skimpy Corporation towels, the manager came to see how we were. Fortunately, the door was locked. He peered worriedly through the frosted glass, but Miss Chadwick called through to tell him not to worry, we were in good hands. It was some time before he could be reassured, but eventually he went away, taking his fatherly concern with him.

The other girl sat chatting happily with the gym mistress and the attendant. Her parents would only show concern. I knew what I was in for.

"I've got a good mind not to let you go again."

"I was only standing there. She grabbed me."

"I don't want no excuses ... you're more trouble to me than all my own kids put together." And so on.

She let me go the following week, after all. She had had the pleasure of issuing the threat, which was the main thing.

I was to leave school, and couldn't be hit any more, apart from a vicious pinch from Winnie, at a Lodge meeting. She would brush my hair, short though it was, for the sole purpose of engaging me in argument. She would say something we both knew to be untrue. I would contradict her, and she would crack the back of the brush against my skull.

I'd die before I'd let her know she'd hurt me, so she would follow with; "Where there's no sense, there's no feeling."

She was quite frank about her hatred of me, and would say, openly, "There's no-one I hate more than you—but then, you don't matter. It's only yo, ennit?"

The usage of the Brummy 'yo' is one much misapplied by many a radio and television actor. It was never used in ordinary, neutral speech, but only as defiance, either real or jocular. In aggression, or affectionate badinage. I know which she meant.

All punishment tended towards the psychological now, and the worst of this was the nagging, saved up for Sunday dinner, as a special treat after a hard week's work on buses, in canteen or in household drudgery. They took turns, barely taking time to swallow their food. The list of my shortcomings would be embarked on, with slight excuse. As one stopped to take a mouthful, another would start.

" ... and another thing she does ..."

" ... just like her bloody mother, a bloody crank ..."

" ... no good to herself, nor nobody else ..."

" ... what that lot needs is a father be'ind them ..."

" ... the Dad would have sorted that lot out ..."

" ... and another thing she does ..."

When I finally broke down, they looked up in bovine astonishment; and as I made my way upstairs to get a hankie, I heard Nellie say, "I suppose we did go at her a bit." I heard them talking in quiet surprise at my reaction. I have always hated Sunday dinner.

I must have become hardened to it, because I can see Mrs Williams now, after a day's frustration, drudgery and ill-health, as I got home from school or work—her heavy head shoved at my face, suddenly launching an attack for no reason I only know it had nothing to do with me, her jaws working frantically, her breath taken in gulps, her sentences short, and her tongue flapping about. As the list went on, my selfishness, my greed, my ingratitude, my family, all I thought was, "Don't we look funny when we talk?" A stirring speech, an eloquent soliloquy, Hitler's rantings; it all comes down to that comic piece of flesh rooted in the mouth, dancing against the teeth.

Still in this distant mood, I thought, "Poor bastard, I can see how she feels." My stony silence maddened her. She wanted drama, and she wanted a fight. I had had more than enough of both. But she needed to keep me dependent, useless, to raise her own stock. That was why she hadn't minded looking after me when I was ill. Her life had been invested in family care, and motherhood was her entire asset. I was "more trouble than my own kids put together," and than the other children she had fostered, of whom she was most fond of the one with the worst temper, as she admitted it. I once, and only once, tried to emulate a bad temper, thinking this was what might have gained affection for me too. It only gave her more fuel, and a whole new sin to be added to the list. She never hit her grandchildren; their mother lived too near. The clichés of young people nowadays, 'too little discipline', and 'they have too much give 'em', had come down to her from her elders, just as they have come down to the present generation of parents, and with the same mindless subjectivity.

The one thing Mrs Williams had never been able to thrash out of me was compassion. There is nothing of the moral high ground here. It must surely be inherent in human nature—we would have all eaten each other by now, otherwise. This has formed the basis of many an argument with my Christian friends; and Humanist friends, too, who ought to know better. Whether I wanted to or not, I sympathised.

Shortly before I left school, I met with two innovations. One was pocket money. For the few weeks before I would have a pay packet to hand over, I was given three shillings a week by each of them, and they took it in turns to top it up to ten. They didn't want it thought that they "never gave me pocket money," if only for a few short weeks.

The other thing was to be attendance at three lectures at school, given by a Health Visitor. The first was entitled, 'Hygiene and Adolescence', the second one the following week was 'Courtship and Marriage'. The third was 'Childbirth'. This must have come as a relief to the Williamses. Mum was to tell me, years later, that Winnie had confided in her, saying how worried they were, and that none of them knew how to approach the subject. It occurred to none of them to get a booklet from the doctor, or the clinic.

On several occasions, I had been taken to the pictures by Nellie or Winnie. I thought this was a welcome sign of proffered friendship. Maybe I was going to be accepted as one of the family after all. But, remembering the conversation either of them had attempted, it was evidently an attempt to raise the matter of sex and babies. They tried to choose suitable films for me to see, but they seemed to be either Victorian murder melodramas, or the kind of adult film to be understood only by those already in the know. Thanks to the Hollywood Hays Code, I thought that all newly weds slept in twin beds, with a space of some three feet between them. As for the film in which the Indian maiden, (no longer, in this case) came running into camp, threw herself to the ground and hurled ash all over her head, followed by an exhausted looking cowboy, I thought, if this is courtship, forget it, I won't bother.

The Health Visitor was a severe faced woman who loftily pointed out that she was not a nurse.

"You are not to refer to me as 'Nurse', but as 'Health Visitor'."

So you're not a real nurse—well don't be defensive about it. (I could be very bold in my silent ripostes.) Do go on.

And she did. So *that* was why the Senior girls had an indoor lavatory and bins and things. It was also why I was allowed to miss assembly when I said I didn't feel well, and was mystified not to be questioned about it. So Jean Taylor hadn't been lying, either. Naturally, I hadn't believed her, she was only a silly kid. I only believed adults.

None of what this grim-faced woman said sank in in one go. Parents and guardians were asked permission to give us the information we needed. Only a few from our class went for the lecture. The remainder were girls whose parents wanted to protect them from adulthood.

They needn't have bothered. When we came back into the classroom, I became aware that the entire class was looking at me. I came out of my customary absent-mindedness, and looked mildly back at them. They all swiftly turned their heads elsewhere. So it wasn't just because I was rubbish at Games that they despised me. It was my sexual backwardness, too.

The Health Visitor invited us to write questions on a piece of paper and hand them to her afterwards. If anyone wrote anything silly it would be ignored, she told us, with a glare. But how would we know if it was silly? At that age, we were aware that our questions were going to sound naive and stupid—we didn't need this extra discouragement. I had wanted to know what the Change of Life was about, as I'd heard Nellie making jokes about it. My anxious questions to her made her thrust it away with even more levity. "You'll learn, soon enough."

But I was worried that it would be like not being able to tell the time. The longer it was left, the less possible it became to admit that I didn't know. There was no way in which I was going to confide in this hard-faced madam. I would have to pick it up in bits and scraps after all.

The lecture the following week was specifically about sex. Either she knew only what she had read from a book, or she was blessed with a very accommodating physique herself. No mention was made of painful deflowering, so she can't have believed in it. The phrase; 'slips into' has stayed with me from that time. Then she said something surprising. She described an orgasm. I thought it sounded very like what had happened to me at the age of about three or four, when I had an enema for worms, and when one or two of my infant dreams had been enlivened by the same thing. I guessed rightly, of course, but I can see that this woman was blinded by optimism in making it all sound so easy.

One of the questions she read out asked if the words 'virgin' and 'vagina' were connected. I wondered what the hell religion had to do with this, and where did Our Lady come into it? The word meant Jesus' Mum, nothing more. It was not conveyed to us at the Catholic School that 'virgin' had the remotest thing to do with sex. And the Health Visitor didn't think to explain it either. So it was no surprise to me when she said there was no connection. And she had said she wasn't going to answer silly questions! As the only Catholic in the class, I hoped no-one thought I had asked the question.

The final lecture concerned childbirth. I relaxed. This would have nothing to do with me. Not only for the obvious reason that raising a family was too hazardous for me to contemplate. I would either have treated my children to the kind of childhood I had had; would have swung all the other way, spoiled them and messed up their lives that way; or made a good job of it and destroyed myself with resentment in the process. Besides, I was no good at anything—I had had that fact drummed into me. So I had better avoid the difficult jobs. I had been told that raising children was no picnic, and that all I was good for was "painting pretty pictures and making up stories for kids and that won't get you a living, my girl." Not a real one, with luncheon vouchers, one supposes. Besides, I thought with relief, there were plenty of women willing to do their duty by the state. They could do my bit for me while they were at it.

So the Health Authorities no doubt congratulated themselves on having done their duty, and the Williamses sighed with relief that their duty had been done by the child. Relief that would last right up to the time when they realised how little help that elaborately thought-out health programme had been.

"She doesn't seem to know anything, after all," Nellie said, in my presence.

"Well, if she doesn't know now, she never will do," her mother said, dismissing the troublesome subject.

We were lucky to be told that much. The boys got told even less. Billy was told the facts of life by a nun—almost as surreal as having the Pope pronounce on sexual ethics. She told him all about pistils and stamens, and how bees fertilise flowers. His position was even more challenging than mine. He had to face the jokes and knowing nudges of young men of a similar age, without knowing what any of it was about.

* * *

1947 was the year that the school leaving age went up to fifteen, some weeks after my fourteenth birthday. I was given the option of staying on for the extra year. I decided, wisely, to get out quick, while I could still read. Any more of it and I would become as dense as the teachers. Miss Peach, our own teacher, didn't know about the application of 'pride' as a collective noun for lions, nor the noun 'converse' meaning the act of conversation—a dated noun, which she might have known nonetheless. The word 'azure' she seemed not to have heard of either; in each case she crossed the word through and put a question mark in the margin. This, again, was nothing. Billy's teacher said he was 'a good drawrer'. He tells me he wasn't, incidentally. Realising how much attention she was paying to her job, I didn't struggle any more with arithmetic, but put down numbers at random in the answers space, safe in the knowledge that she had no time to do any more than skim through the exercise books for marking.

We had mock exams, to see whether we were worth being set the entry examination for Grammar School. The results were pinned up on the wall. Unfortunately for me, there had been only three English tests but four Arithmetic tests. Although my name was at the top of the sheets giving the English results, I came bottom for numeracy. This imbalance led to my being next but bottom in the class placings.

I was very grateful to the girl who came bottom. Mary Pye, wherever you are, I hope you did as well in life as you wanted to. Had there been an equal number of English and Arithmetic tests, I would have come somewhere near the middle.

Miss Peach could not let even this go without public comment. In the middle of a noisy sewing lesson, when I was straining to hear what another girl was shouting over the racket, Miss Peach suddenly screeched, "Don't think you can talk in class just because you've come top in English, Mary Benton!"

Girl turned to girl in mock surprise, gabbling loudly, as if they hadn't scanned the lists carefully days ago.

I was surprised at Miss Peach's habit of shouting, "SHUT UP!" at intervals, when the class was noisy. Not at the shouting itself, but at the vulgarity of the phrase. I would have thought BE QUIET more appropriate in someone wishing to instil ladylike habits in us.

This was left to Miss Jack, to whom we went for housewifery, to some flats in Acocks Green, and at which I learnt only the determination never to become a housewife. I had no desire to be married to a house.

We were given points for how clean we had made the flats. If we had to Ronuk the floor of the bedroom that had the roughest floor, we got fewer points than for the one that had been more recently put in, and which took a better shine.

Did anyone say life would be fair? I'll say they did. From the earliest age, every figure of authority in power over us, that's all. "Behave in this way, and you will be rewarded. Behave in that way, and you will be punished. That's only fair." Not a word about it being unfair.

Poor Miss Jack had pretensions to running a finishing school, not having in a bunch of Council school kids to work as free labour for the teachers who lived in the flats. I recall one rebellious girl, whose handsome face went red and sweaty, and whose hair came out of curl as she thumped away in the steam over the dolly tub, complaining about this fact as Miss Jack walked into the kitchen. Miss Jack spoke a well-rehearsed speech about its being nothing of the kind. We were there for our own benefit, she told us calmly, and those teachers paid the Council for the service, which money went on our education. I have to say that my labour, for one, was wasted. I can't remember one useful thing that I learned. Having learned how to Ronuk a wooden floor, I only need to vacuum or mop. I ironed frocks and blouses then. I buy drip-dry now. Having then pounded away at the dolly tub with a copper-based vacuum washer, I now throw it all in the washing-machine. The art of bedmaking I need not have bothered with. I throw the duvet over it. I had already learned to dust and skivvy at seven. Besides, you don't need several months drudging at the same activity to learn how to do such brainless work. And I can't think what the money went on for our benefit, considering how little education and equipment we got.

Miss Jack's argument convinced me at the time, though. I was young and gullible.

Meanwhile, in line with Miss Jack's social pretensions, she would hold high tea with two girls at a time. She also had two girls every day to make a midday meal with her. This was a hit and miss affair, since only a few girls got the chance to do this. Not a bad little job from Miss Jack's point of view though. Two free meals a day on the rates, under the guise of teaching girls how to cook.

I have to admit that I liked the high tea. My turn came round twice, once as Hostess, and the next week as Guest. Only the Hostess was allowed to begin the conversation, a rule to which Miss Jack kept no matter what the embarrassment caused to tongue-tied youngsters. This was no problem for me, but the following week when I was a Guest, my friend sat dumbstruck while I tried to mouth the word 'Christmas' at her. Miss Jack sat in stony silence, looking grimmer by the second.

Finally the girl burst out with "What do you think of the weather, Miss Jack?"

It was coming down in stair-rods, and this made me giggle. I had a sudden fantasy of Miss Jack's giving a ribald reply. Once the spell was broken, the farce proceeded on its way, and more tax-payers' money was wasted. I couldn't reconcile this turn-of-the-century etiquette with the house-labour we had done during the morning. It was, in any case, not even good manners, let alone etiquette.

I can't imagine my mother tolerating this state of affairs, had she had the care of me. She had joined the Communist Party during the War, and took the *Daily Worker* after the War, when the ban on it was lifted. Never one to be po-faced about her beliefs, she had a pair of earrings in the form of a hammer and sickle, and wore them for years. She tied Winnie up in knots over dialectical materialism whenever she called to see me. On one occasion, we had a game of Twenty Questions, and Mum chose as her Next Object, a Ghost. She declared it to be Animal, as it was a product of the human brain. Since she believed that everything that existed was material, then it could not be abstract. They argued about it for half an hour.

When she left for the bus, refreshed by this intellectual sparring, she left them frustrated and fuming, and I took the brunt. This involved their criticising everything about her, from her politics to her hairstyle. She had recently had her hair, which was black, in a bubble cut, with one curl at the front dyed blonde.

"What does she think she looks like?" was Mrs Williams' contribution.

"She looks like Harpo Marx with the wrong wig on," came from Winnie. For the moment, Nellie contented herself with a delighted laugh at this witticism.

"I wish you wouldn't talk about her like that," I said.

"Don't you take it upon yourself to be so pious," Mrs Williams snapped. "Anyway, you forgot her birthday," she added. After a disapproving pause, she went on; "Fancy forgetting your own mother's birthday! Really, I am ashamed of you."

She dropped this sermon, which she had previously covered in a half hour tirade anyway, and went back to jeering at her behind her back. I did rather wish my mother would not be so hard on them. It achieved nothing. They were not capable of clear thinking, and were unable to point out the flaws in her logic. She could have employed a little undetected patronising. They were hardly a worthy subject for intellectual challenge, after all. She had had no reply for Jimmy, when she had stated, in Winnie's presence, that no statement could be an absolute certainty.

"That must include *that* statement," the teenaged Jimmy had pointed out.

Winnie gave a shout of pleasure at this, and it cheered her up for a week.

* * *

School got several things right, at last. We were taken to the Town Hall to hear the CBSO perform a children's concert. All the popular pieces; Swan Lake, Carmen, and Elgar. I wondered why stuff this good was never on the wireless. It was, of course, but the Williamses never tuned into it, not even out of curiosity. I suspect when they eventually came to own a television set, they would watch mainly game shows, and complain that most of the programmes on the telly were rubbish.

A touring actor brought his one-man reading of Treasure Island to the school. Beginning with a rather aged-up Jim Hawkins, aged seventeen—he went on to personify the Squire, Ben Gunn, Blind Pugh and Long John Silver; all given full make up and costume, then their characterisation, interspersed with more of the story. I thought what a wonderful way it must be to earn a living.

* * *

After Blanche and Lena went back to Hull, and to a woman's wage packet once more, Mrs Williams' two sisters came to stay. They had lived in a back-to-back in Balsall Heath, with gardens, intersected with a service path. Like Adelaide Street, the houses had been condemned before the War, and had a yellow, four-pointed star painted on the door jamb. Not worth converting to electricity, nor worth the expense of knocking down. This was left to the Luftwaffe, who missed.

Sister Annie was someone I could have got on with. She had more common sense that her sister Helen. Less prone to lose her head. She also questioned many of the superstitions and 'traditional wisdoms' that Mrs Williams relied on. One of them was that rendered down goose fat had done her son Bert 'the world of good'. "He didn't half heave, but it was the saving of him."

"How could it have done him any good, if it made him sick?" Annie wanted to know, but didn't get a sensible answer.

I had escaped that remedy, and narrowly missed one almost as bad. Before going to bed with a heavy cold I had been given a cup of warm milk, with a lump of butter in it. I managed to say goodnight like a ventriloquist, before spitting it out into a hankie on the way upstairs. Because children in her day suffered nutritional diseases from lack of essential fats, she thought she must shove as many fats down them once it could be afforded. She had no idea what was good for children.

The oldest, Rose, had never gone to school, and had never married. It was not surprising that she was cranky and childish. She had had, as the eldest girl, to look after the other children, and had neither childhood nor adult life to speak of. As she couldn't read, there was nothing for her to do but sit and watch her sister doing the housework. It might have helped if they had put the wireless on, to a programme of light music or comedy. There was no community life for them to join. Society had changed its shape; the extended family had turned nuclear, and there was not yet the structure to include them in a group. Annie would go out, to the park and to the shops, and make friends, leaving Rose to sit and sniff, a dry sniff, only a habit. But perpetual. It must have driven Mrs Williams frantic.

Annie died before Rose. "It's wicked to say it, but the wrong one died," Mrs Williams said. Of her elder sister, she said, "It's a pity the Lord don't look on her." Eventually, he did. Rose had a less dignified going, and not so swift. She was a big woman, and when the caring of her became too much, she had to be taken to a geriatric hospital. The porters put her in a chair sling. By all accounts, she fought all the way down the stairs. None of her relatives visited her, but eventually I was sent, with some food. She found this the final straw. "I don't want it," she said, "take it back. You needn't have bothered."

When she died, I read the card on her wreath. It began: "We saw her fading like a flower ..."

I deplored my reaction to this, but sometimes laughter is the more profound response. My feeling now is that if I show signs of such an old age, those who love me can take me straight to Amsterdam.

CHAPTER EIGHT

SOMETHING IN THE CITY

One of Winnie's favourite words was 'exterminated'. The word had become prevalent in the 'thirties, with the rise of Nazism, and she still thought it sounded rather smart.

"Men! They ought to be exterminated!" Or, "Women! They ought to be exterminated!" And of course, "Kids! They ought " and so on. It wouldn't have left anyone standing, but I'm sure it would have put the world back on its feet.

Winnie was one of those puzzling people who despised the human race, preferred animals, and yet treated their selected animal friends as if they were human. She would talk to the dog as a mother might talk to a baby, referring to herself as Mommy, when she took the unfortunate brute on her lap. Of the second dog they had while I was there, a white cross breed called Monty, she would say to him, when he was in disgrace,

"Poor Monty, you're more sinned against than sinnin'."

She didn't specify who had sinned against him, or how, but it was another fine, ringing phrase, and its lack of application was beside the point. He would gaze blandly back at her, unaware of what the neighbours had complained of, or of being in disgrace.

"He's only human, after all."

"He's not," I said, suicidally, "he's a dog."

Monty had been acquired after the dog Billy had been run over. I had come home from school, to be shown something under an old piece of carpet on the garden.

"That's Billy under there," Mrs Williams told me solemnly, waiting eagerly for a dramatic reaction.

For a split second, I thought she meant Billy, my brother, and when I realised it was the dog I tried to look sad, but the fact is that the death of animals does not affect me. I don't humanise them, though I deplore cruelty towards them. I don't eat them either, but I don't sentimentalise them.

Monty met his end in disgrace. A bitch to whom he paid his respects was owned by a family with a small child, who must have played with and fondled it, because Monty caught the scent on her. He did what dogs do. He tried to mate with the little girl. She had hysterics and had to be put to bed. The owners of the bitch told the Williamses, who immediately arranged to have the dog put down. I can't help feeling that they need only have had him neutered to ensure that he didn't do it again. Animals live from moment to moment. They don't anticipate to the extent that humans do, and would not miss what their instincts no longer prompt in them. The child's parents had not asked for Monty to be killed, and I can only assume that the Williamses were prompted by notions of respectability.

When drama intruded into real life, the old lady seized it keenly. A twelve year old boy, whom I'd played with once or twice with Jean, had an accident at football, and hit his head against the goalpost. Later, he collapsed at home, and was taken to hospital.

Next day, when I came home from school for dinner, I was getting my apron out of the lobby, when she came right up to me and said, "You know Barry Adams? HE'S DEAD!"

She watched me closely for a reaction, but I stood stupidly, with my apron in mid-air, thinking, "I suppose there's nothing more they can do for him then." In being unable to rise to the drama, I felt I had snubbed her. She really needed these moments of theatre. I ate my meal, but thoughtful and quiet only. She would have to be content with that.

* * *

Winnie, in a mood of skittishness, once asked me if I knew what the oldest profession was. "What do you think it is, Mary?"

"Ooh, don't, our Winnie," her mother remonstrated.

I thought for a moment, and said, "Farming, I suppose." Winnie found that wonderfully funny. I still think it is farming.

Politics was a confusing affair. Winnie belonged to the Transport and General Workers' Union, and spoke scathingly of strike-breakers.

"What does 'blackleg' mean?" I asked her.

"It means SCAB!" she told me, with relish.

"What does 'scab' mean?"

"It means SCAB!" Well, I'm glad we've cleared that up, then. She also disapproved of strikers, depending on whichever was the more impressive stance at the time. Nellie was a canteen cook, didn't give much thought to what went on in politics or industry beyond bearing a general impression that the bosses ripped off the workers; yet, like her younger sister, believed that the work-force should be tame and obedient. Their mother, according to Winnie, supported the Tories, voted Labour, and hoped the Liberals got in. Or any permutation of the three. Each in her declamations might contradict the others, but more frequently, herself.

The two younger of Mrs Williams' sons voted Tory. I gained the impression that the eldest, and more prosperous, took a more radical line. He may have been his father's favourite, and for this reason followed in his footsteps. I was told that, if his sons came lower in their class placings than third, they got the strap. Perhaps the younger ones voting Tory was their revenge for his having made them what they were.

John, the eldest, was in middle management. The second son, Bert, hovered between white and blue collar status, and the youngest, Charlie, worked at a garage. He was a working-class Conservative who believed that if you voted for the boss class, then by some magic means, you joined it. Only Charlie's family kept up their membership in the International Order Of Good Templars. He never made it to Chief Templar, but the man who held that office in 1954 once electrified the Lodge meeting with a proposal that had been formulated by him between some of his business acquaintances; and that was, that apart from Columbia Lodge, which we attended, there should be established a special Lodge, 'for men of repute'. Poor Brother Jarvis! The wrath of Brother Davies descended on his head.

"Of all the undemocratic, snobberatic ideas, that's the worst! It won't get a ha'pny of my money!" he declared, inventing, in his fury, a new adjective.

Brother Davis sat, and rose again. "Anyway, what's wrong with Columbia?"

"That sort of thing does leave a nasty taste in the mouth, you know," said Sister Nellie Williams, in a tone of warning reproof.

Fortunately for Sister Winnie Williams, she was out on a Midland Red turn, otherwise she might well have had one. Sister Benton thought, sceptically, men of *what* repute, always bearing in mind there is more than one kind? And would *women* of repute be admitted?

I heard Winnie talking about Communism and wanted to know what it meant.

"It stands for 'What's yours is mine, and what's mine's me own.' It's all self first, self last, and self always!"

"Like the Tories, then?"

She ignored this, and went on, "Communists like to kid themselves that you can share everything out equally, but let me tell you this, my girl," she said, gearing herself up for the big cliché, "if all the money in the state was put into the kitty, then shared out equally, poor people would only be a penny better off."

"Only if someone was cheating." I saw through this old conjuring trick every time the subject of redistribution of wealth was raised, the mathematical absolute of one man's wealth being the cause of another's poverty was conveniently ignored.

When Charlie came round, and politics came up, it descended into a shouting match.

"Your General strike didn't get you very far ..."

" ... scabbed on by the well-fed middle classes ..."

" ... bloody Urinal Bevan ..."

" ... bloody Churchill, sold our bloody pig-iron to Germany ..."

" ... handouts for the idle ..."

" ... unemployment ..."

" ... appeasement ..."

" ... warmonger ..."

Mrs Williams sat frowning and nodding at all this, then turned and glared at me, to see if I was taking in the Shavian interchange.

"You'll learn a lot by listening to this. You pay attention. You'll LEARN!"

My head ached abominably, but there was no way in which I could get away. My every move was policed and questioned.

When the clever people were not there to hear her, Mrs Williams gave me her interpretation of the matter.

"All Russians are illegitimate baahhstards!" allowing her lower jaw to drop on the long vowel. While I stifled a giggle, Winnie laughed at her and said, "The two words mean the same thing, our Mother."

* * *

Winnie looked through the Situations Vacant column in the Birmingham Mail, and took me for an interview at the Wesleyan and General in Steelhouse Lane. I was given the loan of Nellie's music case to take my sandwiches in, and for months people must have thought I played the piano. When I won a small attaché case at the Wesleyan sports day in a game of luck, the first thing Winnie said on seeing it was, "I can use that to take to work with me." What's yours is mine, etc. She never did, though. I kept it for years, valuing it all the more for having got it for nothing.

The work as a filing clerk was simple, but physically demanding. The insurance proposals were kept in large tin boxes, kept on and under trestle tables. I was all day humping them up on to the top of the other boxes, opening the rusty clasps, getting out or filing away the proposals, humping them down again, and with very little time to sit down. I amused myself reading the small print: "The Society is not liable for civil disturbance or Acts of God." I'd bear that in mind should I decide to insure my worldly goods.

The first day, I came home, ate my dinner, and sat staring into the fire, too tired to answer their questions except by a Yes or No; too tired to knit or even to read. I went to bed early, and heard them talking in sympathetic tones as I went upstairs. It was the milestone in my life that one might expect it to be. I thought, "That's it then. I didn't want to grow up, but here I am, I'm fourteen. Childhood is over. You only get one go."

I was paid £1. 5s 0d a week. Twenty five shillings in 1947 would equate roughly to sixty or seventy pounds, fifty years later. I had to hand the packet, containing five pounds, every month to Mrs Williams, and she gave me back enough for my bus fares and two cups of tea a day, and she put sandwiches for me to take. If I needed money for a swim or the pictures or for my Lodge subscription, I had to ask for it, or I would walk part of the way to work, and save for it. I lost a two shilling piece down the floorboards at work, where the lino was worn away, and had to walk to and from work for three days. I pretended the bus home had been late. I didn't dare admit that I'd been so careless that I'd let the money slip between the joists.

My reputation for carefree recklessness would have been flourished at me. "Easy come, easy go, that's Mary," was one of Nellie's favourite criticisms. It might, of course, have been only an example of her cutting wit and ironic inversion. When I left for work, I slipped out as early as possible, and went the shortest way into the city, cutting across the bus route—along roads that no longer exist, and which have been superseded by super highways. I got to work just on time.

"You'll have to wear a different dress every day," Mrs Williams told me. I don't know where she had got this one from; the 'daughters of the house' for whom she had worked, maybe, who wore several different gowns a day. I only had three frocks, so they had to be interchanged before they had been 'dirtied out'. They were shabby and falling to bits, and should have been thrown out long ago. Winnie would pick up a cheap frock at a sale, for a few shillings. While I had been at school, I needed only a clean white blouse with my gym slip, and I had two pairs of black woollen stockings. This appealed to my snobbery, as school uniform equalled posh schools in my mind. That the other girls beat me up for giving myself airs, was hard luck, but it did teach me to run fast.

I had a rise after a few months, to £1. 8s. 0d., and had to hand over three quarters of it. "*You* can buy the *Daily Mirror* from now on, Mary, now that you've got some money in hand," the old lady told me.

"And it's time you started wearing some lipstick; and your hair will have to be permed." All that, and the court shoes I would have to wear instead of school shoes, was going to make quite a hole in seven shillings.

"Your underwear is a disgrace, it's full of holes—you really should buy some more." This reproof came only half-heartedly. She realised I couldn't afford it, but felt she should keep reminding me to do these grown-up things all the same. Once I'd bought the lipstick, I quite liked the effect, but the novelty soon wore off, and I didn't always bother.

As for my hair, only a schoolgirl could get away with it straight in those days, and I was going to work looking like a twelve year old, so I succumbed to the perm. I had been trying to cling to the shreds of childhood, but I was aware that this was cheating, though I sometimes lapsed. I was taken to a social at Earl Bourne, where Bert Williams worked. His daughter Brenda was there; like me, fifteen by now, but very grown-up and sober. While the dancing was going on, I grew bored, and started playing with Josie. We collected the cigarette ends from the ballroom floor, and put them into ashtrays, then compared each other's haul.

When Mrs Williams got to hear about it, she was scandalised. She couldn't understand why I was such a freak. What had gone wrong with my upbringing, after all they had spent on me, after all the thought and care that had been lavished on me? And so on. No good asking me. I really couldn't imagine. I only know I must have embarrassed the shit out of them. It is my contention, and was my mother's, too, that it is the duty of the young every now and then to startle their elders. This was before green hair and cannabis—I did my best with what was at hand. I was caught climbing trees at seventeen; by a park-keeper who asked me if I didn't think I was too old for it. As he stood there—for some time—looking up my frock. I didn't know there was a clause in the bye-laws about age. Either it was unlawful to climb trees or it wasn't.

Rebellion was all very well—indeed, it was urged on me at one point: "Why don't you be like other gels?" Winnie added to this by saying; "When I was your age, I was smoking behind the shed ... yes, that's something you didn't know about, our Mother ..."

I should have kept to just this formula. I should have joined the Young Communists and got it all safely out of my system, then settled down, like sediment. But that kind of rebellion has far more shock value when it is discovered in a white-haired biddie, as I often find to my glee.

Mrs Williams gave me her husband's Pitman's Shorthand text book. This interested me, but I was hoping for something more exciting in the way of eventual employment. Night school for art and drama had been suggested by the Headmistress just before I left school, and these were entered upon. But it all had a disturbing feel to it. I felt cavernously insecure. After years of denigration and neglect, I was suddenly expected to blossom of my own accord. I was always going to be given this or that facility. Mrs Williams was going to teach me to cook, "but not until I've taught Winnie first," so I needn't set my hopes on that. I was going to be 'overalled' by the doctor.

I was told, "we'll have to get you a dictionary," because I was always asking what they meant by this or that word—words they used without thinking—merely to pad out a sentence to give it more emphasis.

The list of promises eventually took the place of their fulfilment, and the duty was considered to have been done. I was declared ungrateful, without knowing quite what form the ingratitude took. Great plans had been talked about and left at that. I knew they were not capable of them.

"How do I become an actor?" I asked.

"That's for you to find out."

"Where do I ask?"

"If you're keen enough, you'll find out for yourself. Use your initiative. Get off your backside, and stand on you own two feet. Don't just rely on us to do everything for you. I won't always be around to look after you, you know."

"But I want to know how to begin."

"If you're so clever, you should know." I would keep up the frantic questioning, aware of time passing and the opportunity with it. They would throw the matter straight back at me. I was getting anxious about making a living. I couldn't be a filing clerk all my life.

Eventually, the nagging started up again. "Neither useful nor ornamental."

"Big enough and ugly enough."

"After all that's been done for you."

"No good to yourself, nor nobody else." The dreaded words, repeated until they acquired a thudding rhythm, a sing-song tone of sour boredom, seemed to come at me in cycles. They would leave me in peace for several months, then one would start, and the other two would take up the chorus. I got nagged as a husband does by a bitter wife. I could see the years stretching out, grey and pointless. At seventeen I finally took up shorthand.

"Why the sudden Thusness, all of a sudden," Mrs Williams demanded; "you didn't want to do it when I suggested it. Anyway, I don't know whether I'll let you. You are under my guardianship, and while you are under my roof, you have to do things according to my jurisdiction. When you go home, you can do what you like. You can stand on your head if you like. But while you are in my house, you act according to my jurisdiction." She liked the sound of this last word, and worked it in a third time.

When her shouting had died down, she grudgingly acceded to the shorthand lessons, even though I had taken the matter on my own initiative, for once, having set it aside when it had been all her own idea.

Isn't it strange that a decision that you have been mulling over for some time, then taken leisurely steps to put into operation, appears to others as abrupt and headlong? The first pair of glasses I bought drew the comment from a woman in the same department; "This is a bit sudden, isn't it?" She gave an amused glance round the office, to note my eccentric behaviour.

"I've been thinking about it for months, Miss Derby. I can't see the numbers on the buses, and the cinema screen is a blur."

She repeated doggedly how sudden it was to see me wearing glasses. It was obvious that I should have reported to her first. Or perhaps she felt that I should have got them bit by bit, a lens at a time, then the frames, and finally the arms. In order not to startle her from her comatose routine.

I had the perm. I was wired up to the hairdresser's machine looking like the Bride of Frankenstein. The slightest move and the cookers dislodged and rested on your scalp. Being the fidget that I was, they soon did. When I complained, I was admonished by the hairdresser; "You're supposed to sit still for half an hour. Besides, you don't want a steam burn, they're really painful." Well pardon me, I didn't know you provided extras. One of these was to get the apprentice—every time I went, so I had her fumbling and bungling over my head each time.

I could have done without the ordeal of the brassiere. I mean I could really have managed without it, no-one would have noticed. I had very little to put in it, and it felt horrible. Ribs are not meant to have constricting straps round them, and I couldn't take a full breath. I felt dizzy. I used to undo them as soon as I got to the toilet at work.

I can understand most sexual and gender variations, but male transvestism has me completely baffled. They could have had all my pins, belts, straps and toe-pinchers for nothing. They actually *choose* to wear suspenders?

I was at last allowed to bath myself by the age of sixteen, but the first time this occurred I locked the door. I heard Mrs Williams try the handle. She was furious. She'd been hoping to get a good look.

"That's false modesty," she raved, misapplying the phrase, "sheer affectation!"

I heard her go away, and carried on soaping my neck.

Then she came back. "Who do you think wants to look at you anyway?"

You do, you weird bugger.

CHAPTER NINE

REUNION

I began to drift away from the church. The Sunday ritual was getting me down. The pointless kneeling, standing, sitting, then more standing, more kneeling. I skipped it and went to watch the football on the recreation ground. I never quite understood the rules, I still don't, but I enjoyed the skill, and took sides.

After several weeks, I met Father Rhys on my way home from work. He wanted to know why I hadn't been to church. I was too polite to say I was depressed by the dead ritual, so I said,

"Well, it's not doing me any good."

"How do you know it's not doing you any good if you don't come?" Logic was not his strong point.

He stood there, raging and shouting, "You young people, you've no responsibilities, you're thoughtless and ungrateful ... you'll feel differently when you're older and less carefree ..."

Oh, burst into flames, you silly old fart, I thought. I finally got away, already tired after the day's work, and rendered further jaded and tearful by his rage. He hadn't been this bad-tempered since the last time he had requested a silver collection, and got a pile of silver threepenny bits on the plate. He denounced us tremendously from the pulpit the following week, the only enjoyable part of the service.

The last occasion on which I ever willingly went to Mass, the priest, who was old and crabby, ranted at us for there being so few of us there. We were the ones who had turned up, and he was blaming us for those who were not there, the barmy bugger. "Look at you!" he bellowed, "there are barely twenty of you here!"

Mrs Williams didn't make the fuss I thought she would at my giving up religion. I think she had envied me, and imagined it gave me something denied to her.

"Your lot worships statues," she claimed.

"We don't worship them, they're just ornaments."

"Don't answer back! I said you worship them!" She spoke scornfully of small girls on their way to their first Communion.

"They look like little brides," she said, in distaste.

But she was more than happy to come with me to St Mary's in Handsworth, when I was confirmed, to see Canon Bryan Green dab the oil on my forehead. She had scouted round frantically to

Me with Naomi and small boy next door —
3, back of 27, Adelaide Street

borrow a white frock, only to find they had some at the church, for those who couldn't afford to buy one. She took great pleasure in reading out the piece in the Birmingham Mail, describing how we had looked 'like a flock of white birds'. Religion might well have provided her with comfort, drama, and a measure of serenity, as long as she could have kept up the belief all through her illnesses and disappointments. If she could have held on to the illusions until death, it would have gone some way to redeeming itself in my eyes.

* * *

I enjoyed learning shorthand, but I have a bone to pick with Isaac Pitman. There is no way in which the human ear can regard P, T, K, and Chay as soft sounds. Nor B, D, Gay or J, as hard. There is more labial effort in making a P than for a B. This caused a stumbling block to speed writing. I frequently inverted his rules without meaning to. I had eventually to work on a compensating principle—a light stroke for the hard P, a heavy stroke for the light B. Apart from that, I raced ahead.

Consistent with my habit of doing everything arse-uppards, I took the typing lessons after I was well established with the shorthand. By this time, Mrs Williams was getting impatient for me to get a job as a secretary.

"If you don't get a move on to qualify, I'm going to stop you going."

"It takes about two years," I said.

"What about your friend in the Guides; it only took her eighteen months."

"That's because she was on a full-time course. She didn't have to go to work, like me."

"Excuses. You're full of excuses. Always arguing. You love to argue."

l told the tutor about all this, and she looked puzzled. "You're doing fine," she told me, "you're well ahead. Haven't you told her that?" I always found it embarrassing to have to explain how things were at home, so I let the matter go.

The old lady had a taste for indoor spring flowers. There would be daffodils, narcissi and best of all, hyacinths. In the evening, they would be taken off the window sill before the curtain was drawn, and put on the table after tea. I used to sit at the table to transcribe my speed notes. I used a fountain pen that Jack had given me for my seventeenth birthday, and I have a memory set of shorthand homework, the glorious smell of hyacinths, and my first and only fountain pen. By the time the rubber feeder had perished, ball point pens could be bought without having to order them.

One warm evening, I didn't feel like going to night school, and bunked off to the park. The tutor sent a postcard, asking if everything was all right, evidently worried that I had been forbidden to come. I came home from work to find that Mrs Williams had read the card, and she did a big production number on it. "Be sure your sins will find you out."

Resisting the unkind urge to laugh, I said, wide-eyed, "How did you know what was written on the card?"

"What do you mean, ... ? I read it of course." I raised my eyebrows. (I couldn't raise just one eyebrow, though I practised).

She blustered, "I've got a perfect right to read it. Everything that comes into this house belongs to me."

Quite untrue in law, but it did me good to see her face, caught out in her nosiness.

After six months of typing lessons, I thought I was ready for the typing pool, and asked the Lady Controller for a test. I read back my shorthand all right, but the typing is best not thought about. "Give yourself another six months, you should be ready by then." She was sympathetic, but I was distraught to realise that I was not about to take the secretarial route out of hardship just yet, and went back in tears to my filing boxes.

I was working in the basement by this time. It was warm in the winter down there, where all the pipes were, and I worked with two shifts of women clerks now. The previous ones were young men who were waiting to do their National Service, and didn't see why they should be too particular about the job. As the proposals had come back from the departments, they had shoved them into any box that had the space, wholesale, leaving the files in chaos. We sorted out the confusion, checking right through from the earliest ones from the 1850s to the 1950s.

Winnie had bought me a second-hand bike, for a pound. A friend of hers had bought if for her daughter, who had then died, and the bike was never ridden, but had lain in a shed for years. I cleaned it up, de-rusted it, had it fitted with a lamp and a basket, and learned how to mend a puncture. I was glad to be free of bus journeys, and made my way to work on it, parking it in the basement.

The acquisition of a bike, and the exercise if afforded, coincided with the menarche, though I have no idea whether the two were connected. I lost masses of hair, and got a baldy spot that never completely grew back, but I felt that I had at last joined the female race. 'Race' was the operative word, with hurdles. The boys I hoped to attract were too shy, or spoken for. I seemed only to attract the attentions of old men. The Williams' grandson, Colin, called one day, so I nipped upstairs and put some lipstick on. I'd been told, frequently, to "make the best of yourself, you never know who you might meet."

But as I went out of the room for some other purpose, I heard Nellie remark, "You can see what Cleopatra's up to, can't you?"

I went straight upstairs and rubbed the lipstick all off again, and went out for a walk, furious with shame. I wished they would make up their minds between them. I was expected to catch a husband, but must not be seen making the effort. You were either a sad old maid or a scheming husband-hunter. Even if I had been possessed of the girly tricks, I liked men too much to make fools of them. And I saw too many casualties of the sex war. Girls got called nasty names for giving in, and even nastier ones for leading a man on, holding out for a white wedding.

Besides, I had certainly not come all this way to carving out a living for myself, for some man to take the credit as my provider. "Anything that has to be fought for as bitterly as that is not worth having." These are the memorable words of a Shaw character, even more memorably named Lesbia, from Getting Married. One wonders if the virginal Shaw knew what the named implied, or if it was a deliberate tease.

The 1953 coronation was marked by school parties. Our sister, Naomi, who was five, was taken out for a treat, to the Lickey Hills, with Mum and Billy, because they didn't want her to miss out. This fine, Republican gesture was spoiled only by the fact that the corned-beef sandwiches had been left at home.

* * *

Five years before this, Ruby was expecting her first daughter, Delia. While I was sitting reading one evening, Winnie was knitting baby clothes.

"Are those for Ruby?" I asked.

She snapped back, "What do you want to know for?"

I knew that a stern voice was not always indicative of disapproval, or even natural bad manners, but might be a mask for anything from embarrassment, double-dealing, to self-importance. In the present case, if was the last.

"As a matter of fact," she told me ponderously, "it is for Ruby."

Well, I thought, it shows a friendly feeling towards my sister.

"You're quite right," she repeated with even more weight, "these baby clothes are for Ruby's baby."

I couldn't complain of being left in doubt, then, as her mother then found several more ways of saying the same thing.

On one of my child-minding duties with Josie and Michael, they seemed bursting with some information that they possessed, but that I was not to know. "There's something I know that I'm not allowed to tell you," was the taunt that Josie tried to throw my way, as I walked with them to the bus stop. I didn't feel I was missing anything that concerned them, and from which I was excluded. But Josie kept it up, and Michael copied her; then suddenly launched a verbal attack on my mother; gutter language they had picked up at school. I didn't hit them, for two reasons. One was cowardice—the other was even worse. I had become indifferent to Mum; she was just a woman I knew. I told Nellie about Josie and Michael.

"Put it down to where it comes from," she said, with a surreptitious look towards her mother and sister.

Jack used to come to stay at the Williamses during his weekend leaves from the Army in 1947 and 1948. The arrangement was that he would send a card in the days beforehand, and then turn up. One day he arrived at their door, and Mrs Williams asked, "Hasn't your mother written to you?" It seems that she had asked Mum to tell Jack that it was no longer convenient for him to stay. So he arrived there on leave to find a midwife there, delivering Naomi.

He had had no idea that she was expected—Mum didn't show her pregnancy until a fortnight before Naomi was born. I don't think even Billy or Jimmy knew, and they had been living at Adelaide Street since the middle 'forties.

Mum asked Jack to go to the Williamses to tell them, and for them to tell me. So it was that, as I was sitting in the living-room with Jack, Mrs Williams stood before me and said, "Mary, you've got a little sister."

"You mean niece, don't you?"

"No, I mean a sister."

I looked at Jack, thinking this was the first he knew of it. He looked away. This must have been more of a shock to him that it was to me. My emotion was one more of startlement than of dismay. I believed adults when they said that certain things should not be done. At fifteen, I knew what most of them were. It didn't hang together. Cutting across this, was my observation that what adults themselves did was not for the young to question. Since I accepted this unquestioningly, it was easier for me to juggle the conflicting orders.

When Jack left, Nellie said, "Poor Jack." They didn't bother to ask me how I felt, or even to discuss it with me. After all, they had told their own grandchildren before letting me know.

Nevertheless, of all the events I had had to cope with, this was the least traumatic, and after finding to my amusement, that I felt a fleeting jealousy at no longer being the baby of the family, I would have settled down to the fact, and looked forward to seeing the baby. But this was something that Mrs Williams was going to make the most of.

At forty-two, Mum felt she could decide what she did with her own fertility. She could handle any spiteful moralist; she was not, after all, a vulnerable girl of seventeen, fair game for attack and destruction, so few people got nasty with her. Her neighbours, near to the bottom of the social heap, were too busy surviving, and they took this traditional attitude. One just got on with life.

Mrs Williams was in her element—on her high moral stance in denunciation, and outrage, interchangeable with heroic forgiveness when anyone else's frailty was invoked, demanding to know who they were to judge. Whichever pose suited her own sense of worthiness at the time.

* * *

My teenage years trudged on—I reached twenty, and hints were dropped that it was time I left and went home. Hurrying out to work one day, I noticed a button missing on a blouse, and pinned it across with my old Guide badge. The old lady noticed it. "That's dishonest. You're not a Guide any more. It's a lie; sheer pretence."

I didn't explain about the button, I would never have got off to work.

"Have you been opening the big window in your bedroom

again?" came the accusatory question, several times in the oppressive summer.

"Well, I find it hard to breathe, and the transom window isn't enough."

"Don't make things up. It's sheer affectation. Keep that window closed. It might fall off and go crashing into the yard." I had developed a frightening condition in which, as I started to drop off to sleep, my breathing stopped. I would wake up with a jolt and have to sit up in case it happened again. This would happen several times before my breathing became involuntary again. I hadn't heard of Ondine's Syndrome then, so it can't have been suggestion.

Their worry about the window dropping off into the yard can only have been a cover for their fear that I would be listening in to what they were saying about me in the other back bedroom. If so, they needn't have worried; I could hear much better from the landing before they came to bed. Muffled sentences began to drift up … "She'll never amount to anything …" "Well, she's not all that bad, but she's got nothing about her. She's got no flair …" " … She needs to be more like our Brenda …" And then, to my astonishment: "Well, we haven't been that much help to her." This was from Mrs Williams, and was the only time I ever heard it admitted that their influence might not have been all it should.

I quite liked Brenda. She and I went with Winnie to Llandudno. Winnie didn't enjoy it at all. She took the usual licence to hit me when she felt like it. Brenda was shocked. This was a side of her Auntie Win she hadn't met with before.

I stayed at her house for a weekend after the following Christmas. Once again, I got to learn how normal families lived; how young girls were supposed to develop. There were four of them, all girls, much younger than Brenda, and both their mother and father tolerated more noise and disruption than I had ever caused. I compared them with their senior family, and got a better overview of both.

Brenda said to her mother; "I don't understand Auntie Win. Mary gets on all right with us."

Her mother replied, with slow emphasis: "It's not Mary—IT'S THEM! Look at Michael. He's a complete mess when he's with Grandma, but he's perfectly normal when he's with us."

Back at the senior Williamses I was left in the house one

Saturday afternoon. "Don't get inviting any friends in, do you hear?"

As I'd never been allowed to anyway, this was needless. "No, of course not."

So I was rather worried when Brenda and her friend turned up. They were sitting with their backs to the window when Brenda's Grandma came back, and glared ferociously at the intruders as she came up the front path. When she saw it was her grandchild and friend, she could hardly blame me for it. At teatime, the two girls helped themselves to two slices of bread and butter at a time, leaving two slices on the plate. (And she thought my sparrow appetite was excessive). She was so indignant at this that she sat suddenly bolt upright and glared at me, daring me to take one of the remaining slices. Brenda and Lily giggled into their plates.

By way of conversation, Mrs Williams commented on Lily's red jumper. "You look like a Robin Redbreast ... you do." They giggled at the word 'breast' and she repeated, " ... just like a Robin Redbreast ... you do." It was her habit to say the same thing in as many different ways as possible.

I had taken to going to Pype Hayes to Brenda's family nearly every weekend, when Mrs Williams put a sudden stop to it. When I asked why, she refused to be questioned on the subject, and simply forbade me to, 'while I was under her roof'. It occurred to me that one might get up to all sorts of wild behaviour, as long as it was above the tiles and among the chimneys.

Her final complaint against me was that I didn't pay enough for my keep. More than a third of my wages, in fact, for food, laundry and one bath a week. All the rest; clothes, swimming, football, cinema, speedway, holidays, I paid for myself. I suppose the truth of it was that I was an embarrassment to them; too much unlike them to be acceptable.

"Why don't you just tell me to go?" I asked her one day at breakfast.

She mumbled some acceptance of this, then later, as an afterthought, she said, "You don't mean any more to me than a lodger."

I wondered why she pointed out such an obvious fact, and thought no more of it until I told a colleague at work. It wasn't until her shocked reaction; "What a thing to say to you after all these years!" that the idea struck me, and my eyes began to sting. I had got used to the fact that affection had to be earned;

or that it was, paradoxically, something that existed within an exclusive, magic circle, to which you either had or had not the right of entry. I had detached myself from hopes of family affection, and found it jarring to be faced with this sudden thawing.

We agreed on a month's notice, when Winnie told me that, by rights, I should pay two month's keep when I left, because of having a month's grace at the beginning of my working life.

I said, "How much do I owe you then?"

She tried to baffle me with a speech on the lines of; a month's credit this, in lieu of that, further to the amount in hand of something else—leaving out only heretofore and notwithstanding. It sounded for all the world like the Marx Brothers' Party Of The First Part sketch.

"So how much does that mean I owe you, then?" I asked, not even pretending to take it seriously. To her credit, she hadn't the hardihood to keep to this idea, and turned her head away in disdain.

* * *

In October, 1953, I borrowed the suitcase, and arranged to bring it back the following Saturday.

"You will bring it back, won't you?" Mrs Williams was anxious to know. Of course I damn well would. I was only indifferent, not dishonest. She still hadn't got to know me.

When I brought it back, I was asked how I was settling in. I didn't spare them the details of slum living, but I did get a twinge at seeing the old lady silently weeping at what she had sent me back to. The fact is, my concern about my living quarters has only ever been one of comfort, not status. I had no time for materialist snobberies; mine were all cultural and academic. When I told people at the time that my ambition was to have wall to wall carpeting, they thought I was talking fashion and status. I only ever meant warm feet.

There were pluses and minuses in my latest change of address. The minuses included sharing a bed with Mum and Naomi. If you ever have the flu, try and avoid sleeping in a bed with an energetic five year old jumping up and down on it. Having no garden or spare room to escape to in a family row, of which there were plenty, mostly at Sunday dinner-time, just the streets of Balsall Heath. Living in a red-light district didn't help where I would be propositioned on the way to work, in broad daylight, striding along, with attaché case, sensible clothes and shoes, and no make-up.

"There must be a shortage of prostitutes round here," I thought, "if they have to try it on with a frump like me."

The pluses were that I lived near enough to the city to save money by walking to work. Lack of a bathroom was no problem. I lived only a few streets away from Kent Street Baths, and they had slipper baths. But the biggest advantage was that I was left to organise my own life. I could meet young men and get my life started without being made to feel like a scarlet woman, or worse, a desperate old maid.

I had already joined the Birmingham Ladies' Swimming Club, the first one ever for women in Birmingham; that's how old it was. I was in the team, and although we never won a team race, I usually came away from a gala with a set of spoons or a goldfish bowl, for coming second in an individual event, or for a dive rewarded for its height rather than its style.

By means of wearing my shoes out until I had to put cardboard in them between my feet and the pavement, I was able to save up the six pounds for a pair of ice-skates. It cost six shillings a session at the Summerhill Rink. I went about ten times, then realised I was not going to be the second Sonje Henie, so I cut my losses, stopped going, and sold my skates to a dealer in Hurst Street. I was given two pounds for them. Expecting him to ask three pounds on re-sale, I later saw them in the window, marked up to six pounds. Mum had often said that the first law of the market place states that a thing is worth only what someone is prepared to pay for it. I would add the rider; 'or what the vendor is willing to let it go for.'

The best way to warm up the tiny room at home was to light the oven, and leave the oven door open. The cat would sit in front of it, with her head too far forward, and singe her whiskers on both sides. She never learned. All the same, it quickly warmed the room.

Those old places were falling down. We would hear about it on the news. The condemned houses, tired of waiting for the bulldozers or the bombs, succumbed in their rotten state, to the force of gravity, sometimes killing the occupants. One night in the early 'fifties, a tectonic plate a mile beneath us shifted slightly. I was the only one awake when the tremor made its way up through the prehistoric rocks, and the street shook. The sound was barely perceptible, but after two seconds the wave was taken up by the

terrace of houses, sturdy enough in their back-to-back forma-
tion to do nothing more than make the timbers creak.

It was an eerie feeling as I waited for the bricks to fall, but
only the crockery rattled, and the bricks rumbled. We always
know immediately when it's an earthquake, and I sat up in bed
(I'd got my own bed now, though I still shared the room with
Mum and Naomi), waiting for the rotten bricks to crumble. The
door to a small cupboard under the stairs above us had come
ajar. Inside this was a nail on which I hung my three frocks. Two
pairs of shoes went on the floor with the attaché case.

* * *

Tony's Dance Hall, next to the Hippodrome, was free on Saturday nights to girls and women, but I met few young men to
whom I would give houseroom, and I didn't much care for Rock
and Roll. I grew to like it some thirty years later, when it came
back in fashion, but that was only when the better tunes were
played, leaving a huge amount of dross behind. Lesser
musicians had churned out the stuff on the crest of a wave
which had brought a fresh and vigorous popular art form. It
was the rubbish that had deadened my ears to the good stuff,
and prejudiced me. By the way, I couldn't stand Elvis.

I made friends at the Swimming Baths; young men with
motorbikes. I assessed their date-ability on whether they surrendered the crash helmet for me to wear without my having to
ask for it. As I fitted it over my bubble cut, and climbed astride
the pillion, I began to think I might be about to join the human
race after all.

* * *

The first time you ever go abroad is bound to be special. I got
the chance in 1956 to go to a Temperance Summer School in
Sweden. The island of Öland is the long strip of land on the
east of the mainland, shaped like a paper knife. I had had a
year to save the twenty-five pounds, and decided to make use
of the time to learn a bit of Swedish. I was motivated by
curiosity rather than need. Most modern countries, then as
now, spoke English. It gave me an insight into my own language. I hadn't noticed how many superfluous forms there are,
nor the fact that we need only one word for 'is' 'are' and 'am'.

My knowledge of most subjects is broad and shallow, rather than narrow and deep, and I often give the impression of being more erudite than I am. I would write a Bluffer's Guide to almost anything, but for the fact that even that needs a detailed study of what to pick out. I haven't subsequently remembered more than some twenty words of Swedish, but I was struck at the time by how much easier it is to learn than French or German, of which also, I only learned holiday use.

The chief attraction of another country is its physical difference. I like it to *feel* foreign; colder, hotter, drier, damper; where the daylight defies the clock, or dusk begins at noon. Where double storm doors stand in contradiction to a warm summer, and where altitude renders the sky overhead inky blue in mid-morning. What Öland has is a botanical oddity. Splitting the island lengthways, it has lush growth on the mainland side, and stunted shrubs on the other; the same type of plants, but dramatically smaller, separated by only the width of a roadway. A pleasant surprise was the temperature of the Baltic at Malmö. It was the warmest sea I had ever swum in, and the cleanest. I could see through it underwater like a swimming pool.

We stayed at a residential college, about forty or fifty of us, and mostly from Europe. I couldn't say now what was decided about the effects of alcoholic drink, but genetics was discussed and pronounced upon, the result being a state of healthy disagreement.

Sharper in my memory was an Englishman, who clearly had not taken the fourfold pledge, (no drinking, no smoking, no gambling and no swearing), who smoked the whole time, it must have been about eighty a day, stopping only at mealtimes; and even then, he smoked between courses. His fingers and thumb were a deep mahogany.

I had taken the fourfold pledge at the age of twelve; I don't remember being asked, only told, to do it. So it might be regarded as a youthful indiscretion—an immature decision. I therefore had no compunction in breaking it at all points once I was old enough to know better. I didn't become addicted; I've never needed alcohol as an excuse to act silly—high spirits rather than potent will do that for me. Smoking was what I did to kid myself I was engaging in a leisure pursuit while working; repetitive, brain-rotting copy typing. Nicotine did absolutely nothing for me, and I gave it up with no trouble at all. As for gambling, I have a low disappointment threshold and a sufficient grasp of mathematics and the laws of probability not to send my money back to the already well off. I only swear in print, or when there are no ladies present.

One of the speakers had the worst Cockney accent I had ever heard till then. It's notable that the further North or South you go from the Midlands, the more likely that a regional accent is to be unintelligible. None of us knew what he was saying. Even I could pick out only a few words, and I consider myself an honorary Cockney. We were told that he had been a lot worse.

Although the agreement was that everyone would speak in English when addressing the class, that didn't stop a member from making a string of jokes in Swedish, which pleased most of the class — he seemed to be some kind of stand-up patter man. The jokes and the laughter came in rapid succession, staccato and quickly cut off, ready for the next joke. It made for a weirdly humourless impression.

The English were not much better mannered. A member from our group congratulated Bro Arne Goplen on presenting the manner of a perfect English Gentleman. I looked for a hole to disappear into, and the Norwegians murmured to each other, "No, he's not, he's Norwegian." They said it, pointedly, in English.

The most respectable looking Englishman came into our dormitory to say Goodnight to his daughter. He didn't knock the door or ask permission, just walked straight in while we were undressing. Someone must have had a word to his wife the following day, because he didn't try it the following night. What he did in his daughter's bedroom was not our concern, but anyone's guess.

We found the Swedes were irritated to have their country described as the 'Scandinavian America', on account of a surface impression. The obvious prosperity I noticed was more uniformly distributed than that which we observe from the United States. The overall impression I gained was one of cleanliness and luxury. There were even carpets in the corridors of the trains.

Of current interest at the time was the belief that Sweden led the world in licentious behaviour. This hopeful myth had more to do with partners not immediately marrying on the birth of their first-born, an innovation (or ancient practice) that has spread without harm to the rest of the modern world. The other old chestnut concerning Sweden was its supposed world-leading status in the suicide rates. That the lack of an underclass to kick around meant that life was no longer worth living. I suspect that the world could get on without someone who felt that way.

We stayed overnight in Copenhagen on the way back. I had started a period just towards the end of the holiday and was so bad-tempered about it that I went into denial. I didn't bother to buy pads; I pretended that it wasn't going on. This was how I came to dump three pairs of bloody knickers in Copenhagen Harbour. Perfectly good garments, but I'd had enough.

It would be some ten years before the contraceptive pill, and the discovery that if I took it all round the cycle without a break, I could get rid of periods altogether. My doctor was puzzled when I asked him if it was safe to do this.

"Some women enjoy their periods," he told me. I'd remember that next time I was curled up round a hot water bottle.

I had asked a doctor earlier if I could have the new hormone treatment to get my period to come on at weekends. He smiled fatly and asked, "When's the wedding?"

I explained.

When he realised it was not the wish to avoid getting a pretty dress spattered with blood, but a desperate attempt to hold down a job, he went stern on me, and told me,

"We must put up with these things, mustn't we?"

Nice of him to share it, but I'd upset his idea of a woman's place in his cosy world.

Backyard of 23, Conybere Street

* * *

The Council moved us at last from Adelaide Street, in 1957, to a house a few streets away. 23, Conybere Street, still in Balsall

Heath; the road runs off Gooch Street, still only half a mile from the city. The houses were terraced, but not back-to-back. We had the whole of the house to each household, front and back entrances. They were in courts of three houses, and we had a lavatory to ourselves; in a row of three across the yard. No bathroom, but we did have a tiny garden at the back, big enough for two to sunbathe in, and with fencing that almost matched the garden in overall area, like a small picture with a big frame. I planted a sunflower against the wall, I've been told. A huge flower in a tiny garden.

The houses opened directly on to the street, and we shared an entry into the court. The man next door, who had also just moved in, took up some of the ground bricks from the yard, held in common, to extend his garden, but the other neighbour objected, so he had to put them back again. Worth a try, he must have thought. He hadn't learned that only feudal lords had been allowed to enclose common land and call it their own.

There was a telephone in the front room, which we kept. Life was beginning to look up. The stairs bisected the house, and the previous owner had converted the attic into an extra bedroom. Being a builder, he had taken the sink and stove out of the kitchen and built an extra bit on to form a scullery, overlooking the garden from the side. It made a tiny kitchen, and the original kitchen was now a back living room.

I had the attic bedroom; at last, a room of my own. I'd been working as a shorthand typist for four years by now and was able to furnish it, after a fashion. I bought a single wardrobe for seven pounds, was given a table, and bought a record player. I bought Buddy Holly's single, I Guess It Doesn't Matter Anymore, and an extended playing record of Peter Katin playing Chopin, and began to feel I really existed.

Patrick Moore began his Sky At Night programmes on television that year, and because Mum, Jimmy and I were Science Fiction fans, the house began to fill up with copies of Nebula, Beyond, Astounding, Galaxy, If, and Amazing, the story magazines. All quality stuff, no space-cowboys or horror stories. Clarke, Pohl, Asimov, Aldiss, Ley … And the very titles of the stories were enough to set the imagination alight. Thus We Frustrate Charlemagne, a time-machine farce; Billenium, a futuristic nightmare of over-population, and The Nine Billion Names Of God.

The Space Race was under way. The Soviets were secretive,

the Americans paranoid, both boldly going, each determined to get a man on the moon before the other. It was a time of national optimism. The people we had invited from the colonies were arriving, bringing their talents, skills and cheap labour. The cultures circled each other warily, sometimes clashing, sometimes enriching. We stared at dark faces because of their novelty. Asian men at first wore plastic hoods in the rain, until they learned that men didn't wear this sensible headgear, only women did.

These houses were not among the factories, as Adelaide Street was, but near the main road and the shops. Next to us was the

Me in deckchair in 1957 — wide awake, but posing

side entrance to Woolworths, and at the corner below that was the Triangle cinema, a tiny place with just one setting of seats, straight down in a rake of some three hundred seats. It was taken over for Indian films. Jimmy went to one; it lasted three hours; only men were in the audience, and they took food in with them. A man kindly explained the plot to him. A daring screen kiss, when the hero kissed his fingertip and placed it on the heroine's lips, drew delighted shock from the audience. The films were all musical, all escapist, and the music drifted through my skylight.

The house continued to fill up with books. In the 'forties, Mum had bought the sixpenny Penguins, Graham Greene, Evelyn

Waugh, the Mitfords, Saroyan, Steinbeck and Saki. By a fluke, she also had the *Complete Works of Bernard Shaw*, leatherbound. This came about by her having borrowed it from Green Lane Library, was late in returning it, and the Library requested her either to return it or to pay the statutory shilling for its loss. So she paid the shilling, and in return, became the owner of a tome that must have been worth at least three pounds in contemporary value, and some eighty to one hundred pounds now. All on account of an absent-minded librarian.

There were two ground-floor rooms to the house, and two bedrooms, one in which Mum and Naomi had a bed each, and which overlooked the front. The one across the landing held Billy's and Jimmy's beds.

* * *

Shortly after the 4th of October, 1957, Jimmy came running up to the attic and said, "Quick, look out of the skylight, Sputnik is going across." We looked through, and saw a point of light moving among the stars. The Space Race had begun, and we were in on it.

Mum, far left, with two waitresses, late 1950s

CHAPTER TEN

DRAMA SCHOOL

I had clung timidly to my first job for eleven years, when I decided to chance it and take another job. In an era when we could, as we so often irritate the young by saying, walk out of a job on Friday night, and walk into another on Monday, I was still too wary, afraid of being out of work and out of pocket, to sit back for a week and take a break.

Eventually, though, I took a job at Lloyd's Register of Shipping, in Newhall Street. I should have changed years ago. The Wesleyan never had its typewriters serviced. A typist had to get used to every little fault, caused by wear and tear and lack of cleaning and oiling, with the result that only she could work efficiently on her own machine. I had changed departments and asked to take the typewriter with me. It was refused—that simply was not done — so it became impossible to get a decent piece of work out of the one I had to use. The Wesleyan scrimped on its equipment; evidently saving up to build the new, unspeakably ugly building that now disgraces the site. I had been confident that the old building would be listed. It was considered to be the best example of nineteenth-century architecture in Birmingham. In fact, the only thing I liked about the job at all.

Improved job or not, I was still not doing an exciting job. So I bought oil paints, canvases, and a studio easel. What to paint? I lived in a city, not the countryside, and buildings were as yet beyond my skill.

I drew faces in cafes, until the subjects realised they were being looked at. Paintings of horses came next, not because I particularly liked the animals, but they have a satisfying shape. There was, too, always self-portraiture to fall back on. I would arrange some still life and do that when I couldn't think of anything else. I even took my drawing block to the City Art Gallery and copied what was on the walls.

Andre Drucker, a columnist in the Birmingham Mail, announced that he was opening a chain of tea rooms in Birmingham, and wanted some pictures for the walls. He was looking for young students' work. I picked out one that depicted horses plunging about in water, in blue monochrome, and took it to one of his tea rooms in Gosta Green. He was all smiling welcome at first, until he realised I was not a 'real' student, with nothing to do all day but paint, but an impostor who had to work for a living. So he lost interest in my picture. I was about to take my leave, when he decided to give me the benefit of his aesthetic judgement anyway, and called me back.

"This is no good at all," he opined, looking down on it as from a great height, "it's contrived."

All art is contrived, of course. That is what the word means. If it were spontaneous it would not, by definition, be art. But I was not sophisticated enough to say that. I hadn't thought the picture was anything more than a nice piece of colour to brighten up his walls.

"I didn't think it was great art," I said, "I just thought you might like it for one of your cafes."

But he hadn't finished with me yet.

"It's pretentious," he declared, "there's no room in art for affectation." He indulged in more of this high-flown bombast before he let me go.

Never mind that pretence is its very function. When Magritte entitled his picture of a smoker's pipe, This Is Not A Pipe, he meant that it was only the picture of a pipe, a pretence. Perhaps he was satirising such as Drucker. All *he* needed to have said was that it was not what he was looking for, but have thanked me for my interest, and made one or two encouraging remarks in compensation. I humped it back across the city in tears. I've always taken care, since then, never to disparage young people's work. I determined I would never tread on the feelings of insecure youth as did the pretentious, contrived and affected Andre Drucker. It would be a long time before I would take my harp to a party again.

Another holiday abroad came up with the IOGT. This time, simply a holiday, not a summer school. We went to Holland, stayed at the Scheveningen sea resort and took day trips to The Hague, the Windmills, and to Amsterdam, with a night at the Concertgebouw Theatre to see a modern ballet. Very daring stuff, it brought the comment, "There's more to that than meets the eye!" Funny, I thought, not much more could have met the eye without the censor intervening. People don't think of what they are saying; 'meeting the eye' is precisely what ballet does — there's no other message.

We didn't have a visit on our itinerary to any of the Art Galleries. Rather like going to Stratford and not going to the theatre.

* * *

It was while working at Lloyd's that I decided I had had enough of office work. I was going on the stage. This would be possible only after I had rid myself of a mouthful of rotting teeth. I thought this would be a simple matter. I told the dentist, "I want them all out."

"Oh, no, you can't dictate treatment, unless you go private. The NHS ruling is that I have to save as many as possible." I thought I'd let him see what state they were in, then he'd change his mind. No chance. He was out to take my money.

He must have seen they were crumbling away to chalk; they didn't hold fillings for more than a week at a time. But he kept up the pretence. "I can take them out privately, in which case you can tell me what you want done; then I can provide the dentures at the National Health price. And by the way, there is one good tooth, on the lower set at the front. Do you want to keep it?" I could imagine what that would look like, until it, too went into painful decay. I didn't bother to argue, and committed myself to paying extra. He was the one with the sharp instruments, after all. The total cost, including the National Health charge of £1.10s. 0d. came to nine pounds, more than a week's wages.

At least he didn't economise on the novocaine, like the dentist I went to after work one day. I was fourteen, and it cost me half a crown. The cocaine didn't work beyond numbing the surface of my gum; enough to stop me jumping at the first grip. Consequently, I put off going to the dentist for a long time. By the time I was eighteen, they were rapidly decaying, and I had another painful extraction and a series of painful fillings. Every touch on the nerve was like an electric shock. Next time, I had an extraction under gas. I decided after that to let them rot, and hoped that I would never again need a general anaesthetic. It cannot have had the effect it did, and have been safe. The going under was bad enough—I felt as if every atom of me was exploding— slowly. It was extremely painful, all over my body. After that, I was spinning around in eternity. I had no sense of time, nor of who or what I was, only this terrible Forever. Coming round, I could feel sharp blows thudding at me, and I was springing back, involuntarily, only to find that all that was happening was the dentist pushing my eyebrow up and letting it fall again. The smallest touch was perceived in exaggeration as a heavy blow. I wondered, ever since, how anyone would choose to take mind-altering drugs. They must be bored with life to put themselves through that.

I've never been so glad to be rid of anything, as the rest of my teeth, in 1959, and I found, as a bonus, that the rheumatism in my shoulder began rapidly clearing up, now that the carious toxins were no longer flushing through my system.

* * *

The Birmingham Theatre School was a converted garage in Islington Row when I went, with my audition piece in early 1960. Mary Richards, who ran the school, said she didn't see why I shouldn't shape up as an actress eventually, once I had overcome my tendency to gabble my lines nervously; so I paid my fee for the quarter, and arranged to be there three nights a week. On the following Monday, she gave me the script of a short play; an excerpt from a not very good piece. It was typed; not good enough to have been published. She may have made it up herself. It was certainly not worth the minute attention she gave to every word. I would, at the most get three words out, and she would stop me, and have me say them again, in exactly the same way. It was like a master class, but on such a feeble thing, and with no point to it. I had this stop-start treatment until my nerves were ragged. I had learned nothing I did not already know, and nothing of what I needed to know. I took the thing home to learn, but every time I looked at the words, I heard her voice interrupting, jerking me back to repeat it. Consequently, I didn't know the words when next I attended the class, so she gave herself a five-minute treat bawling me out for that.

When she produced Shakespeare, she didn't indulge in any of these displays of expertise. It was important to her to put on a good show when it was the Bard. At these times, she was careful not to upset the actors. Then, she was good-humoured and well-mannered, letting us get on with the reading, and correcting us afterwards in the normal way, with Notes, or fore-warning us of how a phrase or word was to be emphasised. She didn't throw any tantrums nor scream at us to relax, at these times.

"Always remember, dear hearts," said Mr Burt, who took improvisation, "that to do a convincing laugh, you must empty your lungs before the laugh, otherwise you'll get a rush of exhaled air, and a false HAH HAH tumbling out with it."

Once he had got us laughing naturally with emptied lungs, he turned to the subject of corpsing, laughing for real when we shouldn't.

"If you clench your abdominal muscles, it will become physically impossible to laugh," he told us.

That was optimistic of him. The following week, during rehearsals for King Lear, Cordelia and her betrothed got the sillies during Lear's opening speech—the actor playing the King got very upset about it, and suddenly stopped the rehearsal.

"I'm sorry, but I can't do this speech with these silly kids giggling," he announced.

"No, John," Miss Richards agreed, "you're quite right, now let's take it again …"

"It's so unprofessional," continued the man who, on his first engagement at the Rep as the policeman who comes on at the end of the murder mystery, could not remember the three lines he had in the entire play, "and when some of us have taken so much trouble learning our lines …"

"Yes, John, I understand your feelings. Now, I think that speech could be taken more lightly at the beginning …" but Miss Richards' husband, Vic Heath, felt he ought to put his point of view at this juncture, and backed up the actor by pontificating at length on the amateurish behaviour of the two young people, by which time Cordelia became distraught, and fled the stage in tears. Mr Heath was obviously not aware of his wife's rules on Shakespeare rehearsals, nor the fact that only *she* did the temperamentals round here, no-one else.

King Lear, by now embarrassed at the commotion he had caused, and further discomposed by My Lord, the Earl of Kent, who looked ready to take him apart for calling him a silly kid, mumbled on, and the rehearsal dribbled to its finish.

* * *

I had a form to fill in, in connection with my fee, and I did it wrongly—stuck the stamp in the wrong place. Miss Richards gave me a full ten minutes of her most cutting derision, holding the form between finger and thumb in distaste and puzzlement, then, as the other students came in in their ones and twos, she related the story all over again to each of them, polishing her performance each time, until the class was full. None of them was the least interested, but she doggedly relayed my idiocy, in the belief that it became more entertaining at each repetition. She had a very poor sense of comedy.

To balance things up; when we did things the way she approved, she reacted with gross flattery. I was playing Mrs Danvers and pupils in the wings were chatting and giggling. This didn't bother me, but Miss Richards stopped everything to say, "It's disgraceful, here's Mary doing her best—no don't come out of it, Mary!—and you lot are behaving like silly kids! ... Don't come out of it!"

Come out of what, I might well have asked. I found heavy drama embarrassing as it was, without Miss Richards piling on the cringe.

She suggested I hyphenate my first name, but took it upon herself to call me Mary, in the belief that Mary-Rose was an affectation.

I got into her good books on the grounds that one John Benton, a Labour Councillor, had saved her home for her. I explained that, although my brother was a Labour Councillor, there was another such in Birmingham, and that it was he. "Thank him next time you see him, ducky," she said, not really listening.

I have said that Mr Burt took improvisation. He also took liberties with the female students. He made a speciality of breath control. This necessitated him handling the abdomens and rib-cages of the young women in the class. He seemed to do a lot of study on breath control. Until he tried it on a spirited Irishwoman who had not long joined us. She had a splendid, declamatory sense of the theatrical—old fashioned and very stirring. She told Mr Burt to keep his grubby hands to himself, and at volume, then flounced out.

Burty had to vanish for a while; this often happened, allegedly. Then he would reappear when a new lot of students signed in. He'd be back, calling everyone 'dear heart', and trying it on with the newcomers. Allegedly.

The Day School consisted of younger students, who had left school, but whose parents could afford to keep them from work while they 'took up the stage'. This formed the basis of Miss Richards' favourite joke, about the parents who told her their child wanted to take up the stage. "They might find it a bit heavy to lift," she reported herself as saying to them, as we smiled tiredly.

The Day School students had the use of the small theatre next door, which had some three hundred seats to our twenty-odd in the converted garage. There was an electric fire in our room, but as it was fixed to the ceiling, it was not very effective. It didn't feel very safe, either; we avoided sitting under it.

To make sure that we all got a chance to perform, no full-length plays were put on, only excerpts. These were the same every term; mostly late Victorian, and that were popular in Miss Richards' own youth. Her favourite was a piece based on Victoria's alleged statement, "We are not amused." These sketches came round like clockwork. Every term. We had, repeatedly, the same excerpt from She Stoops To Conquer, because she had a few Restoration costumes. Likewise, as there was included among the props a small totem pole given to her from a production of Rose Marie, the variety shows the day school produced *always* included the song, I'm An Indian Too.

More rewarding were scenes from proven masterpieces, like When We Are Married. It was a piece of luck that, when we did the first run-through on this, Miss Richards had been travelling all day, and dozed off during rehearsal. We took the opportunity to get through it, get a sense of the shape of the play, and work on the best lines, without the distraction of her flourished expertise.

Her direction consisted mostly of interrupting in the middle of a sentence, repeating what the actor had said, in much the same intonation and stress, and getting him or her to repeat it. She would do this with one line, repeatedly, until the rest of the cast would sigh and tut and shuffle. The actor was either reduced to a nervous wreck, or finally worked to her direction like a robot. She didn't do this with everyone, only those who put up with it.

She would tell us to lift the pitch of the voice up, on the last word of each sentence or phrase, regardless of whether it was appropriate. I could see where this had come from, after listening to some of the day pupils droning on, their voices trailing down towards the end of the sentence, hitting the full stop with a thud.

"Will you read in for Mistress Page, Mary?" Miss Richards asked me.

"Yes, of course."

Marlene Abbott, who was playing Mistress Ford, whispered to me, "' … if he be of any *reasonable* stature … '" so that I would know that Miss Richards wanted that emphasis on Falstaff's bulk.

"Oh … thanks," I whispered back.

When I got to the speech, I stressed the word quite heavily.

Miss Richards immediately stopped me, and quoted, " … any *reasonable* stature …

The rest of the cast sighed, and she realised that this was Shakespeare she was doing, and began to behave herself from that point.

Reading through another play, I had a problem with my top plate, and this made my mouth dry. The results were obvious; I couldn't sound the sibilants, and I lisped.

Miss Richards corrected me each time, so I said, "Sorry, my mouth is dry."

"HOW YOU FEEL IS OF NO IMPORTANCE!" she suddenly bellowed, thinking, or pretending, that I had stage fright. She raged on, in this embarrassing way, for several minutes, while we stared at her. I wondered what she did with actors who genuinely had stage fright, and how much damage that did them. She was always on the lookout for a chance to show off her histrionics; always quoting the best lines herself, without letting the actor come fresh to them, with his own ideas.

A male student, who had clearly had enough of her, got drunk one day, came in to her office, berated her for wasting his time and money, and told her to put her tenth rate teaching methods somewhere dark. His name was David Lodge, perhaps the David Lodge who is now a respected and successful actor.

* * *

We were encouraged to submit playlets of our own for performance, so I passed this idea on to Jimmy, who wrote a short piece. I left it with her, and the following evening she handed it back to me.

"It's rather political, isn't it?" was her opinion.

"I hadn't noticed, but then I didn't write it, my brother did."

"Well, you see, ducky, it doesn't seem to have a plot—it's not *about* anything, is it?"

"Well, you would have to discuss it with Jimmy, it's his play. Shall I tell him you'll put it on?"

"I don't know about that, I'm not sure what it's about."

In other words, there wasn't a murder in it, it wasn't about Queen Victoria, and it had no comic servants who knew their place.

A young Indian man joined the school. The first part she cast him in, which his parents came to see, was as a turbaned servant to a colonist. He left immediately after the performance and we didn't see him again.

A friend of one of the students, a young man who wrote blank verse, submitted a beautifully written play on the theme of Spartacus. Miss Richards gave the minimal amount of rehearsal time to this, rushed the rehearsals, and advised the cast to "Go and see Spartacus." The Hollywood film, with a cast of thousand and big screen action, didn't bear any resemblance to this thoughtful verse, with its poetic rhythm and rolling phrases. It deserved a good director, at least. After the performance, the author said loudly, "I've never been so embarrassed in all my life!" Then he stomped off.

There would be costume displays, for friends and societies known to Miss Richards, and to which we contributed our free labour. If our help was asked for a pageant or a wine tasting, it was as well to accede to the request, if we wanted the chances to come our way on radio or television. The city theatres would sometimes want spear-carriers. I went to a performance of Swan Lake, by one of the big London companies, and was delighted to see a line of familiar figures walk on, stand there with a spear each for a few bars, then walk off again.

* * *

The best part of my time at drama school was in the comradeship that was formed. The jubilation when one of us got a job; in Rep, radio or television, no matter how humble. It might be as assistant stage manager at the Alexandra, props mistress at the Rep, a walk-on in a TV play or a minor part in The Archers. Of however short a duration it was, the break had been made into the magic world; you were part of the make-believe, where life would run according to a script. It was at once safe and colourful. It existed outside the mundane world, yet had its own structure, and you were included in the community that it formed—a miniature community, without the threat of the larger world. The sentimental send-off if it was outside Birmingham. No more exotic than Birkenhead, or summer season at Bexhill—the end of the pier was yet more glamorous than the desk at an insurance firm.

My social life had begun to look up. Not that I was looking for a boyfriend. I had left behind the motorbike pillion seat. The fact was that I could concentrate on only one important thing at a time. I wanted to be a successful actor. Domesticity would have to wait.

That was how I had come to be instinctively drawn to the gay men in the classes, without thinking about the matter. And they, just as unthinkingly, were drawn to me. The absence of sexual tension meant we could get straight through to the friendship. We camped it up about the city, saw the shows, heard the concerts, took in the latest film. We played like silly kids and had a lot of innocent fun. We found safety in each other's presence, and the world left us alone.

Great excitement! A television cabaret show wanted extras for several weeks running, to sit at the tables and take soft drinks from wine glasses. I went on the second week. We wore our own clothes and make-up. This was ITV so the fee was good; thirty shillings for the day. Among the entertainers was Tony Fayne, who had been one of the duo, Tony Fayne and David Evans. They had, in the '40s, an ingenious radio act, in which they both spoke the same script, together, and in perfect synchronisation. The format was usually that of a sports commentary, and every cough, pause, 'Excuse me' and interjection was done simultaneously. These were simple entertainments, of drawing room level; they were sufficient to amuse us then, and, I suspect, now, for those of us who do not demand constant, numbing shock-horror excitement.

Over the years I was to get these jobs, and while they hardly amounted to a career in broadcasting, they provided a welcome day out, and an insight into how television is produced, and often I would bump into old friends, on their way to success or obscurity. Playing a body double for Jeanette Sterk, all I had to do was to act dead. But the young man who played the doctor pronouncing me dead was so nervous that he couldn't keep his hand still as he lifted my eyelid, and he pressed his finger, sweating and salty into my eye. You never saw such a lively corpse as I jumped.

Shortly after that, I was in a hospital scene in the bed next to Gladys Cooper. Tuppence to talk to me, now. It was a soap opera in the middle sixties, and Miss Cooper's character was publishing her diaries. The actress was said to be inserting some of her actual memoirs as a teaser for a book she was writing. When I told Mum whom I had been talking to that day, she could hardly believe it. Gladys Cooper was from another age; she had fed the dreams of those who had watched her films in the 'thirties, in a cinema in Margate.

Bringing me down to earth with a bump, the floor manager, who would not concede to hair loss, but who let his remaining hair grow in a long fringe, well below the crown of his bald head, down the back of his neck; approached me at a quiet moment and said, "Let's go into a dressing room and discuss your prospects."

I stared at him. So they really did talk like that, then. I told him what *his* prospects were, and turned to do something else.

To hide his discomposure, he called out, "Settle down, studio, please."

There was no-one there. They had all gone to the canteen.

Location work brought the most money, free meals and, if it was filmed at night, double-time payment. On a hot, sticky night in 1976, I was an extra in one of The Shillingbury Tales; The Blue Field. There was meant to be a ritual burning of a caravan, but because of the extremely dry summer, they settled for a tent instead. They had hired two fire engines, the crane of one of them carrying the lights. The BBC was to become less extravagant than this. Quite well-known artists would appear without lines, to economise on fees, and the walk-on parts and extras' parts dried up.

I was not the only family member working in show business. Billy and Jimmy worked backstage at the Hippodrome, and were struck by how much better staged the amateur shows were than some of the professional. There was fun to be had, too. In a pantomime, two minor characters, young men dressed as monkeys, had an argument in the dressing-room, which they took on stage. It got so heated that they began to hit each other with their tails. The kids loved it, they thought all this bitching and scrapping was part of the show.

I heard tell of Phyl Groves, in Carousel, being kicked off stage a bit harder then intended, and shooting past the stage-hands who were supposed to catch her, and of the language, my dear! Professor Higgins was to be seen, stomping off stage, shouting Damn! Damn! Damn! according to Lerhner and Lowe, then striding round the back, effing and blinding according to Tony Britton, to walk back on decorously chanting Damn! Damn! Damn! once more.

Jimmy was to do better than I in getting television parts; passers-by, bar-stewards, with lines. He had a few lines in Cathy Come Home, offering to store Ray Brooks' furniture for him. The TV play about homelessness went round the world, and brought a small cheque for Jimmy each time.

* * *

"You've had your BBC audition, of course, haven't you," Miss Richards remarked to me, casually.

"No, not yet."

"Oh, I feel sure you have, ducky"

She had had it in for me ever since I had told her that I had been offered some overtime at work and couldn't afford to turn it down for one of her costume displays. Her fantasy of me as a carefree, thoughtless youngster with no responsibilities and too much pocket money got in the way of her attempt to target me for her stern tutelage and 'iron discipline'.

It can't have helped that I told her on one occasion that I didn't feel I was getting my money's worth out of her, feeling she needed reminding of who was financing whom.

I rather spoilt the effect by handing her that term's cheque, pre-paid as ever. Of course, as soon as she had cashed the cheque and found it to be sound, she dropped the sweet tone of voice and redoubled the savagery. It would take me a long time to learn.

"You should never be in a hurry to pay her," a fellow actor warned me, "you've seen how she treats you once she's safely got your money."

"I daren't do otherwise, George, I'm afraid I'll spend it on something I need." I'm less neurotic about paying bills before I need to, now.

I evidently convinced her that I hadn't had the BBC audition.

"All you need to do is to go to Broadcasting House, and ask to see Mary Smith. She will arrange the audition," she told me, with a smile.

I went to the Carpenter Road offices in Edgbaston, later moved to Pebble Mill, and asked to see Mary Smith. I was asked to wait in a small office, where two young female clerks were working. They had a transistor radio on, playing the 1961 equivalent of Radio 1, and they went in and out of the office, looking me over thoroughly each time they had the chance.

I can't guess what the people there thought about me, nor whether they checked up on me, and if so, whether Miss Richards disclaimed me or told them not to bother, because when the clerk came back, she told me there was no Mary Smith, but thank you and good afternoon.

I hadn't realised Mary Richards hated me that much. But I shrugged this off. Game, set and match to her. It was her way of reminding me who held the moneybags and the power.

* * *

In the late summer of 1961 she told me, "I've got a job for you, ducky, but I don't think you'll take it."

I wondered what favour she wanted, but felt willing enough to do it, if it wasn't too time consuming. I asked her what it was. "It's with the Osiris Repertory Company, but I don't think you'll take it," she repeated. Oh, *that* kind of job. I asked her where it was, and what it involved. I was expecting something back-stage. "It's acting," she elaborated, "but it's with an all-women company. They tour the schools, performing Shakespeare."

Shakespeare! My mind lit up like a torch. "I'll certainly take it," I said, "tell me more."

Miss Richards outlined the job. Miss Hewins was the Director of the Osiris Repertory Company, and lived in a small village in the Cotswolds. This sounded better all the time. They were based in Willersey, a mile or so from Broadway. Not the Great White Way, of course, but the one over the county boundary into Worcestershire. Fifteen miles in the other direction lies the promised land of all aspiring actors—Stratford. This was getting more promising by the minute.

Miss Hewins usually took about five plays out at a time, packed into one of two Rolls Royces, vintage 1928. The other, a 1930 model, carried Miss Hewins and the other members of the cast. Both cars drew the company accommodation behind them, two caravans. There would be six or seven members of the cast at any one time, with occasional help from former members, who happened to live in the area where the school was. As could be imagined, with such a small company, parts would have to be duplicated; even so, the plays had to be cut.

"Well, best of luck, ducky, but I don't think you'll take it."

* * *

My first impression of Nancy Hewins was her startling resemblance to Margaret Rutherford, though not so well turned out. The cottage she lived in was chaotic—the most efficient item being a small filing cabinet with a file marked 'Girls'. Housewifery was not on her list of priorities, a fact I noted with approval. The kitchen was best not dwelt on. The bath, I was to discover, only ever contained Nancy's laundry; never, to my knowledge, Nancy. Two Belgian Griffons came skittering out ahead of her, as I stepped into the cottage, barking their tiny heads off. The garden was a lovely thing. The gardener cultivated herbs, blackberries and vegetables at the far end, and kept the lawn trimmed.

You got straight off the bus and entered the cottage from the green, and either went in through the drive, where the vans and the cars were kept, turned left through some tall firs, and down the garden path alongside the lawn, down the steps, among the bushes and into the house; or you went through the wicket gate at a point further down the green, past the next door cottage which formed part of the Long House itself. The barn was over beyond the drive, and housed the costumes, scenery and props.

Nancy's father was an overseas Minister in Ramsay MacDonald's coalition government in 1931, and was the first Director of the London School of Economics. Stanley Baldwin was her cousin and Beatrice Webb her godmother. With a gift of forty pounds from Lord Rothermere, Nancy started her professional life as Director of the Osiris Repertory Theatre in 1927.

I had picked for my audition piece, Beattie Bryant's final speech in I'm Talking About Jerusalem. I was too nervous to think about the message of the play. I had picked it simply for

Beattie's vehemence, and the fact that it lasted the required two minutes.

When I'd reached the end of it, Nancy only said, "It's rather political, isn't it?"

"I suppose so," I conceded, only glad that I'd got through it. Like Miss Richards before her, Nancy stressed the political nature of the play rather than my treatment of it. Then she said abruptly, "Do you want the job?"

"I certainly do," I said, not realising that Nancy was as desperate for another actor as I was to break into the profession.

She told me the terms. Rehearsal pay was ten shillings a week, plus food and accommodation. Performance pay was thirty shillings a week, with the rest as before. The insurance stamps were not at the full, employed rate, but were only Self Employed. I was to see how disastrous this was to prove, later, but at the time it was explained that we were taken on as shareholders, and I was asked to sign an undertaking that, should the company fold while I was a member, I should pay one pound into it. I never figured out the logic of this, since as shareholders, we should surely have had a share in the profits.

"Are you a quick study?"

"Yes, memory like a parrot." I had developed a method which involved not just reading the part as often as possible, but reading the first speech ten times on the first reading, followed by the rest of the page just once. Then the first speech five times, then four, and so on, down to once. Similarly with the rest of the page. Then without the book. I would establish as many associations with the words as possible, by taking the script with me in cafes, parks and galleries. When I ran the words through my mind I would have a link, or hook. This cup of coffee, this clump of trees, this picture, would bring to mind the words conned at the time. If I couldn't get out of the house, I would go from room to room, or simply sit on different chairs, still saying the words in my head. I was to take this method with me round the Gloucestershire lanes.

I had been explaining some of this to Miss Hewins, while her eyes glazed over, when she suddenly said, "Can you cook?"

"Oh yes," I assured her, brightly. I could bugger up cornflakes, but I'd let them find that out.

She gave me the history of the Osiris. After she had come down from St Hugh's, in Oxford, she first called her company the Isis. She changed the name to Osiris when it turned professional in 1927. They toured all through the Depression; on through the War, when they used a horse-drawn caravan, during petrol rationing. On they went, through the 'fifties, riding out the competition from the television, the wide cinema screen, and the Rock 'n Roll craze; with their ancient entertainment, now become a novelty once more, to children grown blasé to technology, and affirming the ability of children to suspend their need for sophisticated realism.

I sat in the Midland Red bus back to Birmingham, passing through the September countryside, but I wasn't seeing England in its autumnal glory. I was already in Venice, in Ancient Rome; a wood outside Athens—or on a Scottish plain while Birnam wood marched on to Dunsinane.

CHAPTER ELEVEN

OSIRIS

Back at drama school, I was now the centre of attention. It was my turn, as it were, and amid the mock farewells and the foolery, my friends were glad, because it encouraged the feeling that it would be their turn next. The good luck was catching. Burty came in to ask me if I would be helping out with the Christmas show.

"I hope to be on tour by then, Mr Burt."

His reaction was to raise his open palms to shoulder level and declare, "Oh dear heart, I am glad for you!" Camp as a field of tents, that one. It occurred to me to wonder how it was that it was only the girls he pestered.

I had changed my job a few months previously and had made friends with several of the young women at the office. I was working at the Forward Trust, a credit company at Five Ways, in which my job was the typing of Dear Sir Unless letters. In employment of such stultifying boredom, it was natural that the employees would grab at the smallest excitement. My fellow workers used to ask me about all the new developments at drama school, listened with sympathy when I told them what a dreadful witch Miss Richards was, and were glad for me when I told them the good news. We had a few drinks after my last day there, and they handed me their parting gift, a valise to take with me round the country.

* * *

Because I joined the company in mid-term, I had to go to Abergele to catch up with the company, where they were performing Twelfth Night at a private school, the kind that Miss Hewins would refer to as 'girls' posh'. I would watch the performance as I hadn't yet rehearsed. I had been told to learn only the parts of Viola and Feste so far. The rest would come later, when I had settled in. It was a cold, wet day when I ar-

rived, and I wore woollies and wellingtons, my shoes still in
the valise. When Miss Hewins brought me from the station to
the school, they were putting up the scenery. It was made up of
a silver painted backdrop, with black curtains in front of that,
hanging drapes at the sides, and a pelmet. There was the minimum of stage furniture, and for the box-tree scene, a painted
drape to represent the box-tree itself. Behind this, where Sir
Toby, Sir Andrew and Feste were concealed, there was a bench
for them to sit on, while Malvolio strutted in front. Miss
Hewins was nearly sixty, large and scant of breath. The bench
was vital. I was to be grateful for it myself, on later occasions.

I went off the stage, down a corridor, and made a less than
grand entrance to take my place. Walking down between rows
of quietly behaved young ladies in identical evening frocks, I felt
they might giggle at the sight of my chunky woollies and my
socks — I couldn't leave my wellies on after all. But they were
too well bred for that. The Headmistress showed me to my place
at the front, and introduced me to the Head Girl, whose task it
was to entertain me. How Miss Jack would have loved all this.

As soon as the Head Girl started chatting to me, however, all
the other girls began to talk. They didn't see why they shouldn't,
if she was allowed to. When we stopped, they stopped. The curtain was late in going up. We talked again. The other girls did
so, too, in the same elegant, conversational tone as before. This
provided two firsts for me. My first exercise in audience
manipulation, and the first time I ever felt sorry for a school-
teacher.

After the performance, everyone stood. Waiting for them to
leave the hall, I saw instead a girl making her way to the piano.
She sat, and played the National Anthem. Wishing to show willing, I began belting it out, only to find that they had been
trained to sing it like a chorale. For a few notes, my voice soared
raucously above their softly modulated tones, then I settled
down. A bit of a change from the tin hut school, I thought.

Not all schools were as swanky as this, of course. When Miss
Hewins sent out the circulars, she addressed them to every
school in a given area, and about twenty percent replied. We
might be at a tiny private school, and be dining with the Head,
one day; at a massive comprehensive, housing over a thousand
school students, and queuing up at the school canteen to buy a
meal for one and six, on another. At a village hall in Wales,
entertaining both the parents and the children of the local

school, and making our own meals in the caravans; at a public school the following afternoon, using a basement kitchen as a dressing room; on another day, at an old-fashioned Council School, by that time redesignated County Secondary.

Besides Shakespeare, we performed other classics; The Importance Of Being Ernest, The Rivals, Pygmalion, St Joan, Maria Marten, Arms And The Man, and Everyman.

Miss Hewins surrendered the part of Lady Bracknell, a part any actor would give her very handbag for, to a minor member of the company, and instead played Algernon, because only she played the piano. I think that could have been faked with the aid of a record player—Miss Hewins did not make a convincing young man. She quite artlessly cast herself in the main roles, except for St Joan, and that seemed to be the exclusive property of Kay, who at fifty-seven might not be considered the best choice (pace Sybil Thorndike, who was forty-two when Shaw wrote the part for her), but more on account of Kay's rather stolid performance, than of her being the wrong age.

Miss Hewins was built for Caesar, but at the time I joined the company, she had taken the part of Antony, and got the most lines. It's a matter of personal taste. I preferred the thoughtful, wry observations of Caesar, to the grand, declamatory role of Anthony.

Relaxing back at the caravan after a performance, we would discuss our favourite lines over coffee in the evening.

"I agree with Shakespeare about death," I said, launching into the quote: "'Of all the wonders that I yet have heard, it seems to me most strange, that men should fear, seeing that Death, a necessary end, will come when it will come.' Funny how we waste precious time worrying about it."

"Very profound, Mary-Rose," (Nancy was to be one of the few people who not only observed my double-barrelled name, but enjoyed giving it full value), "but I must say I enjoy the bit that comes after the old chap has declared ... 'for always I am Caesar...' then brings himself down to earth with a bump when he says, 'Come on my right hand, for this ear is deaf'."

A younger member declared herself to favour the blood and thunder passages, 'Strange screams of death ... ' and the sound effects to go with it—we had a sheet of iron that was held with one of its corners on the floorboards, and shaken, to produce a pretty good rumble of thunder.

By these means, we wound down at the end of the day, and I

seldom found nowadays, that I suffered from insomnia. This most ancient of afflictions, shared by Shakespeare himself, and incorporated into his text, had tormented me for years. It was now in abeyance, a tribute as much to the job I loved as to an exhausting schedule.

* * *

Nancy played the flute beautifully. She stood behind the back curtain, playing, as Bassanio agonized over the choices in the Casket Scene. She could also whistle melodiously, but found no way of incorporating it into a performance. I wondered at this. A prejudice against women who whistle, perhaps?

During a hiatus in Midsummer Night's Dream, we would all be backstage, changing costume and make-up to play our third or fourth character, leaving no-one on stage to keep the action going. For this, Nancy had a record of Greensleeves playing, while she faded up the dawn gradually, on the switchboard, all the while shuffling into another costume. She would keep a cool head on stage, too. A footlight began to smoke during the Trial Scene In The Merchant Of Venice. Nancy walked stately over, wrapped her robe round her hand, removed the bulb, and placed it on the boards out of harm's way. If there is no way you can disguise an action, it's better to do so blatantly, but carry on with the speech as if nothing had happened, as Nancy did.

In the past, if a major actor of a small company had to double up in a minor role, he was billed by the alias, 'Walter Plinge'. In The Merchant, Nancy appeared as just such a minion. All this hireling had to do was to bring the bad news of Antonio's ships miscarrying. As Bassanio, I was talking to Portia and Nerissa. Getting near the cue line, I could see the back curtain out of the corner of my eye; this should move as Nancy came on. Getting near the cue line, I was aware of it, hoping it would soon move. It didn't.

Then I reached the cue line: "Our feast shall be much honoured in your marriage." Still no Nancy. I made up some Shakespeare on the spot, something on the lines of:

"I see a servant without, bearing news.
"I will go speak with him."

I strolled off, nonchalantly, then, picking up speed, I tore round the back of the backcloth, making it ripple like a ship's sail;

legged it like a madman along the corridor; turned a corner on a wild swing, raced along the next corridor, and burst into the classroom where Nancy sat, dressed as Shylock, talking serenely to another member of the cast.

I had breath only to gasp, "Nancy, you're supposed to be The Salad," (a composite name taken from Salarino and Solanio, friends of Antonio). Neither of them said a word, just gazed calmly at me, leaving me to deal with it. I spun round, dashed out of the classroom, flew along the corridor, swung round the corner again, sped along the last corridor, then behind the backcloth, which rippled in a gale now. I snatched the first thing that looked like a letter, off the piano; slammed on the brakes and strolled through the wings, trying not to pant, bringing the bad news. I opened the 'letter'. It was the Scenes List. I turned it upside down and 'read' from it.

As I flourished the piece of white cardboard, Portia muttered, sotto voce, "A stiff letter, I see." Happily, I was in no mood to corpse, and the play proceeded smoothly to its finish.

I asked Sue Date, who had played Portia, if the audience had noticed anything. "Apparently not. We stood and chatted in an undertone about the wedding plans, and where they would go on honeymoon. By the way, why did Jenny say Ormskirk?"

Then I had to smile. On the phone home, I had unfairly described the place as a one-horse town, and had upset the operator further by saying, "we got cut off there," when we lost contact for a moment.

"I didn't cut you off," a voice from nowhere spoke. (I hadn't said she had, only that we had *been* cut off, but this was no time for being pedantic). She rather huffily cut me off as I was saying goodbye. I wondered idly how long she lasted in the job.

That's something I have never understood, this identification with the town that one lives in, as if one built the place oneself. It doesn't bother me when people describe Margate as the Blackpool of the South, or London as an abomination. Neither did I bridle when Nancy criticised Birmingham. She insisted on referring to it as the Black Country. I didn't correct her, she would have pretended I was being defensive, rather than precise. Besides, Birmingham was, before the Clean Air Act, pretty black. That was because of its function as the industrial heart of the Midlands, where the wealth was produced. I was even less inclined to point that out to her. I would have got a lecture on the politics of envy.

* * *

Cardiff in the rain, the Isle of Wight in the sun, Manchester in the fog, and the Pennines in a blizzard. As long as I had the right clothes, the British climatehas always suited me, and I was to enjoy it in its infinite variety for the next two years. In the caravan, in a tent, in a gymnasium, on stage overnight, in the Long House, in the house of a friend of Nancy's, and one night in a small hotel, we laid our heads wherever we could. Despite the punishing regime, we managed to enjoy it, too.

Costume shoes would have been an impossibly expensive item, were it not that, for the Shakespeare plays at least, Nancy kept a stock of black socks. Two pairs of these, rolled over at the ankle, made a realistic pair of the kind of cloth shoes worn at the time. Tights had to come in large sizes to fit everyone. They could be shortened with the help of a penny and a suspender clip. Chest-flatteners came in the form of elasticated sun-tops. These had been referred to for some years as the 'manly bosom', shortened to 'manly B'. Some girls needed something more firm. Germaine Marion Crawford made her own flattener with sailcloth and canvas. It came down to the waist and might have stopped a bullet. I didn't even need the sun top.

The wigs had been in the company for so long that they had stretched, and had to be secured with hair-grips. The bald wigs had to fit close to the cheekbone, and you had to bring the make-up over the latex to blend in. On a stressful day it would have been easier to have torn your hair out by the roots. Portia's wig was blonde, and combed out and left loose looked quite attractive, but for the period had to be braided and tucked up. Club wigs were worn only by boys and servants; cut short and with a straight fringe. I had let my hair grow, thinking I could do more with it that way, but now that I was posing as a boy, I decided to have it cut like one, instead of cramming it under a wig. White, wispy beards for old men, and moustaches for swells and villains, had to be stuck on, but for shaven soldiers with a five o'clock shadow, we shaded in blue greasepaint mixed with white, lightly round the chin and under the cheekbones.

Because the giveaway signs of femininity are small hands, we were careful not to make too much of them in gesture, and to concentrate on the voice. Germaine, whom we addressed by her family nickname of Jim, had a very deep voice. It was female-deep, but ideal for a male part. Jim was from New Zealand, claimed Maori ancestry, though she had white skin, and was unabashedly promiscuous. She may or may not have initiated many a sixth-form boy in the ways of the flesh, but once on stage, she treated the job with the utmost seriousness and attention to detail.

In leisure time, she liked to read through the cuts in the plays, taking a great pleasure in the playwright. Jim was in her early thirties, and with her long, thick hair in plaits, made a most impressive Lady Macbeth. She was married to Howard Marion Crawford, the film and radio actor, was never short of cash, and held pole position as Nancy's favourite, until her wild life style became too much. Nancy had a weakness for celebrity, but an even stronger need for respectability.

Reading our parts through, I would quote, " ... but be not jealous on me, gentle Brutus ..."

"Oh, but I am," Jim said, "I'd much rather have the part of Cassius; he's very complex. I like his quick temper, and he's so bitter, there's a lot there I could get my teeth into."

Seldom pleased with what we have, I would have preferred to be the more agonized Brutus, noble and contemplative in the misty morning orchard. Ungrateful of me, I can see now, but I was the resident skinny, so I was granted the part of Cassius.

In playing so many characters, we had to underdress, that is, to wear as many of our characters' costumes in one go as possible. In Macbeth, I began as a rather fat witch, went cackling off into the wings, to stride back on as a still pretty stout Thane; slimmed down further into Banquo, then, once the rubber dagger had been drawn across my throat, I became the Porter. After I'd shuffled him off to answer the door, I threw off his rough hessian and slipped a gown over my head, then glided back on as the Gentlewoman. I had, finally, to take the gown off, leaving a servant's tunic. I rubbed plenty of Number Five on my face for a ghastly pallor, and came hurtling back on as the Cream Faced Loon, bringing the bad news about the English arriving. I have to say that I never craved to play Lady Macbeth, but I would have loved to play Macbeth himself; he has the best poetry in the book.

In fact, I have always preferred to play comedy, of any period. Contrary to what most actors say, I found it easier than tragedy. Not that I don't like to move the audience, or make them sad, but I'm uneasy at displays of noisy grief. It's true to say that I enjoyed a stirring speech, and had a field day with Harry Hotspur, but the most rewarding thing I ever found was to make people laugh.

* * *

Most of the time, we would park on a caravan site, and take the Rolls to all the schools in the area that had booked us. On one of many occasions, though, we had parked on the school playground. I thought it would be rather nice if we faced the other way. I got one of the other girls to take the caravan off its support while I retracted the legs. I began to turn it round by the handle on the back corner, but neglected to notice that we were on a gradient. Two of the other girls had joined us by now and, as the caravan began to lumber gently down the slope, they put their hands to their mouths (a giveaway female gesture, which I hadn't leisure to note at the time). The playground faced directly on to the playing-field, and the van ran towards that, negotiating a steep grass ramp. I ran by the side of it, in the vain belief that I could stop it. At the bottom of the ramp, it bucketed wildly from side to side—we heard the domestic paraphernalia rattling and clanking inside. I held up my arms instinctively to catch it, and heard someone scream. It steadied, and ran on. We held our breaths. It ran to a stop.

We had just one more hazard to overcome. How to get it back up the slope without Nancy finding out. Kay Jones was Nancy's friend from Oxford, who was at Somerville at the same time that Nancy was at St Hugh's, and she had come on this tour with us. By a stroke of luck she happened to be crossing the playground. Nancy was in the other caravan, oblivious and rather deaf.

Not sufficiently deaf, though, not to hear Kay starting up one of the Rolls. By the time Nancy had come out of her van, Kay had got the Rolls on to the playing-field, we had hitched up the van, and Kay was half-way up the ramp with it. This didn't preclude Nancy from bustling around, shouting directions loudly and persistently to Kay, directing her in contradictory instructions, and generally losing her head under the guise of being brisk and dominant. Kay took no notice, said not a word, but continued calmly to negotiate the Rolls, with the van in tow, expertly back on to the playground.

"Just three minutes later, and she need never have known," I remarked to Kay. She nodded in sympathy.

Bizarrely, Nancy spoke no word of reproach to me. That was a first, especially as it was my fault. But she railed at some length to Kay, who was not to be forgiven for behaving more coolly than Nancy herself. Kay remained silent throughout it all, as we all three settled down for the night.

I came in for most of the criticism, for almost anything, most bitterly when I had got something right on stage, and the audience let me know as much, or a teacher would say kind things about my performance afterwards. Whatever Jim got up to, the most Nancy would do was to issue a mild reproof, a subtle warning, and find someone else to blame. Not to analyse it to death, it was as if I had needed to be taken down a peg or two, in order not to become too self-confident. The implication of being pegged too high is one I found dizzyingly complimentary.

In Nancy's defence, it has to be said that she was a warm-hearted person, and would try to be kind-hearted, but only if she considered you to be at a disadvantage—artistically, intellectually or ethically. I could see the humanity in this, but it didn't have quite the result she was after. However, she was not embittered, as was Mary Richards, and she couldn't keep up the martinet facade for long.

"I can't keep you from going to the pub," she would say, reproachfully.

"What a shame," murmured Elaine, satirically. Well, Willersey was not a thriving cultural centre, much as we loved it, and we did want to talk to others as well as among ourselves. She would worry, too, about our going to Stratford, and told us not to pick up any fanciful ideas. But as long as we put those ideas into practice while she was not on stage, or within earshot, we could avoid upsetting her.

She never discovered my Porter's Scottish accent, and would no doubt have said, "Now why?" in a confrontational tone, to which I was wont to answer, "Why not?" The fact is, we don't know how Barbaric Scots spoke, except that they did not speak Standard Received twentieth century English.

* * *

The two caravans were occupied in this way: the larger one, named Dame Sybil, but called Dame, held Nancy, her two dogs, Boué and Polly, and the two senior members of the time. The smaller caravan, a tall, straight-sided affair, was called Sudbury, on account of having been bought in that town, and housed the newer members, four in all. Shift would be made on occasion to squeeze in a former member, or a temp. on loan from Mary Richards, and who would bring me the latest news, and return with my own communique to the drama students.

We had one such, when we were short of a member to play Clara, in Pygmalion. When Nancy told me who was coming, I burst out with; "What a cheek! Fancy sending you such rubbish!"

But on reflection, I had to admit that she was the ideal choice. This girl *was* Clara, brainless and twittering. We made her welcome, but she behaved like visiting royalty, accepting our friendly overtures with unsmiling superiority. She didn't even watch the other plays we presented, merely waited to do her turn. After she left, the other girls told me she had passed on gossip about me from the Theatre School. People who hardly knew me had settled among themselves that I was a lesbian. It may have been the case though, that the Osiris girls had made that bit up, to sound me out about my orientation. However, I was as neutral about Sapphic women as I was prejudiced in favour of gay men. So I gave nothing away by my reaction, eagerly looked for.

"Silly cow," was all they got.

Sometimes the hierarchy of occupancy would skip a member or two, and a newcomer would be awarded the envied berth in Dame. This had happened, before I arrived, in the case of Jim, she of the exotic background, and the husband in Ealing films and broadcasting. As I settled in, the departing member was still grumping on about this; muttering, "It isn't what you know, it's who you know."

However, there were advantages to living in the Sudbury van. It was better insulated; warmer in the winter, cooler in the summer. And you didn't have to make breakfast if it was your week to cook. I was asked, warily, if I insisted on a cooked breakfast.

"All I can face, first thing in the morning, is a cup of black coffee with two sugars," I told them. Anyone who wanted anything more elaborate, like toast, was welcome to make it herself. Nancy, on the other hand, always insisted on the full English breakfast though she seldom did any cooking.

I had had two questions to ask: who was the prompter, and what was a typical day? The answers to both were the same; there wasn't one. Anyone near enough to you on stage would prompt, or steer you around to the right position. They would prompt your lines, or even speak them for you. I did this, myself, for a former member, who came back to help out, and who forgot a major speech. I said it for her, transposing the pronouns as I went.

Following this, Shylock addressed me: "Why, look you how you storm," then turned neatly to Antonio, " ... I would be friends with you and have your love ..." Later on, I lost a few of my own words and skipped a bit. All the thanks I got for this was the tart remark, "It's all very well filling in for someone else's lines, but I would appreciate it if you would remember your own." I thought this was a bit thick, considering that she hadn't apologised for forgetting to come on as the Salad on that memorable occasion; not even a "Sorry about that, m'dear."

As for a typical day, it's true to say that the domestic arrangements necessitated a certain routine. Once on site, there were the Elsans to empty, water to fetch, grocery for seven, plus gas mantles, to get. On a winter morning we might have to go out and give the gas bottles a shake before we could make the coffee, then the routine would begin for taking the play to the school. The food boxes had to be filled, a flask of hot water for drinks in each car, and everyone's hold-all stowed on board.

In the black Rolls, called Clare, Nancy would drive, with four passengers and the dogs. In the cream and black Rolls, called Madame Gruchy, shortened to Madame G., most of the room was taken by the gear, with the long rods that took the back-drop, on top. There was room left only for a driver and passenger. Sue would drive this until Jim got her English licence.

Clare did only twelve miles to the gallon, so that meant frequent stops. Once at the school, there were the Head and the English Teacher to see; the gear to unpack and carry in; the stage to examine, to see if it had beams from which to hang the drapes. If it had, I would throw a rope over each of them in turn, with a tennis ball on the end, and haul them up. If not, we would have to put up our own structure, with interlinking rods. On only one occasion did I erect those rods without hysteria—and once with a wrenched thumb. Nancy couldn't understand it—they were supposed to be easier, and I couldn't convince her that my gifts didn't lie in engineering. The term 'verbal, not spatial', was not current at the time. Nancy saw things in black and white, not multi-coloured, as they are. If you were good at one thing, you must be good at everything.

We would borrow a table and six chairs; cover the table with a painted cloth, and to the chairs we tied painted pieces of wood, with mitre shaped tops, to fit most periods. If we were performing Maria Marten, we would bring in a tow-rope to hang William Corder with. If St Joan, a bed for the Dauphin was got together with whatever was at hand, and so on.

Whoever was on Scenery and Props would put the props in their place. Wardrobe would lay out the costumes and make-up boxes and towels. Nancy fixed the lighting schedule and the music, and dealt with the takings and the accounts.

After the play, we would strike the set, and pack Madame G. The switchboard went on the floor, directly behind the front seats, and as precisely amidships as possible. The bench for Twelfth Night would be placed upside down and boxes of shoes, boots and socks placed within it against the back seat. The box of wigs and the one containing the make-up boxes were distributed around the floor space. Floodlights and spotlights were placed up against the far window, with the box of colour filters. Next the back seat was filled—with the backdrop, the costumes, with the costumes for the next play uppermost; chair backs, then the drapes, which brought you very near the roof. In those old cars, built high and roomy enough for a man to enter with his top hat on, there would be a glass partition which the grand people in the back would draw closed for privacy. Essential in this case, to prevent the entire show from cascading over the driver and passenger.

Very occasionally, we could take a shower, if the school had them. After that, the week's cook would distribute from the food box. Then back to the site for the evening routine. If we didn't have to travel on to the next site, we could relax. Jim would go for a drink, and anyone who had the cash and the energy would go with her. The spare wheels would be put in Clare for the night. But if we had to move on, they went in the caravans—two each, along with the gas bottles, water carrier, and the tin tubs from under the water outlet.

Having driven the British countryside for nearly thirty-five years, it was seldom that Nancy could not find her way, not only from one town to another, but by intuitive reasoning, along the best route and on to the required site. When she did go wrong, it was usually owing to my dodgy map-reading.

I took us all twenty miles out of our way on a motorway. "Find the blue line on the map," Nancy said.

Unfortunately, there were two blue lines. I directed her by the A roads instead of the motorway. A new girl, who had been auditioned in a hurry, signed up in desperation and regretted at leisure, kept saying, "Can't we do a U-turn, Miss Hewins?"

"No, Marlene," we told her, "it's illegal, and we wouldn't live to be prosecuted."

Then she would suggest it a short while and several miles later. We explained again. After several more miles in the wrong direction, the idea would occur to her again, in renewed novelty.

"Well, can't we just turn round?" Nancy went rigid at the wheel.

Once at the new site, the last duty of the day was to park, un-hitch, let the legs down, put the steps at the door, hitch the gas bottles up and place the tubs under the vans, then bring the steps in and fall into our bunks.

That was the nearest we got to a typical day. They were not always as smooth running. Nevertheless, I had got on to the stage at last and, humble touring rep though it was, and not-withstanding the complexities and mishaps of the co-operative in which I worked, Nancy's freaks of behaviour, and the clash of personalities, I was doing a job I loved, and if it got no worse, that was fine by me.

CHAPTER TWELVE

WALTER PLINGE LIVES!

During the spring holiday break of 1962, I took some temporary secretarial work, and managed to build my bank account up to ten pounds. As a temp, I made about £8. 15. 0d. a week, and gave Mum £2. 10. 0d. So six pounds five was enough to pay for clothes, soap and shampoo, with a bit left to scrooge away for a week's rest.

On the Saturday before returning to Willersey, I went into the city at lunchtime, on a No. 8 bus, and came back later on the same route, then thought no more about it.

Back at Willersey, I heard on someone's radio that there was a smallpox scare in Birmingham, and that everyone who had been on a No. 8 at lunchtime was to go to the City Clinic at Congreve Street for vaccination. I discussed this with Nancy, and told her I'd like to go back for the jab, but she was keen to get rehearsals started with the new girls, and persuaded me to wait and see.

As we settled down in our bunks that night, Nancy rang the handbell from the cottage door, and called me to the phone. It was Jimmy.

"Did you go into the city on a number eight on Saturday?" he wanted to know.

"Yes, I did, but I had a smallpox vaccination when I was two."

"That's no good, they don't last; you'd better come back and have another one."

"Well, I would, but Nancy wants to take the plays out, and I'd miss the first booking, then have to make my own way ..."

"She WHAT? Isn't your health more important? Let me speak to her." He did. As she listened, Nancy stiffened.

"Now look here, young man, just calm down ..."

After a while, Mum must have come on the phone, because the conversation calmed down. Then I spoke again to Jimmy. As Nancy heard me making sounds of assent, she went upstairs to listen in on the extension.

"OK," I said, waiting to hear the click on the line and speaking loudly so that Jimmy wouldn't hear it and talk angrily to Nancy again, "I'll get on the first bus tomorrow, go straight to Congreve Street, then stay the night at home."

Back in the van, I told the others what it was about. They kept what distance they could in the little caravan, and bitterly decried having to share space with a smallpox suspect.

"Thanks a lot, girls," I said, "I knew I could set my hopes on your kind nursery."

"No good quoting Lear at us," remarked Jenny, who shared my sense of humour, "but we'll know whom to blame when the pustules start breaking out all round."

We all giggled nervously, and I tried to sleep, but what with their attitude, and the to-do on the phone, my head began to feel light, my mouth became dry, and I felt I was running a temperature. I lay awake imagining myself ringing the handbell to warn off the villagers from my contagion.

Before I had even got up the next morning, Nancy came to tell me she had phoned Dr Rosser, who told her there would be some serum waiting for me at a clinic in Pershore. I phoned home and explained that I would get it and have it safely in my arm in a tenth of the time that going back to Birmingham would achieve. So Jimmy's outburst had evidently done the trick. Nancy must have paid Dr Rosser privately, because she came to the Long House with her black bag as soon as she could get away. We breathed again.

Nancy couldn't quite let the matter drop. "They panic so, don't they, the gentlemen?"

I kept a diplomatic silence.

"At all events," she continued, "you didn't have to return to the nest of contagion." Nancy tended to think only of the company, and to regard people as commodities, until they spoke up on their own behalf.

Dr Rosser vaccinated the rest of the company, and as they sat round recovering, I took them through their lines.

Back in Birmingham, the queue at the clinic had gone round the block. The Health Authorities had decided to give everyone the jab. In fact, we were to find that no school would take an un-vaccinated visitor. As children trooped into the gym, we saw a plaster on every little arm. I felt vindicated. The episode drew to a close when Jim rejoined us for the tour, with the wry observation that her vaccine hadn't taken.

"The alcohol in my bloodstream swamped it before it could get to my immune system," she told us, dead-pan.

Macbeth is held to be the jinx play for every company. Not so with us. Julius Caesar was our unlucky play. When the costumes on the back seat of Madame G. began to smoulder from some conflagration beneath the floor of the car, J.C. was held to be responsible, being the play for that day. Loss of props, cancellations, gastric flu, car breakdown, dire combustion and confused events;' put it down to the chap in the toga. Common sense, and the laws of probability, make it obvious that there was an equal chance of cussedness striking whichever play was on. But human nature looks for a pattern, and finds one. It was harmless, and gave us something to blame.

* * *

We were to do Twelfth Night at Windsor. Dame had been parked at some point between there and Willersey. To make sure that both vans and cars eventually arrived at Windsor, Sue had to take Madame G. with Sudbury to where Dame was, unhitch Sudbury and leave it, then take Dame on to Windsor to the school. She was then to drive Madame G. back to the place where Sudbury had been left, hitch up, turn round and go back to Windsor with it. It would take about twenty-four hours.

Sue had wanted to go on her own, but Nancy had insisted on a volunteer; Sue had been subject to fainting fits; though I have to say I'm not sure what I could have done had she slumped over the wheel—veered the steering wheel to the left, perhaps, and hoped we got stuck in a ditch? But I was keen to get away, the rest of the company were getting on my nerves. Two of them had left home for the first time at eighteen, and still thought the world was their nursery. Then they learned to make their own coffee, and felt they now knew all there was to know about life — and were ready to lecture the rest of us on the subject.

Sue had taken some getting used to. On my first stint as cook, I had taken my valise into the nearest town to get the groceries. It was laden, and weighed half a hundredweight. As I began to trudge back with it, I saw Sue in town and asked her to give me a hand to get it back to the site. I still had rheumatism in my right shoulder, and the bag was heavy enough to need both my hands.

"Oh no, I don't have to do that," Sue said, with a bright smile, "that's the cook's job." Then she walked off. In fact, she was never cook. "I'm a driver, and drivers don't have to cook."

I would have found that fair enough, but thought she could have bent the rules a bit to help me back with the groceries. She did, however, redeem herself in my eyes by displaying the same silly sense of humour as myself. I could forgive many weaknesses in one who promised to be fun.

To break the monotony of the journey, we went through a few lines. I sang, having found that shouting my head off from stage had the effect of strengthening my voice to the point where I could carry a tune. Sue passed on valuable tips.

"When you play Bassanio, take your time over choosing the casket. Make the audience think you are going to take the gold one. Even though the audience know which one you are going to take, it's surprising how much you can get them on edge and wondering."

Another hint concerned death by sword. "It's too easy to get a laugh," she said. "The trick is to deliver the thrust upstage, with an upward strike, and at close quarters. It avoids that risible effect you get with the sword sticking under your arm."

"What about running on my own sword?"

"Ah, now that requires you to be on good terms with the servant who holds it. He can make you look very silly by thrusting it so far forward that the audience can see his hand grasping the hilt."

We counted up the parts we had played until then. Mine came to: Casca, Cassius and Calphurnia. Gratiano, Bassanio, Old Gobbo and Portia. Feste, Viola, Malvolio, Fabian and Sebastian. All three Witches in turn, a Thane, Banquo, the Gentlewoman and the Porter. I was later to play Harry Hotspur and Bardolph; Quince, Lion, a Rude Mechanical and Lysander; Caliban and Stephano. Any number of servants, boys, and military nobles bearing the names of several English counties. These were only from the Shakespeare plays. The other playwrights were taken on in their turn. In this way, Sue and I whiled away the miles.

Like Clare, Madame G. did little more than twelve miles to the gallon. We had allowed for an average speed of twenty miles an hour with the caravan in tow, and thirty without, and had timed it all too nicely to allow for being stranded. After filling up, Madame G. was reluctant to start. We would need a tow of five yards to jolt her into action again. There was a heavy truck in the forecourt ahead of us, and I asked the driver if he could help. He was happy to do as much, and only grumbled about his own vehicle as I tied the tow rope on.

"It is 'eap," he said, his Brummy accent suddenly reminding me of how changed my social surroundings had become.

We were grateful to him and listened sympathetically. "There ought to be a proper test got up for these motors before they go on the road." It was to be a good five or six years before the MOT, and this was the reason for the state Nancy's cars were allowed to get into.

In motion once again, I discussed this with Sue. "Nothing gets mended," I grumbled. The door of Sudbury had been wrenched off by Kay's scraping it against a lamppost, assisted by my direction — I had left the door open without mentioning it to her. It was now tied on with rope. Jean had become hypothermic in the back of Clare on the previous tour. I had wound the window down a few weeks ago; it had stuck, and would have broken if I had tried to wind it up again. It now had a piece of spare curtain fixed up against it. I would, the following winter, lose my right thumbnail, slamming it in the door of Clare, in transit, because the inside door handle had broken, and I had closed it with both hands. Madame G. had lost an outside door handle in a small accident. Jim was driving at the time—sober, it must be admitted, but none of us would continue the journey with her. Her passenger came in Clare when the two cars met up at a garage, and we were all piled into Clare, cowardly waving off Jim as she stoically carried on alone.

Whenever I mentioned these things to Nancy, she made her usual reference to not killing the goose that lays the golden egg. "Geese," I mentally corrected, but Nancy would have thought the revolution nigh if I had voiced such a collectivist idea. I never engaged in even the mildest of political exchange while she was driving. We discussed Nancy.

"You have to make allowances," was Sue's feeling on the subject. "She was brought up surrounded by servants. They would attend to these things. She considered it her right."

"Like she considers it her right to have our wages back when she hasn't got change for petrol?"

"Has she done that?"

"Several times. She was quite high about it being our duty to lend her money. All in the spirit of co-operation."

Sue was silent at this.

I couldn't see her handing over her wages for petrol. I was to learn later, however, that she sometimes did pay for it when she was driving.

Nancy did give me a holiday at Willersey, during the summer break of 1962, groceries included, when I was able to get some painting done. I did a triptych on a screen. As I remember, it showed Kay as Hamlet, Nancy as Caesar, and another member, Anne Harris, as Macbeth. The images were not all that well done, and it may have been discreetly put to one side. I got a better likeness of Kay, taken from a photo of her as St Joan, which I set against a background of flames. I let Anne have the picture.

When Kay saw it, she said, "You've made my hands look like bunches of bananas."

It was true, I had rather rushed it. I took it back to Birmingham, and gave her a decent pair of hands. I welcomed her frank criticism, much more constructive than polite flattery.

Kay asked me, mischievously, "I suppose you paint what you see?" a sly dig at arty pretension.

"No, I paint what I'd like to see," I said, then we both laughed, realising I had painted her in flames.

Nancy was unworldly about money. She grumbled about the fact that the Inland Revenue described the royalties she received from some music written by a deceased relative, as unearned income.

"Of course it's been earned," she said, quite seriously, "It's just that it wasn't earned by me." When I wrote home to tell them that one, Mum shrieked with joy, and cackled for a week.

I expanded on this to Sue, as the roadway slipped along beneath us. Nancy would put the performance takings into any paper bag that came to hand, with the result that coins got dropped into Clare's upholstery. She asked me to clean it out once. I collected about five pounds in florins and half-crowns, and took the money in to her, in Dame. I placed it in neat, one pound piles on the sideboard, and hovered hopefully.

"Quite a haul," I remarked, pointedly. Nancy gazed into space, saying nothing. When I called back later, the money had been taken off the sideboard.

It was a good thing I had kept back four shillings for my trouble. My own fault, in a way; I realised I was supposed to have kept all the money and said nothing. But when it comes to money matters, I have always liked to have it above-board, agreed and settled. I found this leaving it to chance and opportunism distasteful.

Had I said *that* to Nancy, she would certainly have thought the Glorious Day had arrived, comrades. She used to quote a young member of the company who considered herself a Marxist, and would tell us how this youngster held forth on matters of distribution of wealth. "But when I suggested she share out her bar of chocolate, she went quiet." She would make this announcement with a flourish. I didn't like to point out that Marx had meant *everyone* to share what they had—that was the whole point.

* * *

Early in 1997, I went down to London to do some research in the archives of the Theatre Museum, in Covent Garden. Searching through the Osiris files, I came across correspondence between Nancy, her solicitors, and an organisation concerned with children's theatre. The letters were dated 1962.

Nancy had wished to sign a contract with them, but she wanted to draw up the terms herself. They tried, diplomatically, to explain to her that it wasn't done that way. Several letters went back and forth and nothing was agreed upon. In one of their letters, the representatives of the Children's Theatre pointed out that, as members of their group, the cast of the Osiris would have to be paid at least £8 a week.

This triggered a memory. It was in 1962 when, after a performance, Nancy told us, as she sat on the edge of the stage, that this was a 'meeting'. Just routine, she said, and all we would have to do was to agree to a few propositions, and sign a form. Tantalisingly, I cannot remember what these propositions were, except that they were phrased in such a way that they seemed no more than a routine affirmation of the way the company was being run. I don't recall anything innovative in any of it. Nancy's offhand manner, and the fact that she explained nothing, and indeed, encouraged us to continue striking the set and packing the goods while it was going on; allied to the fact that she didn't stop the younger members from treating it as a joke (they tended to frolic rather, after the strains of a performance); all this failed to alert me to the possibility of a missed opportunity.

As I continued to read through the yellowing files, I came across a letter from Nancy, expressing the opinion that her girls did not wish to be part of the Children's Theatre; that we were quite content with matters as they stood, and had signed the organisation's form to that effect.

I would be more on the ball nowadays, of course, but I was young and trusting then, and believed that my elders and betters had my interests at heart.

* * *

Expanding on her theme of sturdy independence, she once said she didn't see the necessity of queuing; it was too regimented, too tidy minded, for her. I didn't bother to ask her whether we should all claw our way to the front and trample over each other. I could see that it was her undisciplined mind taking her reactionary nature to its inevitable conclusions.

To tease her, I said, "I think you would make a good Communist, Nancy. After all, you run a co-operative."

After a shocked silence, she said, "I don't think that's a very nice word, Mary-Rose." For a second, I wondered which word. Then it struck me. She meant 'Communist'.

As Sue and I lumbered on, and the rest of the traffic flashed past us, we fell to reminiscence. "I never thought I would manage without a prompt," I told her. "Not that they are always up to scratch. A girl was prompting at drama school. The actor, who was acting a chair-bound invalid, suddenly dried. The prompter said, helpfully, 'The … ' nothing else, just that one, disconnected definite article. The actor filled in with a few invalid groans. The prompter repeated, 'The … ' slightly louder. This went on for several goes, until the actor cut to another part of his speech. I'd love to have heard what he said to the bloody girl after the show."

"Constance could improvise Shakespeare," Sue told me. "Rather like you did in Merchant, except that she could make up whole verses of the stuff, full of 'wherefores' and 'whenceforths', 'by my halidame' and 'a pox on't'. Wonderful stuff, it had the audience fooled. Some of them will have their text with them — they'll sit there, checking on us."

Sue had a lot of these minor incidents to tell; how Constance's teeth suddenly shot out, and she caught them in mid-air, and popped them back in quick. How someone else, with a gastric bug, just made it to the wings before losing her dinner. How Boué had been trained to do a dance with Nancy: she had been left in her basket with her leash attached to it. The dog heard the cue come up, and rushed on, dragging the basket with her.

We reached the garage where Dame was parked, unhitched Sudbury, and hitched up Dame, then carried on towards Windsor. We talked about Constance. I had seen her one-woman show when we were in the same part of the country as she was performing in. The first part of her act was for the small children, for whom she recited Beatrix Potter. The next piece would be for the Juniors—perhaps *Wind In The Willows*. This was followed by an Anna Russell monologue, very dry and witty. Interspersed with these was a routine of her own. She had, years before, fallen off the stage while in the Osiris, and had sustained an injury to her hip, which never properly healed. She made this the butt of her own comic talent, as she manoeuvred her costumes on, in a sitting position. At one point, she swept off the character's wig, and in a startling moment of theatre, revealed a shock of thick white hair. The spotlight caught it, and I couldn't take my eyes off it for the rest of the performance. I borrowed a company photograph of her, and painted a portrait from it in oils. It still goes into all my exhibitions, marked NOT FOR SALE

We eventually reached Windsor, sought out the Head and the Head of English, and explained ourselves. They were about to make us comfortable, but we explained that we had to go back to a garage some fifty miles back and bring the other caravan.

"I wish I had your energy," a member of staff observed.

So do I, I thought, as we parked Dame, stopping only for a wee and a cup of tea. We rattled off again, lighter now by one caravan, and took that much less time as we re-traced the route in the setting sun. We planned to stop at a transport cafe somewhere on the road back to Windsor. However, as we drew into the forecourt of the garage where we'd left Sudbury, a prosperous-looking man in country clothes was waiting for us; he had seen the Osiris label on the car when we first arrived, but we left before he could speak to us. His wife used to be in show business, and he felt sure she would like to meet us. He asked us if we had time for supper, then phoned his wife to expect us. He drove us to his farm half a mile away. A cooked meal, on a real stove, made by someone who wasn't us. After being in the company for this long, domesticity had taken on an almost exotic aura. We were met by a pretty woman in her early forties, and the encouraging smell of real coffee. She was as hungry for theatrical news as we were for the fry-up.

"How do you disguise yourselves as men?" she wanted to know.

Only too happy to talk about myself, I rattled on about make-up, gesture, voice control and the manly B, at some length. "The most complimentary remark I heard from the audience was, 'He's still breathing', as I lay gasping from the fight that had killed me," I went on, "so at least one small boy thought I was a chap, even though I wasn't realistically dead."

I stopped talking about myself long enough to learn that our hostess had worked on stage with Sid Field. I tried to remember what I had seen of him on film, but could only remember the golf scene. I felt the obligation to repay their kindness with some entertaining repartee of my own, some story against myself — there were plenty of them—but my mind was shutting down with tiredness. Improvisation had fled.

Welcome though the break was, we had to get on. "It is so late that we shall call it early by and by," I quoted, never missing a chance to pose.

We took to the road again. "Remind me where that quote came from," Sue asked me.

"Romeo and Juliet—but I don't suppose Nancy would stage anything as blatantly sexy as that, would she?"

"Oh, yes, some time ago, before I joined, so I don't know who played what, except that Kay was Romeo."

Kay, though a small woman, was very mannish looking and sounding, and took the precaution of always wearing a frock or a skirt, to avoid being addressed as a man. One or two girls had developed a crush on her, as girls routinely do. Nancy had never come to terms with this part of human nature. I overheard her saying to Kay, as we settled down for the night,

"I fear you have an admirer, Kay."

"Oh, I don't think so," came the reply, "she's just thrilled about the same things that I am. She's taking the same subjects that I did, and wants to know all about Somerville before she goes up." Nancy's upbringing had been very insular; she would have held the same viewpoint as Queen Victoria on these matters, had not thirty years of working with some hundred or so young women unavoidably brought her face to face with them.

We did not discuss any of this as we drove on, feeling as if we had been driving for ever. We began to look for a lay-by. Sue was developing a cold, and felt dreadful, as we pulled in.

"Don't go too far along," I said, "leave room for something heavy in front of us; we might need another tow." I undid the ropes that held the door on; we climbed in over the spare wheels, gas bottles and draining tub, tied the door back on, each took a bunk, pulled a few blankets over us, fully clothed, and tried to sleep. We had just half an hour in which to rest. Sue set the alarm clock. She managed to sleep, but because she had felt too tired to park the vehicles straight, the back end of Sudbury protruded diagonally, several inches, into the road. Every heavy truck that lumbered past rocked the van with its passing breeze. I lay tensed, expecting us to be struck from behind at any moment, and sent splintering across the highway.

The alarm went off. I was still awake, and still cold. It was still dark, and five o'clock. We dragged ourselves out of bed, climbed over the wheels, gas-bottles and so on, as before, got out, and tied the door back on. I was right, Madame G. wouldn't start, but by one of those strokes of luck that drop by just when you need them, there was a large vehicle in front of us in the lay-by. I got the tow-rope out and approached the driver with a smile.

The first pull got us a few feet, then the rope snapped. I cleared the shreds of rope away, and we tried again. This time Madame G. coughed into life. I untied what was left of the tow-rope, waved thanks to the driver, and got back into Madame G.

"Who's playing William Corder this time out?" I asked, stuffing the hempen remains behind the partition.

"Jim, I think."

"She'll have to stand on her toes in the hanging scene then," I said.

After a few more miles, Sue said, "You can doze off for half an hour if you like." A kind thought, but I was quite unable to by now. I was in that state of wide-eyed exhaustion in which I felt I could go on for ever.

"Thanks, Sue, but I can't. I'm running on empty." That reminded us both that we should look for a garage, and a transport cafe.

It was an ambition of Nancy's to hold an Osiris anniversary in a transport cafe. The modern version of the wayside inn, it epitomised for her the romance of the road, its inhabitants passing each other by chance in the warmth of the tavern, before joining the cold road again. A paradigm of life. It was one with her empathy for Travellers, more usually termed Gypsies then. As they sped by in the other direction, they would note the old cars, and wave, taking us to be Travellers, too.

When we stopped for breakfast, Sue stayed put and kept the engine running, while I brought her a substantial snack from a cafe. Eating while travelling: lesson number one: never eat a fried egg sandwich without a knife and fork. The front of your jacket gets the best of the nourishment. It was still too early in the morning for me to face anything more than toast, so I still looked relatively ladylike. For me. We sat in the car, while Madame G. ticked over, our noses in a mug of coffee each. Powdered and Instant, but it had never tasted so good.

Our eventual arrival back at the school in Windsor, the setting up, making up and dressing is a blur in my memory. We got through Twelfth Night as well as we could—my head was light from lack of sleep; I felt I was walking two feet above the ground. Jenny, whose drastic dieting had brought on anaemia, forgot her lines, smiled and shook her head sadly at me. I cut to a point further on, and somehow we got through the play. I made a wish that we would never again have such a protracted and exhausting journey. Such is the optimism of youth.

* * *

One of Nancy's friends, Essex Barter-Spencer, joined the company for a tour; she was a pretty, middle-aged woman with a youthful outlook and kind heart, who would be playing a witch, a Thane, the Goddess Iris, Worcester, Lady Bracknell and of course, Many Others. It's a compliment to her acting talents that she played so many characters the very opposite of her mild-mannered self. Her fiercesome Lady Bracknell was the same woman who took everyone's duty at walking the dogs; (her sister Sautelle, who bred Belgian Griffons, supplied Nancy regularly over the years with her tiny friends), she replenished our water supply and hitched up the Aqua-Roll to Dame when it should have been the duty of one of us younger members. The hideous witch who threw eye of toad and wool of bat into the cauldron was the same person who cooked dinner for us in Sudbury when we had energy only to eat it. It was also Essex who demanded of Nancy that Boué should be taken to the nearest vet when the little dog was blind and in severe pain. Boué howled grievously when she tried to pass a motion.

Essex made a principled stand about the matter. "Nancy, if you don't take this little dog to the nearest vet, then I shall get on the next train home." We were within a few hours of going up. Nancy had no choice.

Nancy came back from the vet's alone. She said nothing to anyone, except her lines, and we completed Twelfth Night. Nancy performed the song at the end; The Wind And The Rain, including the moves which had allowed for Boué running between her feet and round her legs in a figure eight. The audience may have thought these were simply part of a jig, not realising that they accommodated the ghost of a small friend, one who had been her only constant in a period of rapidly changing casts, personal loss as friends died, and a society to whose changes she had never quite adjusted, and whose upbringing had never prepared her for. She had never been able to commit her emotions to humans and only had her dogs.

I couldn't help thinking that she could have arranged for treatment a lot earlier, and maybe an operation. She could well have afforded it. She must have known that their lives were short, but she never got used to it.

Essex was to take the full force of Nancy's grief and bitterness, and was told to leave the company.

The next school holiday came, and with it the Labour Exchange or the Office Staff Agencies, then we returned to Willersey to face another upheaval in cast change.

CHAPTER THIRTEEN

CROSS DRESSING

My favourite Shakespeare play is A Midsummer Night's Dream. While heavy drama, exciting action and elegiac verse never date, comedy is perishable goods and needs a modern reference. Not so much in the way of topical allusion, though I think that is legitimate—but a modern slant on what taboos there are to break. Shakespeare did it, much to our bafflement, and he also presented his period plays in contemporary dress—Caesar is described: "He plucked me ope his doublet," long before the doublet was designed. Slapstick doesn't date, of course, but it has to be presented with skill, and has to surprise.

Nancy took the parts of the Duke, and Bottom. I played Quince, a sprite, a rude mechanical, and Lysander to Yvonne Guest's Hermia. Kim Stamford doubled Puck with Hippolyta. An Australian girl, Christine, played the Fairy who sings Over Hill, Over Dale. I believe it was she who was tall enough to play Helena, but without studying the entire play, I can't remember who was at liberty to double what with what.

As summer came on, we toured Scotland, the first time I had been there. This brought us to Edinburgh; glorious scenery on the way to every venue, reading without the lights on at midnight at Grantown on Spey, swimming in the Firth of Forth with Yvonne, and rather fewer performances of Macbeth than usual. (Scottish royalty behaving as badly as the English in the other plays).

The swim was my idea. From my early twenties I intended to swim in as many forms of water as possible. In the Cut at Knowle; in as many of Birmingham's public baths as I could; in rivers and streams at camp with the Young Crusaders; in as many seas and estuaries surrounding the British Isles as could be managed. In the Adriatic during a twelve-day holiday in Venice (a last fling extravagance before drama school and uncertain employment), and of course, the Baltic. I didn't analyse why I wanted to make myself part of the landscape in this way. Maybe, like Burt Lancaster in The Swimmer, who swims through all his friends' pools on his way home, it was a statement of "I was here." At Gretna Green I went to the cinema for the first time since we had had the television at home. We saw The Bridge On The River Kwai.

"I thought at first," Nancy said, "that Alec Guinness' stiff-necked performance was overdone, but I realised that it was the character who was like that." Nancy was not a subtle actor. She tended to 'act' in inverted commas.

We didn't take Sudbury to Scotland. It was left behind to have the door refitted. In Dame, there was Nancy, Kay, me, and Kim in a bed on the floor between Kay's bunk and mine. Yvonne, Merry Marshall, who went on to RADA, and Christine shared a tent. The pitch at Edinburgh was a big, crowded holiday site, with a toilet block; luxury enough to be able to empty the Elsan without having to take it through the school lavatories, but with that ultimate in civilised living—showers.

After a long lie-in, we woke to find ourselves the centre of attention, divided between the vintage cars and the travelling theatre. I was often to meet this interest, waiting in the car at the kerbside. I would be burbling on about the company, only to find that it was the cars the bystander was interested in, or I would rattle on about the year of the motors and the short mileage, to be told that it was show business that took their interest.

How odd that a tour of Scotland should elicit memories, not of the magnificent scenery, but of conversations held about past events of my own life. I told Kim about Venice.

"How extraordinary to go alone," was her reaction.

"Well, I was determined to do something out of the ordinary before I got too old to do anything but make what living I could. I hadn't the time nor money to work on some grand plan for my life, so I tended to save for a long time, then grab the chance, whatever it might be."

"Couldn't your family have supported you while you worked out a career?"

"They have no money to spare at all." I replied.

What I found most irritating of all about being hard up, were the cosy assumptions of others. When I first played Alfred Dolittle, I asked Kay how to knot my tie.

"Surely you know how to do that?"

"No, Kay, I've never had occasion."

"You must have done! Surely you used to tie your brothers' ties for them when they went to school?"

There was no way in which I could have combated this attitude. If I had said, "Kay, they didn't wear ties," she would almost certainly have said,

"Oh, don't talk like a fool!"

And if I had told her half of the rest, she would have thought I was lying, for effect. She did believe that such an underclass existed, but they were a sub-species to her, who could barely string a sentence together. Certainly nobody that she would have shared living space with. Her carefully constructed picture of me was wrong on another two counts. That I was the eldest, instead of the youngest, and that we were all brought up together, and at a time when the War was splitting up families all over the place.

* * *

While we were in Scotland, I didn't stress the Porter's accent too heavily. The real McCoy, as it were, were sitting in the audience. I gave him just a hint of rolled Rs and moderated the vowels a bit. The matter of regional accent is a modern worry. Miss Richards used to say that a Romeo with a Brummy accent would not sound very romantic, but the likelihood is that the first boy to play the part had something approximating to the Midland accents we now hear.

It was unfortunate that The Merchant Of Venice was a popular choice as a set study for 'A' levels. It contains the most repellent racism; and as Portia, I had to speak the vindictive lines. I found them embarrassing and shameful. Shylock is castigated not just for being cruel and greedy, but for being Jewish—why else would Portia insist on his conversion? Times change, Portia's bigotry, like bear-baiting, would not be found acceptable now. It might be portrayed, but not by the hero. Scholars have evidently decided that the play has more to offer by way of poetry, dramatic structure and tension than Julius Caesar or Macbeth. I deferred to their expertise and contented myself with making the most of the comedy scenes.

This matter was taken up by a newcomer, Mary Eastham; a strapping, energetic young woman who joined us while we were touring, and who watched the performance. We had travelled a very long way, and had not made up our capital of sleep. Even the younger dog, Polly, when we stopped en route to get something out of Dame, hopefully jumped into her basket, which lay on Nancy's bed; only to be told by her mistress,

"Sorry, Poll, there are many weary miles to go yet." The little animal, like the rest of us, braced herself for the rest of the journey.

Mary, coming to us fresh and rested, watched the performance, and criticised it afterwards without stint. On our return to Willersey, she continued her assessment of Shakespeare's troublesome play, as we curled up for the night, exhausted.

On the following day, while Nancy stayed in for a well-needed rest, we all went to Stratford for the day. We couldn't afford to go to the theatre, so we went round the town. Because my company Shakespeare was falling to pieces, I bought another cheap one of the same version, and decided to get some autographs on the flyleaf.

We strolled towards the stage door of the Memorial Theatre during the afternoon, and saw some people coming out, including a very tall, slim young woman with blonde hair. Yvonne said, "Look, there's Vanessa Redgrave."

"No, it's not," Mary told her, impatiently, "It's nothing like her."

I approached the young woman and asked her for her signature. She wrote 'Vanessa Redgrave', smiled, and went on. The next three actors, I admit I could not identify, but I asked them, anyway, and they wrote, severally, Bill Travers, Tony Richardson and Ian Holm in my book. About to turn and hitch a lift back to Willersey, I saw Ian Richardson coming towards us, and told the others who it was. This one I was sure of.

"No, it's not!" Mary snapped. Nevertheless, when I asked him, he was happy to sign. I now have Ian Richardson's autograph alongside the others.

"How did you recognise him?" I was asked. (He was not then as famous as he is now). "I painted his portrait from a photograph, when he played Hamlet at Birmingham Rep, three years ago. It was the first portrait I had ever painted, but he seemed to like it, and sent it on to his Edinburgh flat."

"You should have told him who you were."

The truth is, I had been struck by uncharacteristic shyness. I had already invaded his privacy, on both occasions, and didn't like to push things further.

Mary was still bad-tempered and prepared to find fault. What with going to Stratford, which involved a lot of hitchhiking and walking, we were pretty bog-eyed by the time we got back to Willersey. The buxom Mary, however, had stamina enough for twenty, if not for helping with the work, then for debate. Back at the Long House, we sat drinking coffee with Nancy in companionable silence, when Mary decided to put the case of Shakespeare's anti-Semitism. Nancy gave her opinion that it was for the conscience of the audience to judge for themselves, and to balance it with the consideration that it was the drama of the time.

Mary came back at her with great vigour. Nancy, trying to keep her eyes open, said tactfully, "Mary, you must surely have been aware that the play would be in the repertoire when you applied for the job." Mary changed tactics, and tried soft-voiced reasoning, her voice getting quieter and more reasonable as she went on. And on.

"I can't hear you, I'm rather deaf," Nancy told her. This merely brought Mary's voice up again, fresh for the onslaught. "I have to go to bed now—Goodnight," Nancy finally said, and went upstairs.

We trooped off to our own beds. Yvonne and I were in Dame, she in a sleeping bag on the floor, and Mary in the bunk opposite mine. As we closed our eyes, Mary resurrected the argument.

Despite my agreeing with her, she wouldn't let it go. Back and forth it went.

"Mary, we'd been driving a long way before you joined us," I said, in desperation, "and we must get some sleep." She made a sympathetic "Oh," briefly at us, then after a few seconds, began again. This happened again.

By now hysterically tired, I shouted, "You're absolutely right, Mary!"

Yvonne screamed, "GOODNIGHT EVERYBODY!" and we were finally allowed to sleep.

Next morning, Nancy rang the handbell and called for Mary, who went into the Long House. A few minutes later she came flouncing back, hurled her clothes back into her suitcase, clomped out and slammed the caravan door. Waiting until she had got through the gate, Yvonne and I put our noses above the blankets, looked at each other and laughed.

"Quiet!" I hissed, "she'll come back again and tear our heads off."

Nancy came over later to tell us that she had told Mary she had no time for half-baked intellectuals, and that she might as well go back home and put the world to rights from there.

I longed to tell Nancy that Mary's high principles were for show only, and an outlet for her excess energy. No doubt she would grow out of them, make a virtue of self interest, and lecture her children on what she imagined to be the realities of life. But the thought was only forming in my mind. I would, like Manny Shinwell, become more revolutionary with age.

* * *

The best thing that ever happened to me was my fiftieth birthday, but twenty years before this happy occasion, Nancy found me taking a lie-down in the wings, for a vital few minutes before bounding back on as Bassanio. As she frowned over me, I pointed to my wrist and held up three fingers.

"You can't just drop out like that," she reproved me, later. "It's irresponsible."

"I hadn't dropped out, Nancy, I was making use of a break. There would have been no point in my standing about, feeling worse."

"Women didn't have this trouble when I was young," she claimed.

"Oh, they did, you know, but they just didn't discuss it. My landlady in Birmingham used to tell me she had no end of trouble. She ran the bar at her husband's working men's club, and she'd be behind the bar for hours, with the blood running into her boots, unable to get away to clean up or make up another pad." As an afterthought, I suggested, "I'd better wear black tights with the white tunic, don't you think."

"It won't look very romantic," she said.

"It will look even less romantic ..."

"Quite so. Well, what about red tights?"

"I appreciate the thought, Nancy, but the reds are not the same. I should the multitudinous seas incarnadine ..." I left the quote in mid-air, as it didn't quite apply unless I'd had green tights.

It was always good to find that I was not only accepted as performing as a male, but sometimes to be genuinely mistaken for one. We had been successful in making the ring scene in Merchant funny. The audience, all teenage girls, had relished

Bassanio's discomfiture as I tried to hide the ring from Portia. Sue's air of "Get out of that, Bassanio," had struck a chord in the girls' own developing sense of manipulation, and after the performance, they came round to ask us for autographs. As they each saw my name in their autograph books, they gave a small expression of disappointment. They had thought I was a boy, even at close quarters. Well, I was clearly not worth flirting with, (except in the minds of a statistical few), but we all enjoyed this opportunity for girl-talk. I felt quite affectionate towards these trusting young people, eagerly looking for a lead in life, from someone they imagined to possess the sophistication and poise they sought. I felt a complete fraud.

* * *

On a trip home, Naomi excitedly told me that she had told all her school-friends that "My sister's an actress." She also wanted to know if I got a lot of money, like actors are supposed to get. Oh well.

We didn't always get time to wash our hands after putting up the scenery. Sitting out a performance of Merchant on one occasion, when a newcomer was being given a chance, and the parts were shifted around, I noticed Jim's hands as she sat across the table with Nerissa, discussing her suitors, and from the audience the palms of her hands were pale black. Elegant Venetian lady has to hump the furniture about before queening it before the public. It's a glamorous life at the top, one thought, with a sigh.

* * *

Hitch-hiking home on one occasion, I found myself walking by the river at Evesham, looking for a bench to sit and eat a sandwich. I strode along, in slacks, my hair cut short, and with no make-up. A young woman of about eighteen came towards me, then suddenly began to veer over to my side of the path, swaying her hips and humming a tune. I scuttled off in panic — I didn't want the deception to be quite that realistic. Something else came as a pleasant surprise though. I found I was deferred to in matters of personal space. I was not jostled on the pavement; no-one let doors swing back in my face. And older men left me in peace. (The statistical minority, in this case, would not try their luck in broad daylight). The only drawback was the difficulty in getting a lift. A young man with a suitcase is something drivers tend to be wary of.

It was a mild summer day, with a cool breeze, so I didn't mind walking, and after three more miles I stopped at a mobile sandwich van. The crowd standing round were all men, and the sharp-eyed woman behind the counter said to her husband, "Serve that lady next." He looked at, over and past me, searching the crowd, so I raised my hand and smiled. He was still not happy about it though, as he served me. Neither was the woman, who stared unsmilingly. Perhaps she suspected me of being an effeminate boy.

I must have walked on for five more miles, when I finally flagged down a light open truck. It was driven by a boy just old enough to drive, and with several other youngsters in the cab; he invited me to get up into the back, assuming rightly that I didn't want help. I stretched out, exhausted, watching the treetops going past, for another ten miles, pleased with myself. With the black slacks I was wearing a long-sleeved blouse that passed for a shirt; and although the driver looked in the mirror now and then, it was to look at the road, not at me, lying there, with only a buttoned blouse standing between the world and my secondary sexual characteristics. Once back on the Midland Red route, he dropped me off, and I thanked him.

"OK mate," he called, and drove off.

* * *

Another school holiday came and went; a few more pounds were saved from office work; several more firms gave me work for a week or two at a time, and my fellow workers dumped on me the work they found most difficult or time-consuming. Some were paranoid about my sitting in their friend's chair, as if I had no right to be there. Others regarded me as a fly-by-night with no sense of loyalty—yet others hinted at the higher fees I took per hour than they did, ignoring the fact that I had no sick pay or holiday money. Put another way, they felt tied to their jobs.

There were though, always people who welcomed me with friendliness and good grace, and bosses who offered me the job I was covering. I was almost sorry to get back to the Osiris.

Not sorry enough to want to miss playing Harry Percy,

though. Vehemence and bluster, and a dying speech to fetch the ducks off the pond. Although the sentiments expressed in much of this hot air were those of a bunch of greedy nobles, audiences love a bit of belligerent declamation and macho flourish, and I got a rousing send-off from the boys at the Douai School; as I went crashing to the floor, they raised a cheer. Maybe they were just glad to see the back of this aggressive bore, but we don't tell ourselves that when we hear the music of applause.

Sue, who played Prince Hal, asked me why I always threw my shield upstage as I went down. I had to think about that. We often do things on stage for no obvious reason. "For dramatic effect, I thought," was my initial explanation, "or because I didn't want to trip over it, or send it below the curtain line. But I may well have done it today because I was startled at your sword piercing my chainmail." Blunted though it was, it had gone through everything but my skin, leaving a red mark.

It's easy to forget the names of so many schools, but one or two stay in the mind. The Douai, run by monks, one of whom felt he should direct the raising of the scenery; "All right, boys, take it up and look sharp!"

They whipped the drapes up on the ropes, nearly bringing it all tumbling down, when I shouted, "Gently, please! Stop—I have to check it." Which I had to, anyway.

We gave The Importance Of Being Ernest at Les Oiseaux Convent, at Newmarket, where we set the caravans down in the drive—and where we got up early in the morning to see the horses trotting out in the mist, crossing the road running through the Heath.

The Haberdashers' School, I remember only for the name, and the fact that in recent years, pupils of the school were on television, being asked what haberdashery meant. None of those asked knew. Cotton gloves, veils and modesty vests are not exactly up to the minute items of young people's wardrobes, but I thought the schoolteachers might have told them what the school name meant, not to mention the history of it.

St George's School, in Ramsgate, was a Council School, but no doubt referred to, by 1962, as County Secondary; the name far grander than the school. When I wrote and told the family about it, I was told that it had been Mum's old school, and that Granny had paid sixpence a week for her daughter to attend. When I told Nancy about the run-down school we had just performed at, she looked at me oddly, but remained quiet on the subject. She, too, could not fit me and my family background into a neat compartment.

At a County Secondary School in Stafford, I hadn't had time to explore the town to see what changes had been made since I was last there. I know it must have been Pygmalion that day, because, as Alfred Dolittle, I came to the line, "See you in St George's, Eliza," and the audience went wild.

The penny didn't drop straight away. Then, between scenes, I asked one of the boys helping backstage, why they had laughed. "St George's is the name of the local hospital," he told me, tactfully. This only puzzled me further, then, as I was getting changed, I was mentally revisiting parts of the town; Gaol Road, Crookedbridge Road, towards the bottom of which was the mental hospital, St George's. Of course. The image of the charity shoes, sailing over the wall, allegedly. The very phrase itself, "See you in St George's!" flung derisively from child to child, as children do. I wondered if the Head of English realised the line was included, when the play was selected.

St George's was in the news only recently, in an item on run-down hospitals. A section of it is a modern psychiatric unit, but the remains of the old building are now derelict. There had been plans to make it into a youth centre, but these fell through from lack of funds. Much of it is vandalised and, poignantly, used for rough sleeping by former patients abandoned to the community, and trying to get back to the security of having a hospital wrapped round them.

We were at a Girls' Posh with the entire school watching the play. I was the only member of the cast not on stage at one point, when the telephone rang. The staff were all Spanish, and none of them spoke English. A girl's father had lighted on that very moment to phone his daughter before taking a taxi to the airport, and home to America. I slipped into the hall, and told a teacher, but she didn't' seem to think it mattered. I wondered if father and daughter got together again, the only link having been a wandering play-actor.

Kay and I were travelling back from the Immaculate Conception School in Darlington, when we needed to get some shopping. We parked in the only space available, outside the offices of the local newspaper. When we got back with the groceries, we found a photographer by the car, with a notebook. The outcome was a write-up, with a photograph. There we are, we three, Kay on the right running-board, me on the left, holding on to the long rods

Theatre Rolls along *1962*

ONE part of the Rolls Royce-borne Osiris Repertory Co. at Darlington last night after giving a performance of Twelfth Night to children of the Immaculate Conception school.

Miss Kay Jones (left) and Miss Mary-Rose Benton are members of the seven-strong, all-female company from Worcestershire. The 1930 Rolls Royce carries them and all the props—costumes, lights, curtains, scenery. "Fitting it all in is like doing a jigsaw puzzle," said Miss Jones.

The five other members of the company travel around in a 1927 Rolls Royce.

The company, run by Miss Nancy Hewins, was formed in 1927 and is based at Willersey, near Broadway, Worcestershire. It specialises in giving Shakespearean productions at schools.

Newspaper cutting of Kay and me, with Madame G

strapped on top, and Madame G. herself, with her enormous headlamps, characteristic radiator, wheels like something on a heavy truck and, for the interest of Rolls Royce buffs, her registration plate WX 4868.

* * *

With Jim in Clare, travelling from site to town; something began to knock under the floorboards. We looked at each other and raised eyebrows. It only made us giggle at first, as people began to stare a little more than they usually did. By another half mile, we were in subdued hysterics as the knocking rose to a rapid banging, becoming more and more frequent. And louder.

"Wake Duncan with thy knocking, I would thou could'st!" I shouted, over the racket.

"It's no joke," Jim called back, "I'll have to look out for a garage."

By the time we got to within sight of one, the banging was a machine-gun.

"I'm not driving this cow another yard," she finally decided, and switched off the engine. This was quite cautious for Jim. She had taken to filling the petrol tank with the engine running, in case we couldn't get started again. "A short life, and a merry one," was her attitude. Then Clare rolled obediently into the only garage in the town that serviced Rolls Royces. I swear that heap of scrap metal must have known.

When Jim went to collect Clare in due course, she was told that the back axle had broken. It was the broken ends that were knocking. And "half the teeth were missing from the disc." I merely repeat what I was told. The horseless carriage was ever a mystery to me. I do not drive.

Madame G. gave Kay and me some trouble the following tour, when she gradually slowed down in mid-countryside, and ran gently to a stop. Nancy was behind in Clare, and she stopped, to prod around in the engine for half an hour. A passing old gent stopped his car, and offered to go back to his hotel for help, which Nancy did not hear, with her head under the bonnet. Then he said, several times, "Women will never make mechanics," and went on his way.

As the rain drizzled on, I looked under the car and, after a few seconds, said, "There's a little pool of petrol in this puddle, does it mean anything?"

While Madame G. had a new petrol tank fitted, we put the gear into Clare, and Nancy pressed into use a little car she called Fleance, after Banquo's son, shortened to Flea. Not such good publicity, but more economic on the petrol.

Shortly after this, Clare broke down on the A1. Nancy rang the RAC, who rang a garage. We waited for over half an hour, and Clare was persuaded to get going again. When Nancy phoned the RAC the next day, they phoned the garage, wanting to know why no-one was sent. The receptionist said, "Oh, we didn't believe it—a 1930 Rolls Royce stuck on the A1 with five women in it."

That was a great comfort, knowing that they thought it was a hoax, while we stood and shivered. This was at the time of some notorious A1 murders, as it happened.

* * *

Although we happily made do with minimal facilities; a one-entrance stage with no structure to fix the back-cloth on; a tin hut in a valley; a huge, echoing gymnasium; a hall too small to take our own free-standing structure, and yet with nothing to hang the drapes on; a rickety platform; an elegant Tudor hall to which it would have been a shame to add any of our own scenery; a modern school hall with huge windows, and no way of blocking out the broad daylight—although we met these contingencies these were a challenge and a novelty. They kept us on our toes and encouraged innovation. What undid us was to turn up at a school that had spent thousands of pounds on a specially designed stage, and that had never been used in the two years since it was installed. It had sophisticated push-button controls to move the flats and travellers, and a lighting system that would have delighted Nancy had she had the time to study the workings of it. The flies were too high to hang our drapes from. They would have hung up high like black washing. So we had to set up our own rods, on this great stage, with our own humble drapes, like a post-Medieval band of players in a baronial hall.

I have been asked by other Old Osirians what impact the Osiris had on my life, and how it changed it. It certainly changed my attitude, from one of acceptance to one of challenge and confrontation. It showed me how the other five percent lived, and opened my eyes to the broad band in the middle. I was to meet those who could throw money at any aspiration; who thought the world owed them the privileges they took for granted, and the removal of which would herald the Apocalypse. In the words of Bernard Shaw's St Joan: "Ee, laddie, I didn't know there was that much money in the world!"

The term drew to a close. We had again to think of the Labour Exchange and the agencies. I hadn't been able to save enough for more than one week's rest when I got home, and would, after that, have to find what temporary work there was in the winter.

So we found ourselves, in November, 1962, shivering in togas, waiting to go on in our jinx play. As we looked out through an open door backstage, we saw, from a leaden sky, the first large flakes of snow flurrying down in Northern England, in what was to be the worst winter since 1947.

Photo of painting of Rolls. Madame G (*left*), Clare (*right*)

CHAPTER FOURTEEN

CAST LIST

I thought I would treat myself to a much needed holiday, and draw the dole for a week or two. I thought in vain. Nancy gave us the money for Self Employed stamps; I was to find that these were worse than useless. There was no entitlement to dole money from them, and they didn't even cover sick pay. I would have done better to have put the stamps money in the bank. I could, in theory, have bought a few Non-Employed stamps at the higher rate but, not only could I not draw on them until half-way through the next term, but they would have put me badly out of pocket. I liked to give Mum at least two pounds ten a week. The sympathetic young woman at the city Labour Exchange told me she couldn't give me anything but my bus fare home. I felt so demoralised, I didn't even accept that.

So it was that I came home to that other world, the one with the radio, television and a regular newspaper—Billy's Daily Worker and The Times that Mum took, for the crossword. To Steptoe and Son, and to a daring new satire show on TV called That Was The Week, That Was. And to news of the Vietnam War. The first two I enjoyed; the other seemed to have nothing to do with me.

One of my temp. jobs took me to Lucas in King Street. As I was able to fix my own hours, I chose one day to leave at the same time that the factory turned out. It would be easier to get a bus. There was a fleet of them lined up outside the factory gates. As I stepped out of the office, I heard what sounded like a clattering stampede, looked behind me, and found it was exactly that. What seemed like hundreds of young women swept down in a joyous rush. There is a peculiar look on the faces of people in this rushing horde. A joint hysteria.

I got pushed, jostled and thumped by the Lucas workers as they thundered past me. I wanted to hit them for their brainless rush. But, on calmer reflection, I could see that if you were stuck at a bench all day, bored out of your mind, you needed to dash out in that mass celebration of liberty.

I more recently heard Robert Robinson refer, on radio, to the fact that disabled workers are allowed out five minutes earlier than the rest, for safety's sake. "I can't believe that," he chortled, from his ivory tower, "people don't behave in that way." Oh yes, they do, I wrote and told him.

I got a few weeks' work nearer home and saved on bus fares. About ten pounds went into the bank by the time the Christmas break was over. I bought a copy of The Stage. Still the same list of Artists Wanted, Professional, calling for exotic dancers. Still the same Catch 22 impossibility of getting an Equity card. You couldn't get a card until you had done a certain amount of professional work, and you couldn't get theatrical work until you could show your Equity card … .

I heard of young women working their way to an Equity card via the exotic dancer engagements. Having learned how to take their clothes off in public, they could then be trusted to play Ibsen's heroines.

At about this time, I saw a member of a famous theatrical family in a television interview. The interviewer turned to Nancy Burman and asked, "Should it not be possible to get into theatre work without having to go through the back door?"

Miss Burman mumbled in a dull voice, "Oh, but it's much more fun that way." Neither she nor the interviewer were frank about what they meant by the back door. Nor did this daughter of the rich impresario elaborate on what fun was to be had this way, and by whom.

If she meant that, instead of a part being thrown open for audition, and the most suitable applicant being cast, someone influential slipped his relative into the part, then it's hard to picture what fun and colour that would bring to the production.

* * *

With Christmas over, I returned to Willersey, and two new members. We were now: Nancy, Kay, Elaine, Janet, Joyce and Linda. There was little we could do in the cold but rehearse, try to keep warm, get to know each other, and have a drink at night in The Bell. And watch the snow fall.

Joyce introduced us to the Spirit Glass Game. Elaine, who claimed Marxist credentials, disapproved of it, but rather spoilt her rationalist stance by declaring it to be dangerous. I asked her, "You mean psychologically?"

But she couldn't elaborate on what she meant. Janet asked her point blank what she meant. "I just think it's dangerous," was as near as she got to a dialectical analysis. She had obviously meant that we might "summon up spirits from the vasty deep," a most un-Marxist superstition.

It must be pointed out that Nancy was not at these sessions, as she lived in the cottage, and Kay stayed round the corner at Anne's house. Both would have disapproved of these seance-like goings on. At thirty, I was the senior member there, and was taken to stand in loco parentis for girls of eighteen or thereabouts. However, I had never heard of the Spirit Glass Game, and was fascinated at the prospect.

We wrote out the alphabet and a Yes and No, on little pieces of paper, and arranged them in a circle on the table. Joyce and Janet sat on Kay's bunk, Linda and I sat on mine; Elaine stood by, not wishing to be a part of it. The glass took some time to yield results. Joyce and Janet sat patiently with a finger poised lightly on the top of the upturned glass within the circle of letters, for some ten minutes. Janet sighed.

"Why won't it move?" she said, and immediately the glass shot across the table.

Janet shrieked, and the pieces of paper flew off and fluttered to the floor. Apparently you were supposed to ask questions, which is what Janet, by default, did. We all joined in then, except Elaine, and the glass moved round, giving answers.

We all wanted to know the answer to the big question: "Will I be famous?" A NO every time surprised no one. Joyce asked several questions, and was told she would have a baby when she was twenty-seven. This depressed her. We tried to cheer her up.

"Can I powder its bottom?" Janet asked.

"You might want one by then," Elaine suggested.

"You can take steps to avoid it," I pointed out.

Elaine, whose parents took the Daily Worker, claimed to be a Communist, as had Mary Eastham. I would believe it when I saw it. I had heard too many people make this grand statement, only to be found subsequently to be profoundly lacking in co-operative endeavour, generosity and altruism. In its place was a feel for making a few quick quid and a degree of self-interest that would make Margaret Thatcher gasp with admiration.

Elaine was tall and beautiful. At five feet eight, her weight of some ten stones was about right, and impressively proportioned. Nevertheless, she worried endlessly about her looks and her weight.

"Look at this bump in my nose," she complained. We peered at it closely. None of us could detect a bump. Mealtimes were a misery. As soon as we sat down to eat, she would announce, loudly and petulantly, "I'm FAT, aren't I?" and would keep it up, rephrasing the same sentiment until everyone's appetite was ruined, except hers.

"How is it you can eat anything you like," she asked me, "and never put on weight?"

"Because I CAN'T eat anything I like," I said, for the umpteenth time, already under-nourished and ratty-tempered for that very reason. She would keep asking me this question in the hope that I would eventually give her the answer she wanted.

For a vegetarian, she ate a large quantity of animal fats; cheese, milk, cream, butter and (unfertilised) eggs. If that week's cook accidentally used the same spoon for the mashed potato as she had used to stir the gravy with, Elaine would refuse to eat the mash, and would sit and look lugubriously martyred.

"You've got to admire her tenacity in keeping to a vegetarian diet," was the opinion of one.

"Tenacity in drawing attention to herself and keeping the rest of us on the trot," I snarled.

I was to see her, years later, as a walk-on in The Singing Detective; as beautiful as ever, and with as splendid a figure. I found myself wondering if she ever appreciated her luck.

Joyce worried about old age. She had been talking to Kitty Chidley, the old lady who lived next door to Nancy, in the smaller part of the Long House.

"She has white eyelashes," Joyce said, appalled. "I dread getting white eyelashes like hers."

"You won't care by then," I put in, without thinking.

But Joyce wasn't listening, and missed my lack of tact. She stared ahead, seeing her body disintegrate. I can picture her now; not exactly thin, but with a nervy, wispy look about her that gave the impression of fragility. She piled her light red, flyaway hair on top, which added to the effect. Her eyes darted about, seeing disaster. Her manner and speech, in contrast, were elaborately casual.

She told us something of her history. The breakdown she had been treated for. The little bird-like woman in the bed opposite, recovering from peuperal fever, and how comical Joyce had found her querulous, frightened eyes, "like a startled sparrow." The psychology test she had taken, and which she got us to take.

Joyce's psychology test was this: we had to imagine trees, of any kind, in any number or form. You were walking through them, and were to describe them. You encountered water, and were asked to describe its form and volume, and what you did about it. You had a key with you, explained what it looked like, and what it was made of. Finally, you came to a door, described it, and what you did about it. The key, it was emphasised, had nothing to do with the door.

My trees were spindly birches, the water was a clear pool, which I paddled in. The key was important, but plain. I kept it in my pocket. The door was set in a wall. I stopped at it, not wishing to go through, nor round the wall.

Joyce was not going to tell us what it meant until we had all told our piece. Linda saw the water as a deep lake, into which she dived. Her key was very ornate. Janet saw the water as a rushing stream. Elaine's key was ornate, the water, like mine, a clear pool.

Joyce then told us that the trees represented the subject's own body and state of health. The water meant sex—that figured, I thought, thinking of my shallow pool and timid paddling. The key was religion or ideology, and the door stood for death. Very few people, Joyce told us, spoke of going through the door, or of wanting to. Linda said that she tried to look over it. When I later tested other friends about it, one said the water came from a tap, and he drank it. I still haven't figured that one out.

* * *

As the snow of that extraordinary winter continued to fall, the Cotswolds turned white. This made Joyce turn lyrical.

"It's as if all the mess and dirt of the world were covered over, and everything was clean again."

"But you still think it's all dirty underneath," I asked her.

She thought about this, then said, "Yes, I suppose it is, after all," and sighed.

She told us how she had worked as a model at the Ecole des Beaux Arts, and how she had befriended a male student who was so poor that he was eating only cucumbers, which he got for next to nothing from the market. The other students laughed at him during class because he kept burping. I wondered what became of him, and of any of those young artists starving in their Parisian garrets. And of the bisexual young man she told us about, and who used to make her laugh at the antics he told her of—one of which involved a public lavatory, purple socks, and a note slipped under the cubicle. "He was the oldest queen I've ever seen," had me cackling, Linda smiling, Janet scoffing and Elaine disapproving. The ensuing farce, with the young man falling head-first through the door panel, was Joe Orton with bells on.

For someone who could relate comedy so well, Joyce lacked humour as applied to herself. All ills could be cured by sex, she thought. "Sex is laahvly ... laahvly," she would intone quitely, in a dying fall, shaking her head gently as if in surprise that no-one realised its healing properties. She was aware of Kay's disapproval of her wild ways, and she pitied hers and Nancy's spinsterhood. She was not so serene the night she came back into the caravan, snarling, "the bastard ... getting me all sexed up, then losing interest." Then bitterness would take the place of dripping and drooping over the subject, followed by several hours' reflection on "the irony of fate."

* * *

The garden had disappeared under the snow, as it was falling nearly every day, and it became clear that the tour could not begin yet. Cancellations began to be marked up in the diary, and we learned more about each other.

Janet had the most ferocious energy. Sturdily built, she too was concerned about her weight, but not so obsessively as Elaine. She took up vegetarianism, following Elaine's example. Elaine relaxed a little under this compliment. On stage, Janet was to show more go, and more pace, than the others. Her Dunois had more spirit, it had to be said, than Kay's St Joan. Janet would have been ideal in the role.

At the time she joined us, she told us that she had had to turn down a vacancy at RADA on account of having failed a medical test. She had a cardiac condition, which she didn't elaborate on. But exertion was out of the question. Would we do her share of the cleaning, she asked? I looked at the others, but they all looked downwards, and said, "Oh, yes, of course," in quiet voices. Janet, who had energy enough to stay out late, drinking, jiving and twisting to the jukebox at the New Inn at the top of the green, and who would come back to the caravan and keep us awake till the small hours talking about life, the universe and everything, thanked us all in a sincere, low tone.

"By the way," she added, lighting up another cigarette, "you won't tell Nancy about my heart condition, will you? She might tell me I'm unfit for the life."

A chorus of "Oh no, of course not," followed. Perish the thought. She might even be asked to take a medical test.

I was in the middle of telling them how a former member, Phyllis McMahon, used to try to get the rest of us to learn her lines for her. "Remember this line for me," she would say, and the fact that she had asked would fix it in her mind. Unfortunately, we would get it stuck in ours, too.

As I said the name McMahon, Janet gasped slightly. Then she told us about a boy of that name, in a class she took as a student teacher. It should be pointed out that Janet had a strong influence on susceptible males, and I can picture her, in a tight jumper, and with her sturdy good looks and her energy, strutting about in front of a class of teenage boys. "McMahon was fidgeting under the desk, and the other boys were looking at him." Janet related her story. "I said, 'stand up, boy, let me see what you are doing.' So he stood up, and I said, 'You disgusting boy, stop that at once!' But by that time, he couldn't."

"Poor McMahon," said Joyce, softly, and I began at last to warm to her.

Janet snorted. "He was a dirty little devil. He should have had more control." I wondered, briefly, what a sharp smack to the head would have done for Janet's putative heart condition.

As the snow continued to fall, we rehearsed in the far end of the Long House, by the huge open fire, where the chimney was so broad that you could see daylight when you looked up into it, from the open fireplace. We sorted out the costumes in the barn, sifting through the racks for the plays we would take out when the snow began to melt. A pile of scripts sent up a cloud of dust as we disturbed them, and the ghosts of a thousand performances.

"The Cotswolds are full of ghosts," Joyce told us. I had previous memories of Broadway, where I had camped with the Young Crusaders, at sixteen then at twenty-two. Those six years represented a longer time in my perception than those that flash by in middle age, when you blink and another ten years have gone.

For exercise, we would sometimes walk into Broadway and have a pot of tea between us in a tea-room. This world was new and exotic to me; upper middle-class ladies and tinkling tea-cups. I savoured an experience that some of the others had joined to get away from—that they found stultifying.

In a further attempt to avoid cabin fever, we would go tearing round the country lanes in our wellies—fooling about in the snow on the green, going snow-mad. Joyce, falling to her knees in laughter, as Janet called, "Come back, Captain Scott, we can't go on without you!"

Poor Joyce, still vulnerable, had had a few drinks and fancied that Kay would detect her knee prints in the snow, and condemn her behaviour. Even sober, her mind would spin off in a whirlwind of its own. In the Spirit Glass Game, she would push the glass round quite forcefully, and try to rationalise it by saying, "I know I'm pushing it, but it's the force in the glass that's directing me."

We would be treated to drinks at The Bell, by the locals, but only after we had spent half our rehearsal money. At the New Inn, older men would let us put their shillings in the jukebox and choose our own tune. By this time I no longer knew what was Top Of The Heap, and had to ask.

"Arr, it is 'eap, an' all," an old chap told me, "but try Mike Sarne, singing Come Outside, that ain't bad." The teenage Wendy Richard sharing the disc—now the matronly Pauline in Eastenders.

Still the snow fell, and our lunar cycles began to synchronise, as so often happens when women live at close quarters; like peas growing, as the tendrils begin to curl round the sticks in the same direction, and in concert. Except Elaine, who at eighteen had still not begun. Hence, maybe, her height of five feet, eight inches.

Elaine expounded on the principles of Marxism; Janet declared, at revealing length, how she enjoyed a challenge, but panicked when faced with walking the five miles from Evesham back to Willersey. The next time she went on about enjoying a challenge, I told her she could clean the van out then.

"That's irrelevant," she told me, reproachfully. Joyce told us her boyfriend called her La Vulcan—The Volcano—in bed. She couldn't understand why Nancy told her her acting lacked energy. She shook her head gently and repeated, in the same dying fall, that she was La Vulcan.

Crying off from some expensive undertaking, I griped; "I could do with more money."

"You just have to make a financial effort," Janet said, briskly. She could be very bracing about other people's weaknesses.

"What the hell is a financial effort, robbing a bank?" I snapped. "You do talk baloney, Janet."

Linda told us about herself. I think this was the first opportunity she had had to step outside her introversion, and as she told us about the mother who had no interest in her and whom she could never talk to, or be close to, she quietly wept. I had come in after a walk round the lanes to get warm, and I found them all, drawing her out in this way. Being helpful, I asked if she had ever thought of turning her mind to writing.

"We've gone over that with her,"Janet said, as if I thought I was being original. Linda did begin to keep a journal, filling it in every day, and commenting on every performance.

* * *

The weather became warmer. It was nearly March. We were at last going to tour. Then a gastric bug struck, but we dosed with oil of peppermint and went anyway. I rang home from the school to say where we were, and mentioned the sickness.

"Couldn't you have put it off until everyone was better?" Jimmy wanted to know.

"It wasn't convenient," I said, without thinking. Kay was standing nearby and gasped at the blatant statement.

"What!" Jimmy exclaimed. "She's still treating you like serfs — the bloody tour is more important that your health!" He was right to be indignant, and we should have stood up for our human rights, but Nancy couldn't have encompassed such an idea.

We took out the usual five or six plays with us, this time including St Joan. I found myself in the unusual position of playing only one part in this play, that of The Dauphin. I was still on Scenery and Props, so I had plenty to do. It was the play with the biggest props list: the ever-useful bench, chains, alarm rattle, bed-linen, books, candles, Albert the halberd, which travelled with the long rods on top of Madame G., a parchment, which was ordinary paper yellowed up with motor oil, and sealed with red wax, the Recantation, which I had to write out every time, as it gets ripped up, the pennon, with which I had to indicate the change of wind from backstage. Two reels of cotton attached to the pennon; which were played out to the separate wings. I stood in one wing, jiggling the cotton reel, gradually letting it drop as the wind dropped; then, as the cue came up for the boy to sneeze, I had to nip round the back and start gently jiggling the other reel of cotton. I heard a child in the audience say, "Ooh look, the flag's waving the other way!" The simple effect more fascinating than the special effects of trick photography.

There was the basket that carried the eggs that the hens miraculously laid at the end of Scene One; the same basket that Eliza Dolittle carried her violets in; and any ceremonial baubles that Bernard Shaw had seen fit to fill the production with.

The rehearsals had been rather rushed, and in the Epilogue, when I got out of bed and swung the rattle, I lost a line. I had to go to the window anyway, and just below the stage in the left wing, I saw Kay. "Prompt!" I whispered, as loudly as I dared.

Kay had ears like a Pipistrelle bat, but she pretended to mishear, and whispered back, "That's all right, carry on."

"PROMPT!" I hissed frantically—everyone in the hall must have heard.

Kay's face was inches from mine, but she ignored me completely. I would have preferred her to admit that she too, had forgotten the line.

* * *

On this tour, we had gone straight from Willersey to Oldham, to stay at the house of a former Osirian, Wynne Griffiths, who would eventually inherit the Osiris effects, and who now runs a costume hiring service at the Long House.

We parked next to the house on the moor, but because of the long journey, we were invited to spend the first night in the house, a nice old-fashioned place with plenty of elbow room.

Wynne had a settled job as Wardrobe Mistress at Oldham

Rep, and Nancy felt prompted to say to me, "You know, Mary-Rose, you need to get a steady job in the theatre."

That was one of the many batty sayings I've treasured over the years. Another was, "Bernard Shaw died of pernicious anaemia." (Nancy was not happy about vegetarians). In fact, he died after falling out of an apple tree. He should have known better, at ninety-four, but it was a pretty impressive feat to have climbed it, at that age.

"You know, Bernard Shaw could write really well when he tried." That one made me giggle, but the following one did not.

"Black men, working-class men and students, have less control over their sexual urges than white men or gentlemen."

She often told us that; "At Oxford, they taught us to THINK." She redeemed herself with the potty statement, "You'll never be an actress if you can't cook."

I hadn't heard her saying it, but had heard Jim laughing loudly. When I asked her what it was, she told me what Nancy had just said to me. She knew I hated cooking, though she didn't know it was the association between that and shortage of money, the nagging that I got instead of the school authorities, forever on the scrounge for us to take pennies for this and for that. She liked simplicity in all things, even if she had to invent it. Elaine's slowness was put down to her not eating meat; though Yvonne too, showed a certain languor in her delivery, but she ate mostly meat. Janet, another vegetarian, was as dynamic on stage as ever. None of this stood in the way of Nancy's conclusions.

Stage mannerisms were a problem. At drama school, some actors could only get their words out with the help of a swinging arm or a nodding head. I played Mrs Hill in Pygmalion, and all through one of Eliza's key speeches, she rocked back and forward, with her eyes on me—I could hardly look elsewhere—until I felt quite dizzy, as she went back and forth, back and forth. All Nancy told her was to look at other members of the company now and then. She said nothing at all about the rocking. I tried to tell 'Eliza' about it, but she brushed it aside with a bad grace, as if I was being funny with her. We could have done with a camcorder, to show us what we really looked like.

One of our Maria Martens played her own murder scene with an embarrassed smile on her face. Nancy made a mild protest at this and said she thought Maria ought to look afraid at this point. She was being murdered, after all.

I wondered if Nancy's direction had always been so inconsistent. She would tear into me most savagely—or stare me out during rehearsals while I spoke, trying to disconcert me. She would nag me pointlessly until she had me in tears, my performance would then be dull, and she had failed to get the best out of me. The fact that I can't remember what these tirades were about is evidence they were of no value. I had no real trust in her judgement. I began to rely on the audience for that.

Back in the van, the other girls rallied round 'Maria Marten' in support, in the most unhelpful way, criticising Nancy behind her back, for presuming to complain of the girl's cheerfulness in the face of death. I wondered sometimes if they ever listened to themselves.

I would frequently get the feeling I had at drama school, that of having to drag another performer around with me, willing the sluggish words out of them, and a little spirit into them.

'Eliza' would misquote, spoiling the point that Shaw was making. No matter how many times Nancy would tell her about it, she would say " ... than I am ..." when she was meant to say, ungrammatically, " ... than what I am ..." It made nonsense of Higgins correcting her English in his next line. Nancy was helpless to get the girl to say what the author intended. The girl knew it, and the play plodded on.

To my ears, a pronounced Cockney accent is the worst sound a human can make. There is a phrase in St Joan, "We will never govern England." The girl who had to say it would try instead to say, "We will never be able to govern England." The final 'l' in a word is peculiarly difficult for many Londoners to sound, as anyone will know who has heard a news vendor selling the Evening Mail. 'Mail' comes out in a noise like a strangled cat. "Maai-oo!" is the nearest one can get, or wish to. The reader might like to guess what she made of 'able to', the troublesome phrase coming out as 'ah to'. Nancy would confide in me, telling me how difficult a director's job was. She was troubled, too, about the casting of the plays, and hinted that that too, was an impossible thing to get right. I wondered if she was trying to tell me she would like to cast St Joan differently, but didn't like to upset Kay by giving the part to a younger woman. How I sympathised—but Kay had *always* played Joan.

One of the girls took to eating with her mouth wide open. Slap, slap, went her jaws, inches from my face, as she stood one day in front of my bunk. I remembered David Newbold's barnyard manners. I suddenly shouted her name in protest.

"Whah?" she said, her mouth full and gaping.

"Noises!" I said pointedly.

Satirical indignation was her only response. "Oh. Huh. Is it all right if I breathe? We're not even allowed to breathe now," she said, appealing to the others.

This time they couldn't be bothered to back her up. Each, in her turn, away from home restraints, behaved like a small child, testing the limits. This happens in a small group. They will do as much as they can get away with. They will take on roles, obliging each other to strike an attitude in response. Antagonisms arose. Loyalties shifted. Alliances were formed.

* * *

High in the Pennines, deep in snow, Clare got a flat tyre, and in the bitter cold we changed the wheel. It took three of us to hold it steady. Later, in the middle of Portia's speech, " ... as the gentle rain from Heaven ..." I found my mind drifting, and wondered, even as I said the words, if this appalling winter would ever end. I love the snow, and at first I had enjoyed the way it cast the light upwards, enhancing the dark days; but this was overdoing things. It was now worse than cold and uncomfortable; it was boring.

I was with Sue, at the same altitude, when Madame G. stalled yet again. I stood in the inky night, waiting for something heavy to come over the hill, holding the tow rope high in my left hand, as big headlamps lifted over the brow and went rumbling past us.

We seemed to be permanently exhausted. Now and then, we would get a few days in which we had no performance nor the need to travel. "You can lie in your coffins all day tomorrow," Nancy would tell us. I often wonder how long I could live that kind of life nowadays.

I think even more about how I could have played a part better. Made this or that gesture. Held complete stillness on this or that phrase—put a different emphasis on a word. Timed something differently. Now and then, a performance would be a total success. The audience's response would leave us in no doubt. And it makes me realise the loss—how much better it all could have been.

Just before a performance of Henry IV, Part One, Nancy decided I should pause, and look about me before saying "Where is the map?" Jim hadn't been at the rehearsal, she had just got back from the South of France in time for the performance, didn't know about the pause, and kept prompting me. With hindsight, I realise I could have whispered to her, in character, but didn't think of it at the time. That's the trouble with acting. It's the one art that can't be amended—until the next time, and there's no point in brooding on it.

* * *

On one of those rest days, Joyce told us all about her visit to a palmist in London, by the name of Mir Bashir. She had been very impressed by him. He seemed to know all about her past life, and had some positive advice about her future.

From what we heard from her, he had obviously got information out of her, built on it, and fed it back to her in the form of questions and suppositions, which she had grasped at, confirming the right guesses and letting the wrong ones pass.

I had, the previous summer, had a tax rebate, and with a few pounds earned pea-picking in Willersey, and waiting on table at The Hunters' Lodge in Broadway, I had saved enough for a treat. My treat was to annoy the hell out of Mir Bashir. At the end of the next school term, I got in a few days' agency work, made an appointment with the phoney in King's Wood, and prepared for a day out in London.

As he led me along the hall, he said pleasantly, "Nice to get away from the house and children, isn't it?"

As I made no answer, he swung sharply round and looked at me hard. I smiled absently. I wasn't going to let this crude attempt lead me into giving anything away.

When he had finished inking my palm, and pressing it on to a white pad, I brought out my notebook.

"You will not need that."

"Yes, I will, I won't remember what you say, otherwise." I stuck to my notebook.

"What I have to say about you will amuse you," he chuckled, trying to soften me up. "You will recognise quite a lot about yourself." He began making guesses.

"You have had trouble with your ankles."

I frowned in concentration, then shook my head. "No, not particularly."

"Your shins, then—you have had a problem with your lower leg."

I looked thoughtful, then shook my head again. "No."

"Well, your knees then … your thighs." He was working his way up, and was beginning to lose his temper. He abandoned that one.

"You came of age at fourteen."

Came of age? I thought. "We come of age at twenty-one."

"I mean *physically* you came of age." I was no wiser. "You started your periods!"

"Oh, I see!" I'd never heard it called 'coming of age'. His English usage was what you might call Colonial Edwardian.

His face cleared. I said, "No, in fact I was sixteen."

He scowled again. "You have just had a love affair." He was a rotten guesser. He went on to tell me what was in the future for me. All vague stuff. You'll have a problem, go on a journey, lose a loved one. None of it had anything to do with the theatre, nor earning any kind of living. He didn't even touch on marriage—was he hoping I would ask?

What else he told me, I've forgotten. I didn't keep the notes, but it irritated him to see me writing it all down, and eventually he declared that that was all he had to say, and he saw me to the back door. He must have had someone waiting in the reception room, and was worried about what I'd say to them as I passed.

At the door I turned round. "Actually, I did have an affair a short time ago," I lied. "With a woman." If you are going to tell a lie, make it good and scandalous.

"That is very bad!" he raged, "it is very wrong!"

"I know," I leered, and bade him a cheerful Goodbye.

When we re-assembled back at Willersey after the break, I told them all about it. They only looked thoughtful, though I was fleetingly sorry to see Joyce look crest-fallen. At least, that was what I thought she looked.

After a few days out on the next tour, I found myself travelling in Madame G., with Kay.

"A little bird told me …" Kay began.

How very twee, I thought, and how surprising to hear Kay talking like this, since she always made a point of expressing a dislike of precious talk. Apparently, a little bird had told her that I had been spending my money on frivolities like palm-reading.

"A little bird?" I asked.

"Oh, I can't remember who it was," Kay said quickly. An uncharacteristic lapse of memory, from one who thought the piece of information worth remembering in the first place. But she left it at that.

The poor are not supposed to spend their money on luxuries, not even those they have saved up for. It was our place to drudge along, and because we had to pinch and scrape, then it was right that we should do so. No jollity, no nonsensical expense. It was not our place. When I pointed out, as the matter arose, that what others took for granted, I had to go without, I was immediately in the dock to justify myself when I did have a treat. "You are not so poor as you are trying to make out," was the peevish attitude. I tried to avoid having to explain my penury, partly for this reason, and partly because people simply didn't believe it.

I asked the girls who had been talking to Kay about my extravagant lifestyle, my rakish recklessness. They all looked quietly puzzled, shook their heads and looked elsewhere. So it must have been Walter Plinge who informed on me.

* * *

I began to sense that this would probably be the last year of the Osiris as a company. Nancy's health was not of the best. She had to stay at home while we took a local tour with Kay directing. That is to say, letting us get on with it, with the least interference, but without guidance either. It has to be said that it all went more smoothly without Nancy criticising and fretting. She was getting tired. She was no longer suited to driving long journeys and wearing herself out. Her extraordinary artistic experiment was drawing to a close. She had done what no woman had done—taken a group of female players for more than thirty-six years round the country. Young women of private means, in the first instance, who had families to rely on, and without the immediate necessity of earning a steady living. Mostly, at any time, girls who would marry and raise a family. One or two would become well known: Mary Wimbush, Jane Freeman, both kept busy by the BBC; Jim went back to New Zealand, Elaine, Janet and Linda started up a small theatre in a London suburb for a while; I was to share a bedsit with Linda in the capital for a season, and one or two earlier members of my acquaintance would pop up on TV now and then.

It used to irritate Nancy to have her company described as a 'social experiment'. I suspect that sounded too much like Socialism to her, so it had to be brusquely dismissed.

I wish I could remember my last performance with the Osiris. It might well have been the broadcast for an evening news item, slotted in the Midlands news. We gave them the Cakes and Ale scene from Twelfth Night, in Broadway village hall, and threw in extra interest with footage of us driving round the lanes linking Willersey with Broadway and the Evesham Road. Then making up, putting up the scenery, and enacting the short extract, with Nancy in taunting mood as Sir Toby, Elaine as the buxom Maria, and me as the spoilsport Malvolio, scolding the merry-makers until Sir Toby threw the pot of ale in my face. I always looked forward to that cold splash of water; Malvolio's rantings made me hot and dry.

* * *

Apart from Broadway, we could claim to have performed at Stratford, too. At the County Secondary School. We had travelled the length of the United Kingdom, from the Isle of Wight to Edinburgh and further north. From Ramsgate to St David's. In Manchester, and even London, where we parked in a quiet field in Liphook, and travelled every day into the capital. We saw Wales in the rain, Kent in the sun, bleak grandeur in the North, splendour among the Scottish heights, and the serenity of the Norfolk flatlands. Then back to the Cotswolds, soft and pretty with its honey-coloured stone.

We went our ways, and found what work we could in show business. We didn't find fame, but we had achieved something that we were unlikely to do either in rep or on television; played the roles that most men have only dreamed of.

Some progress is being made in sharing out the thespian goodies between the sexes, and an interchange of gender. I look forward to the more progressive companies continuing to shake and startle us, holding only to the spirit of the text, and letting the words take care of themselves.

I had not finished with touring, that day I went from Willersey home to Birmingham, and on to London, but that was to be in another year, and another company.

EPILOGUE

The company continued to tour for the best part of a year with Nancy and the younger of some of her friends of the past. She thought of writing her memoirs, and I took a few shorthand notes, but her mind was not yet set for the task. Her un-published book lies in the Theatre Museum at Covent Garden.

She later took a teaching post at the Birmingham Theatre School, and then re-tired to run a costume hire service from the Long House.

I was to see her several times over the next few years; we talked for hours on the phone, sometimes when she rang to tell me that a former member had died, sometimes be-cause either of us just felt like talking.

Nancy Hewins

Nancy had been quite strict with the young women over their social lives in the early days, in the 'thirties and 'forties, and must have mellowed by the time I joined. It's true that when I finally took the domestic option and fell, exhausted, into subur-bia but not into marriage, she wrote to me to express her sorrow that I was living in sin, but I jollied her out of these final shreds of Victorian values by reminding her that marriage had nothing to do with morality. That it was a commercial undertaking, and had been ever since it was invented, by fathers with saleable children. Although the upheavals of the 'sixties were to pass by her as the idle wind, I think she accepted with equanimity the way things were done by then.

My last memory of Nancy Hewins is seeing her come across the green to greet me from the bus, with the last two of her Belgian Griffons, Polly, now old and breathless, but who still recognised me with pleasure, and a younger dog, Lizzie. Nancy was wearing the red balaclava I had knitted for her in the winter of 1963, by this time held together with safety pins. A genuine eccentric, she had, at an early age broken away from the life set out for her, and I suspect would eventually have agreed with me that staying single was the bit that we had both got right.

ACKNOWLEDGEMENTS

My thanks for material to: Billy, Ruby, Jack, Stanley, Ken, Mark Rose, Sue Date, Kim Taplin, Mary Collins and Margot Thomas.

Photographs processed by Stourport Photo Centre.